ON THE ROAD TO PERDITION

BOOK 1: OASIS

writer
MAX ALLAN COLLINS

penciller
JOSÉ LUIS GARCÍA-LÓPEZ

inker
JOSEF RUBINSTEIN

letterer
BOB LAPPAN

PARADOX PRESS   NEW YORK, NEW YORK

PARADOX PRESS / DC COMICS
Mike Carlin, VP-Executive Editor · Andrew Helfer, Group Editor
Harvey Richards, Assistant Editor · Amie Brockway-Metcalf, Art Director
Paul Levitz, President & Publisher · Georg Brewer VP-Design & Retail Product Development
Richard Bruning, VP-Creative Director · Patrick Caldon, Senior VP-Finance & Operations
Chris Caramalis, VP-Finance · Terri Cunningham, VP-Managing Editor
Dan DiDio, VP-Editorial · Joel Ehrlich, Senior VP-Advertising & Promotions
Alison Gill, VP-Manufacturing · Lillian Laserson, Senior VP & General Counsel
David McKillips, VP-Advertising · John Nee, VP-Business Development
Cheryl Rubin, VP-Licensing & Merchandising · Bob Wayne, VP-Sales & Marketing

❖

On the Road to Perdition: Oasis, Book 1 of 3. Published by DC Comics,
1700 Broadway, New York, NY 10019.
Printed in Canada.
DC Comics. A division of Warner Bros.-An AOL Time Warner Company

❖

Cover sketch by RICHARD PIERS RAYNER
Cover pencils and inks by DAVID MICHAEL BECK
Colors and separations by DAVE McCAIG

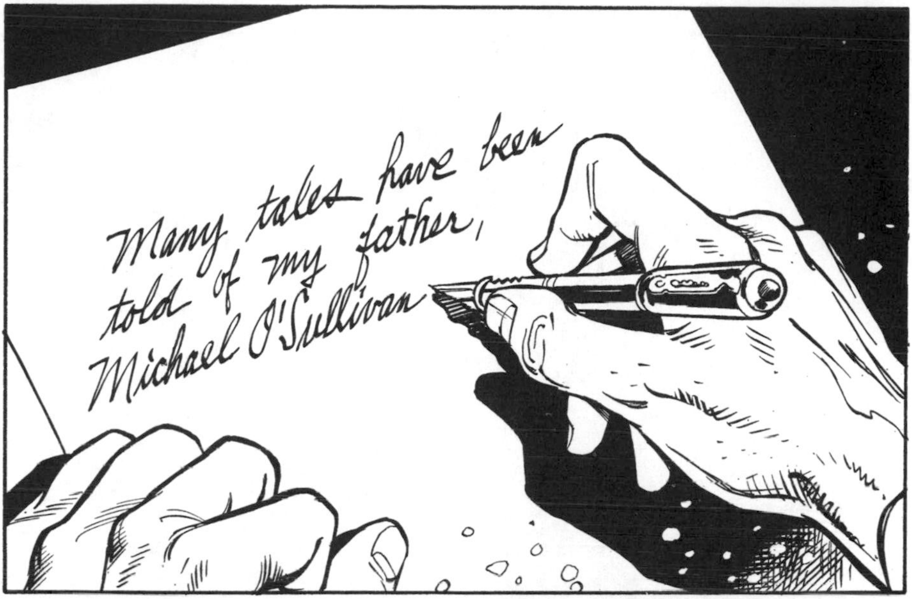
Many tales have been told of my father, Michael O'Sullivan

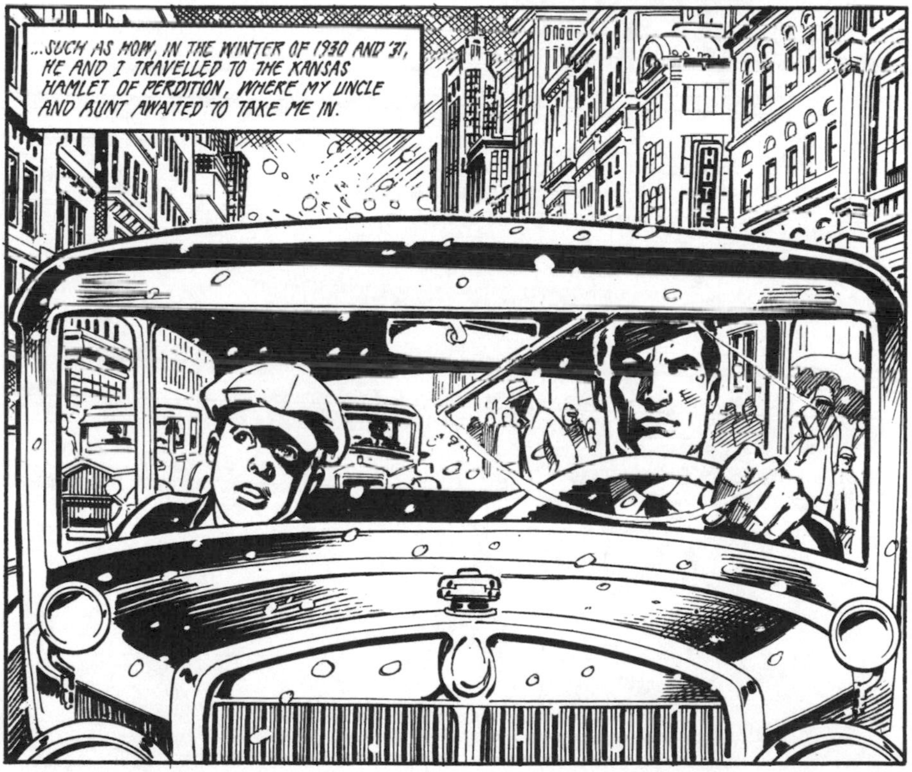
...SUCH AS HOW, IN THE WINTER OF 1930 AND '31, HE AND I TRAVELLED TO THE KANSAS HAMLET OF PERDITION, WHERE MY UNCLE AND AUNT AWAITED TO TAKE ME IN.
HOTE

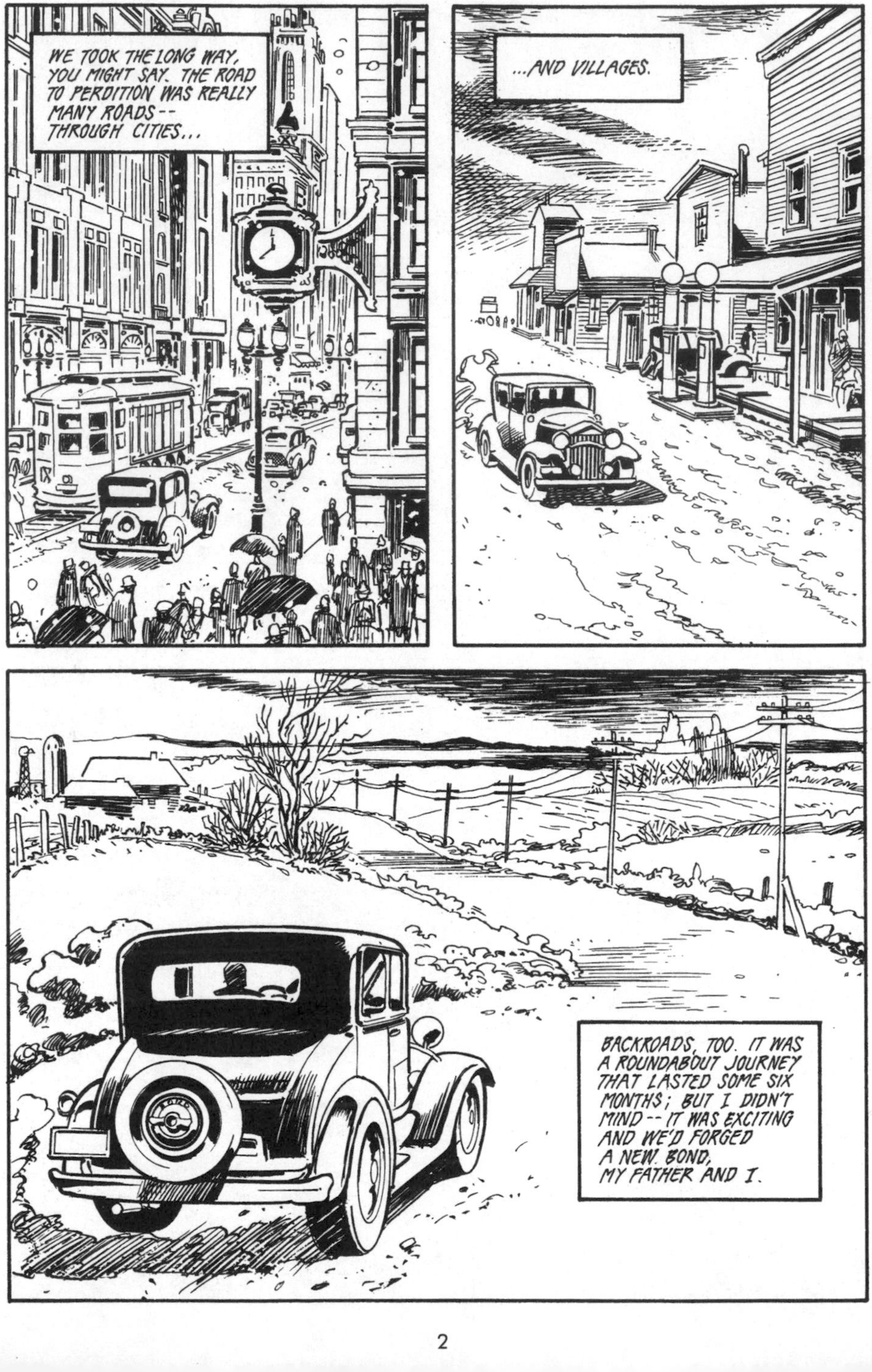
WE TOOK THE LONG WAY, YOU MIGHT SAY. THE ROAD TO PERDITION WAS REALLY MANY ROADS -- THROUGH CITIES...
...AND VILLAGES.
BACKROADS, TOO. IT WAS A ROUNDABOUT JOURNEY THAT LASTED SOME SIX MONTHS; BUT I DIDN'T MIND -- IT WAS EXCITING AND WE'D FORGED A NEW BOND, MY FATHER AND I.

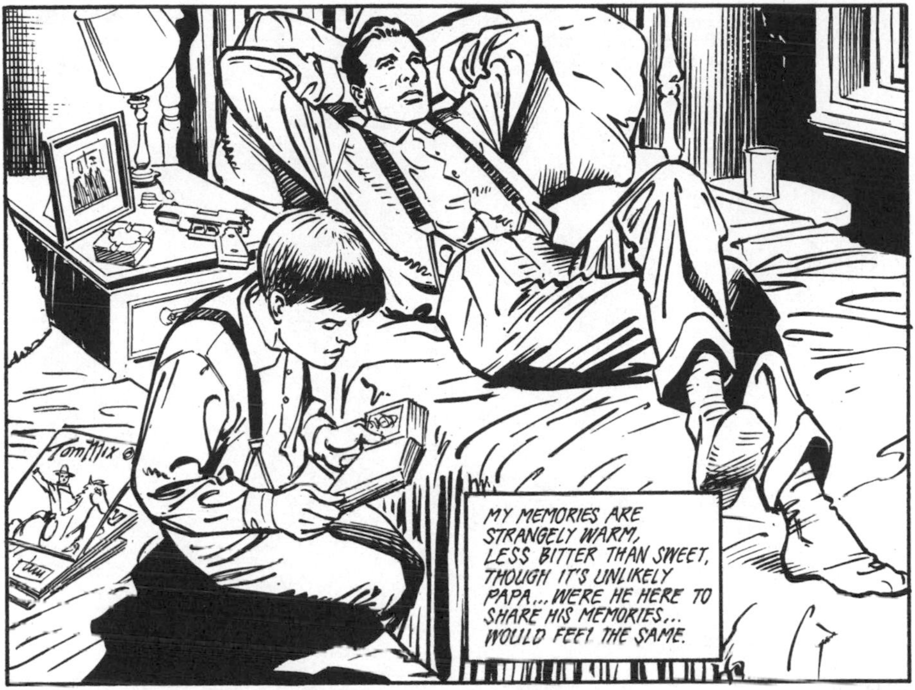
MY MEMORIES ARE STRANGELY WARM, LESS BITTER THAN SWEET, THOUGH IT'S UNLIKELY PAPA... WERE HE HERE TO SHARE HIS MEMORIES... WOULD FEEL THE SAME.
Tom Mix

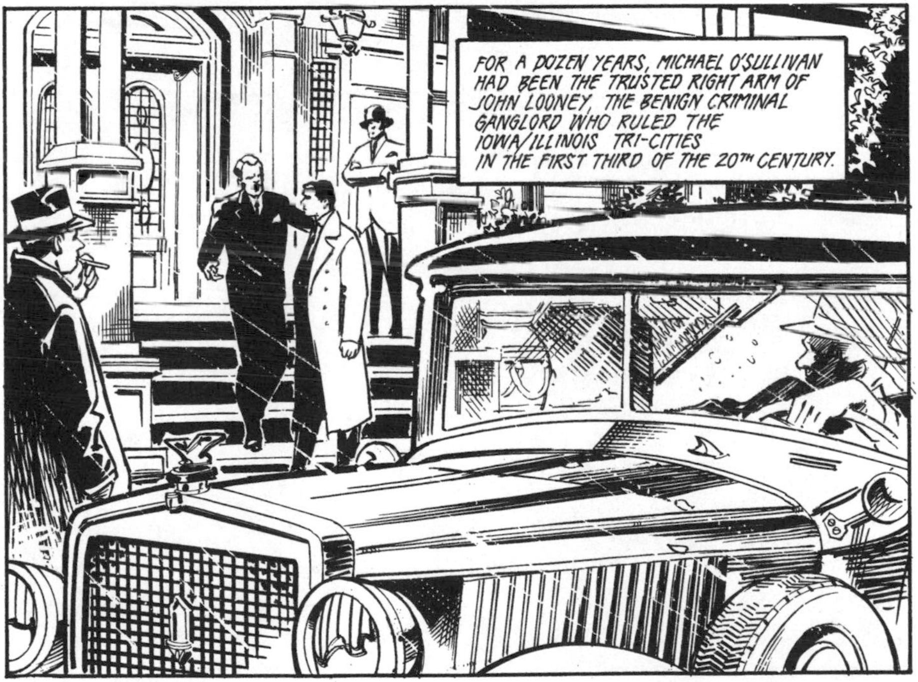
FOR A DOZEN YEARS, MICHAEL O'SULLIVAN HAD BEEN THE TRUSTED RIGHT ARM OF JOHN LOONEY, THE BENIGN CRIMINAL GANGLORD WHO RULED THE IOWA/ILLINOIS TRI-CITIES IN THE FIRST THIRD OF THE 20TH CENTURY.

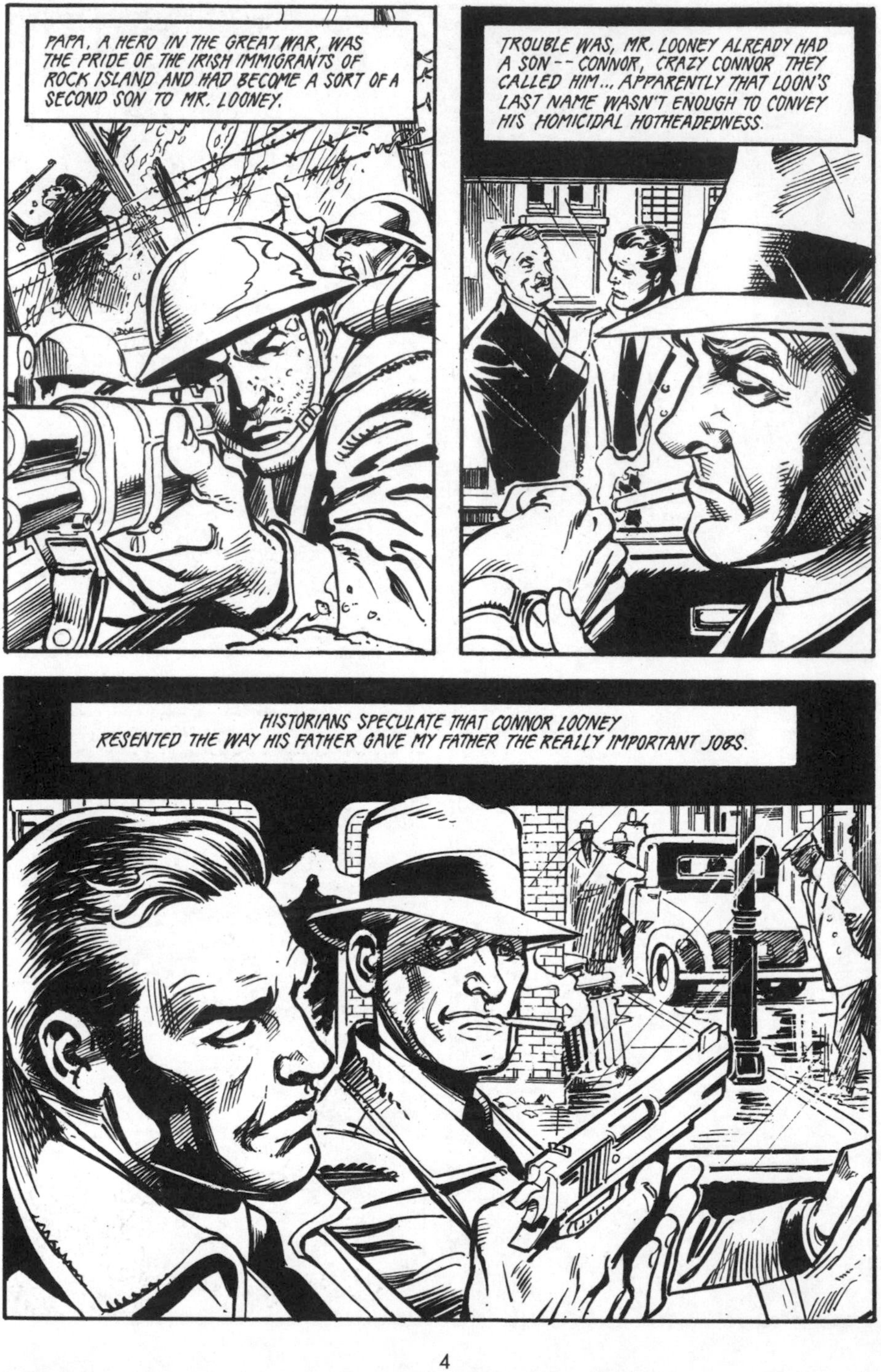
PAPA, A HERO IN THE GREAT WAR, WAS THE PRIDE OF THE IRISH IMMIGRANTS OF ROCK ISLAND AND HAD BECOME A SORT OF A SECOND SON TO MR. LOONEY.
TROUBLE WAS, MR. LOONEY ALREADY HAD A SON -- CONNOR, CRAZY CONNOR THEY CALLED HIM... APPARENTLY THAT LOON'S LAST NAME WASN'T ENOUGH TO CONVEY HIS HOMICIDAL HOTHEADEDNESS.
HISTORIANS SPECULATE THAT CONNOR LOONEY RESENTED THE WAY HIS FATHER GAVE MY FATHER THE REALLY IMPORTANT JOBS.

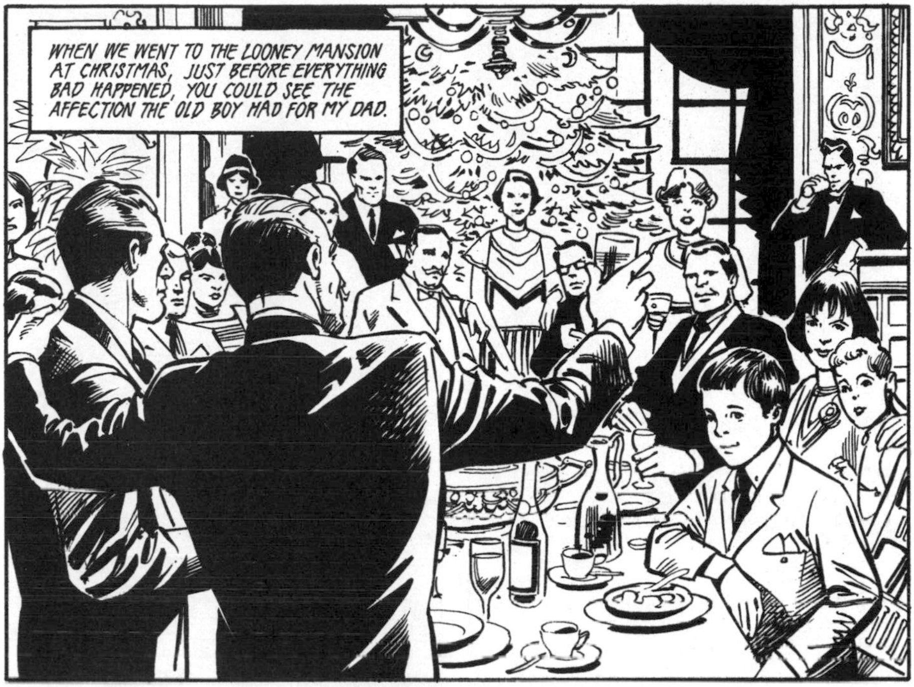
WHEN WE WENT TO THE LOONEY MANSION AT CHRISTMAS, JUST BEFORE EVERYTHING BAD HAPPENED, YOU COULD SEE THE AFFECTION THE OLD BOY HAD FOR MY DAD.

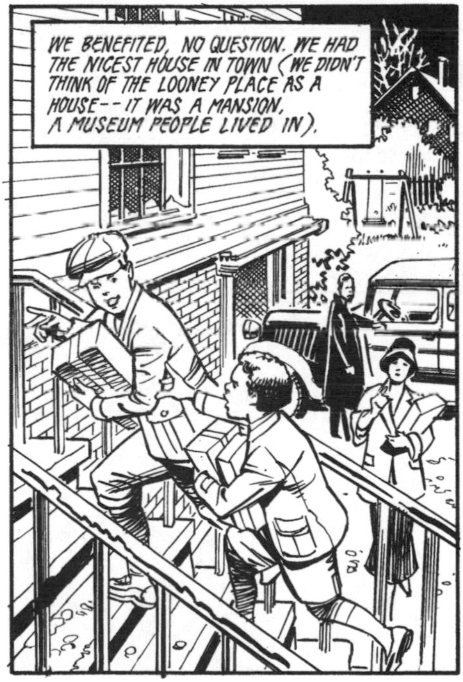
WE BENEFITED, NO QUESTION. WE HAD THE NICEST HOUSE IN TOWN (WE DIDN'T THINK OF THE LOONEY PLACE AS A HOUSE-- IT WAS A MANSION, A MUSEUM PEOPLE LIVED IN).

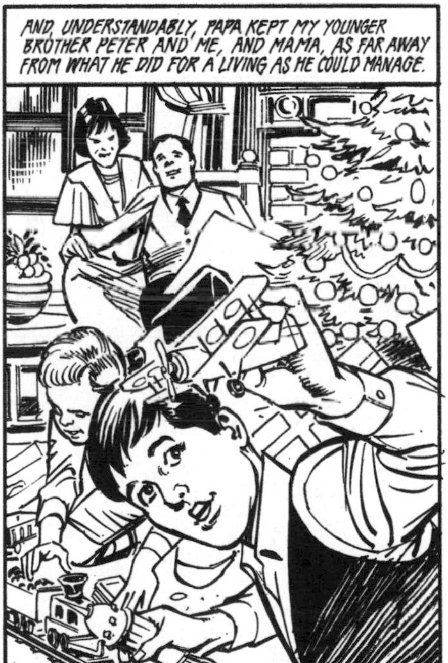
AND, UNDERSTANDABLY, PAPA KEPT MY YOUNGER BROTHER PETER AND ME, AND MAMA, AS FAR AWAY FROM WHAT HE DID FOR A LIVING AS HE COULD MANAGE.

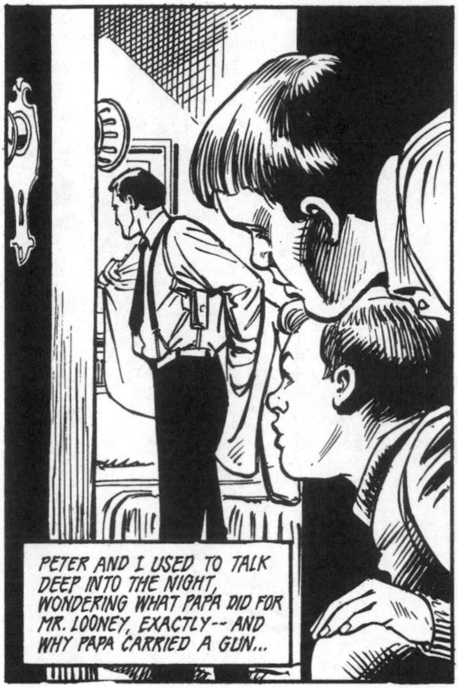
PETER AND I USED TO TALK DEEP INTO THE NIGHT, WONDERING WHAT PAPA DID FOR MR. LOONEY, EXACTLY-- AND WHY PAPA CARRIED A GUN...

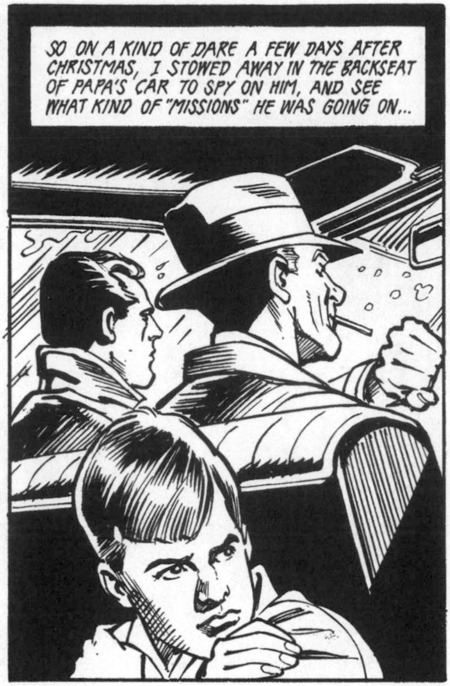
SO ON A KIND OF DARE A FEW DAYS AFTER CHRISTMAS, I STOWED AWAY IN THE BACKSEAT OF PAPA'S CAR TO SPY ON HIM, AND SEE WHAT KIND OF "MISSIONS" HE WAS GOING ON...

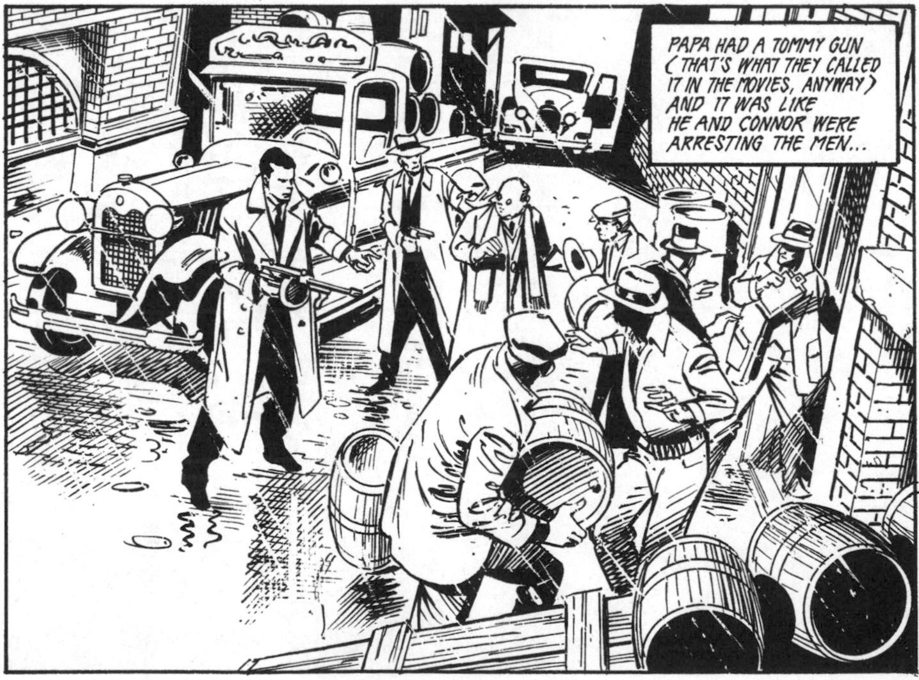
PAPA HAD A TOMMY GUN (THAT'S WHAT THEY CALLED IT IN THE MOVIES, ANYWAY) AND IT WAS LIKE HE AND CONNOR WERE ARRESTING THE MEN...

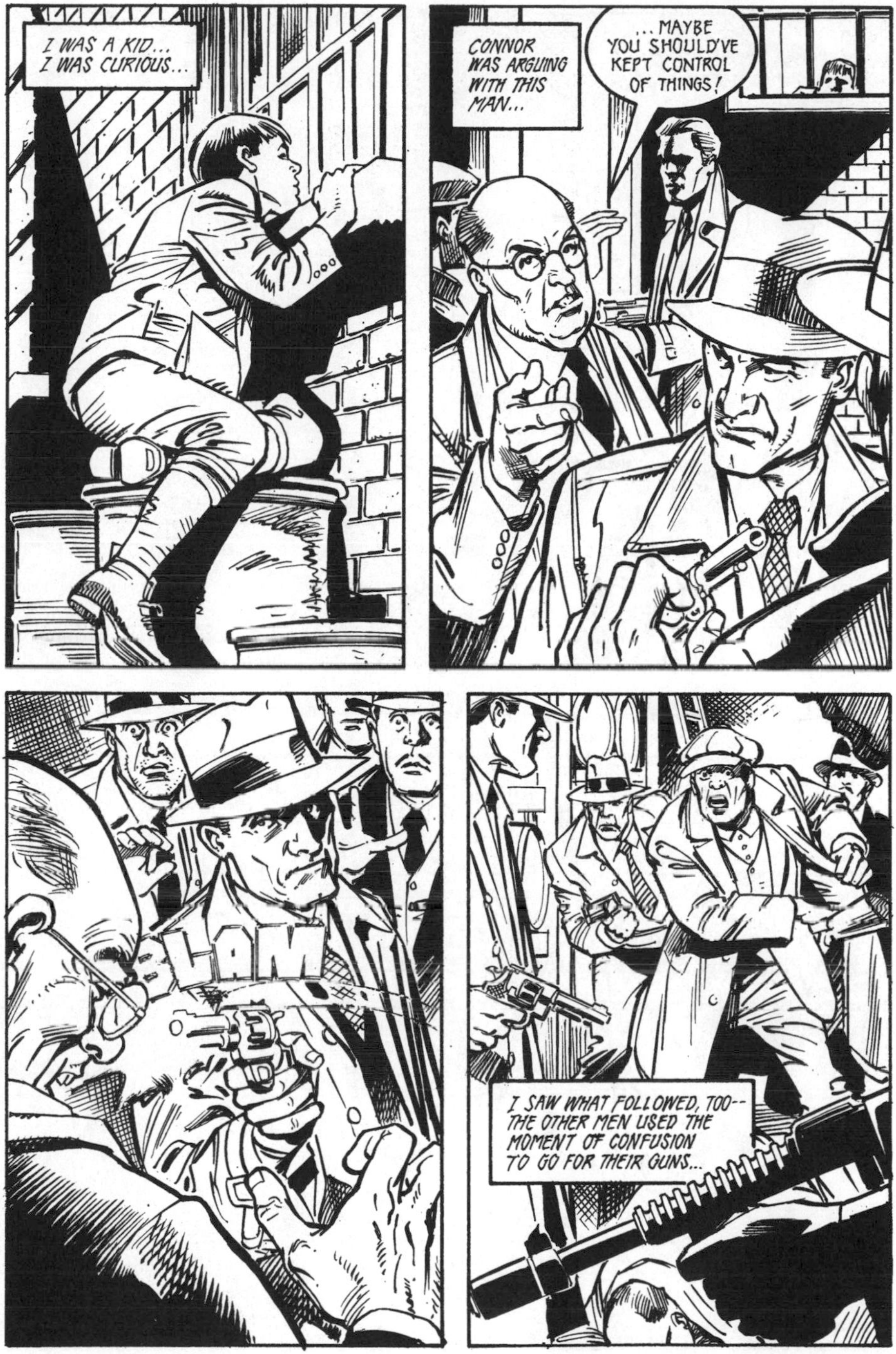
I WAS A KID... I WAS CURIOUS...
CONNOR WAS ARGUING WITH THIS MAN...
...MAYBE YOU SHOULD'VE KEPT CONTROL OF THINGS!
I SAW WHAT FOLLOWED, TOO-- THE OTHER MEN USED THE MOMENT OF CONFUSION TO GO FOR THEIR GUNS...

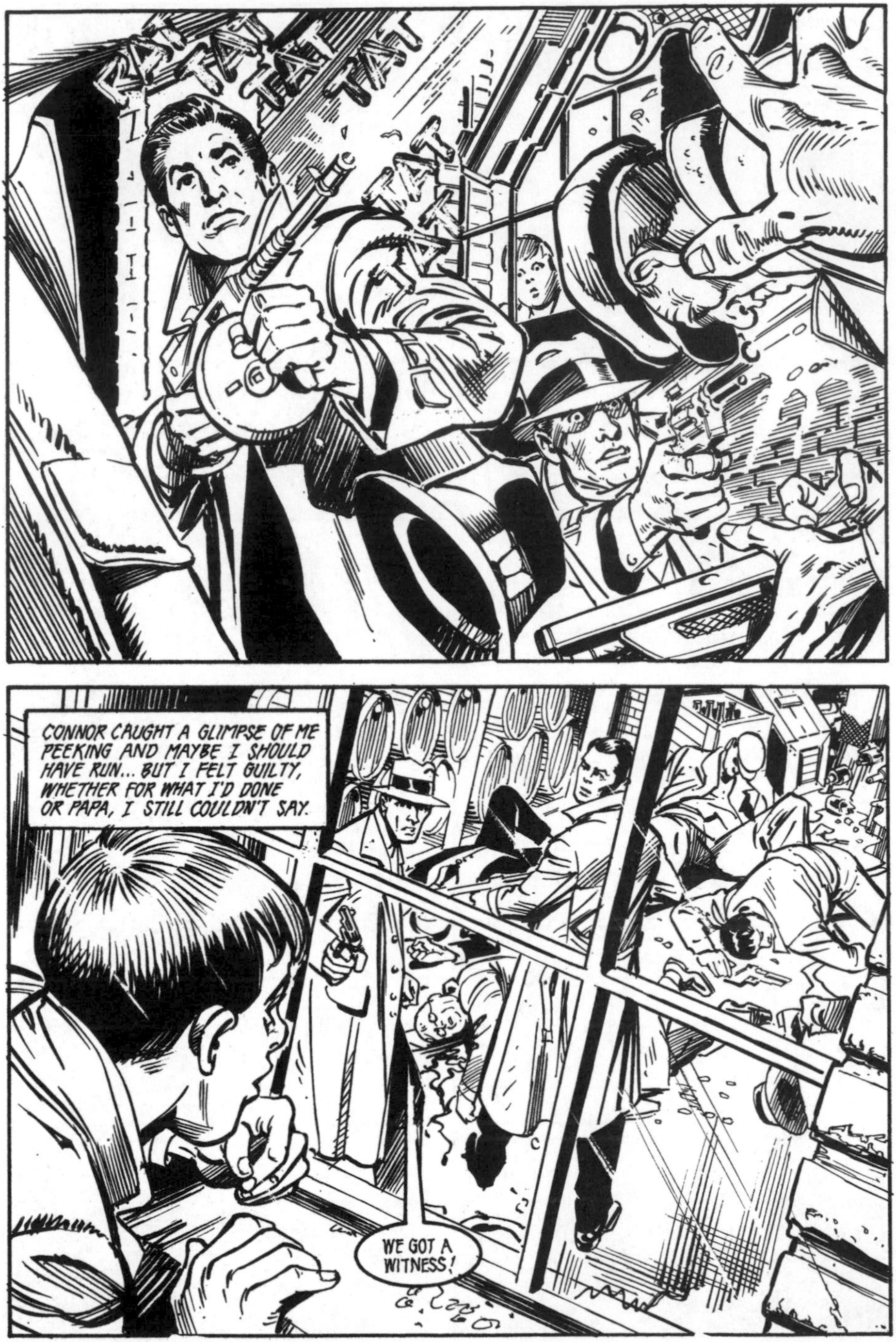
RAT TAT TAT TAT
TAT TAT
CONNOR CAUGHT A GLIMPSE OF ME PEEKING AND MAYBE I SHOULD HAVE RUN... BUT I FELT GUILTY, WHETHER FOR WHAT I'D DONE OR PAPA, I STILL COULDN'T SAY.
WE GOT A WITNESS!

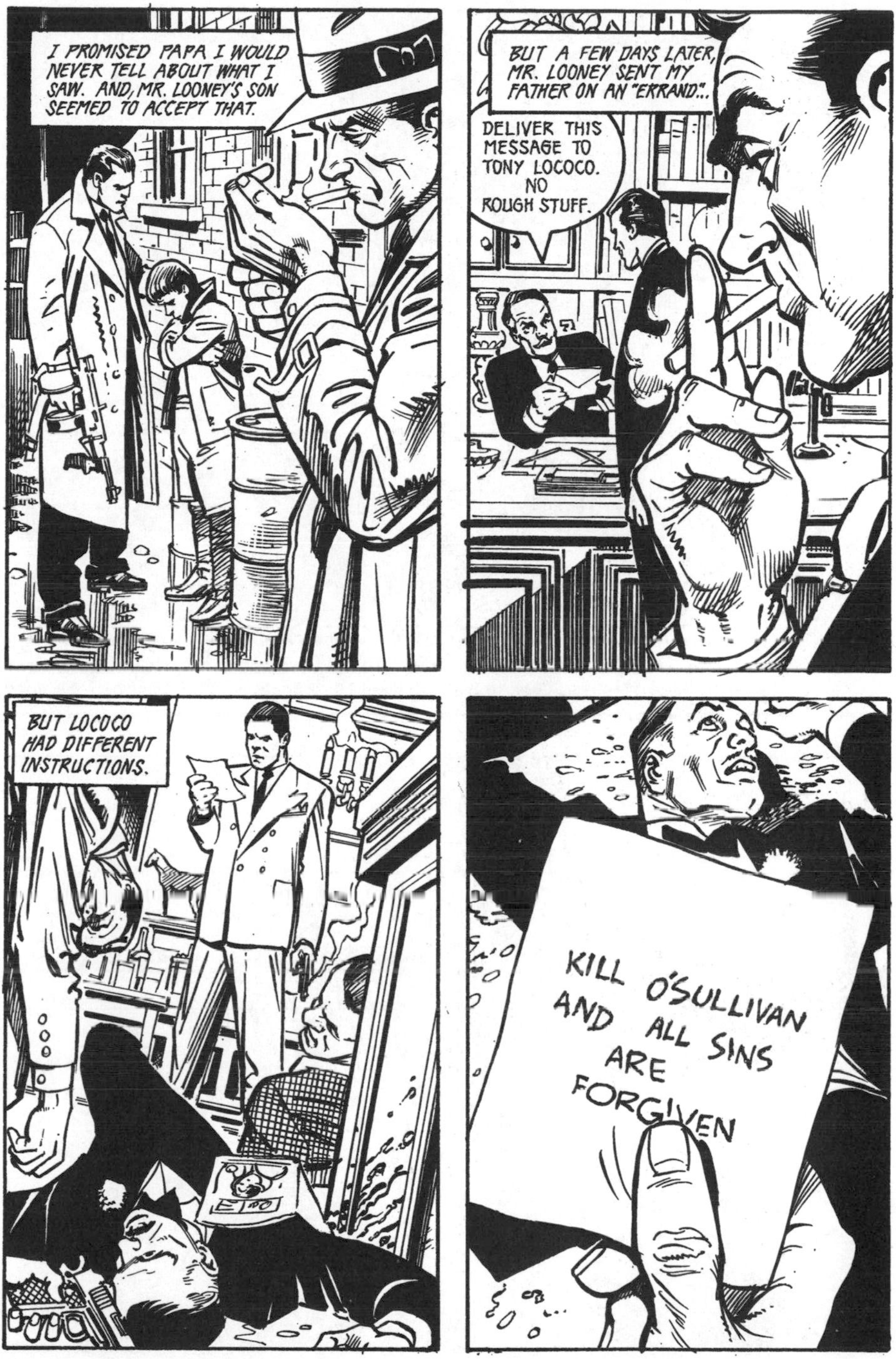
I PROMISED PAPA I WOULD NEVER TELL ABOUT WHAT I SAW. AND, MR. LOONEY'S SON SEEMED TO ACCEPT THAT.
BUT A FEW DAYS LATER, MR. LOONEY SENT MY FATHER ON AN "ERRAND"...
DELIVER THIS MESSAGE TO TONY LOCOCO. NO ROUGH STUFF.
BUT LOCOCO HAD DIFFERENT INSTRUCTIONS.
KILL O'SULLIVAN AND ALL SINS ARE FORGIVEN

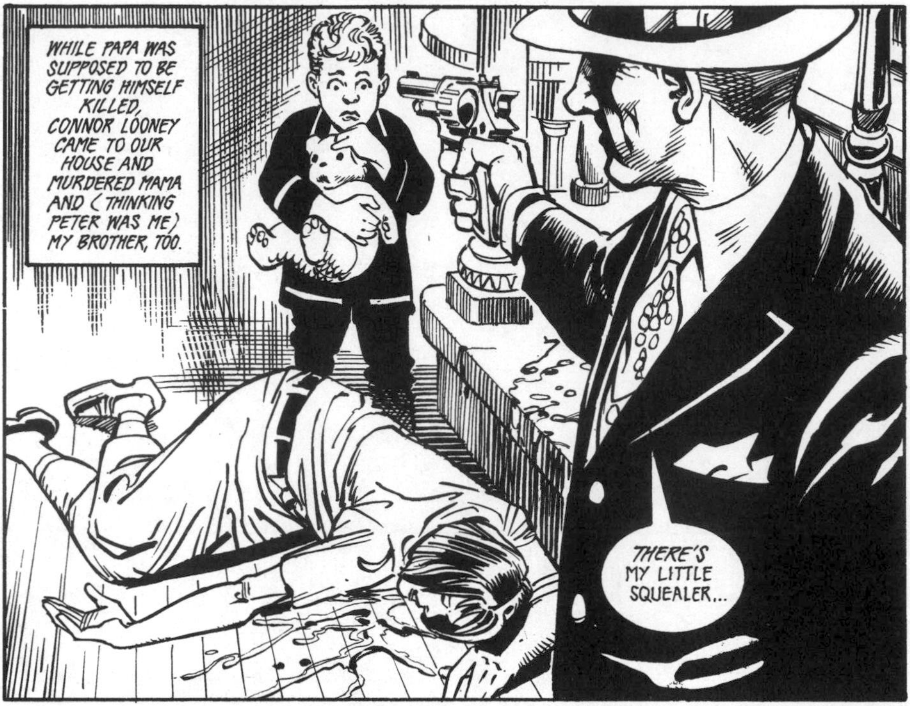
WHILE PAPA WAS SUPPOSED TO BE GETTING HIMSELF KILLED, CONNOR LOONEY CAME TO OUR HOUSE AND MURDERED MAMA AND (THINKING PETER WAS ME) MY BROTHER, TOO.
THERE'S MY LITTLE SQUEALER...

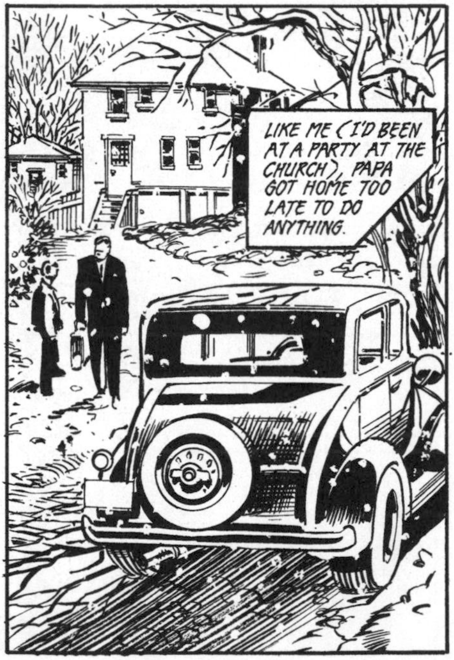
LIKE ME (I'D BEEN AT A PARTY AT THE CHURCH), PAPA GOT HOME TOO LATE TO DO ANYTHING.

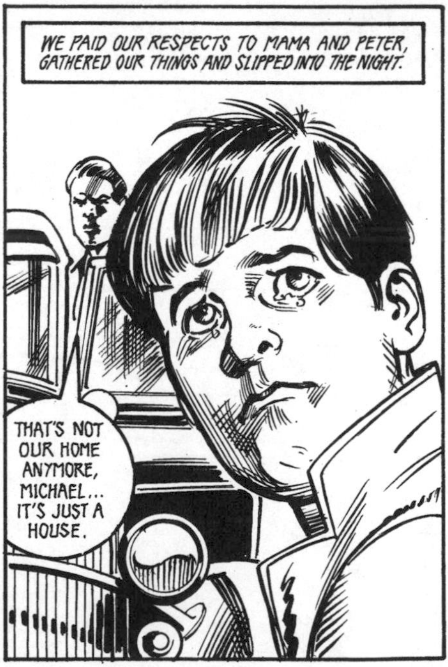
WE PAID OUR RESPECTS TO MAMA AND PETER, GATHERED OUR THINGS AND SLIPPED INTO THE NIGHT.
THAT'S NOT OUR HOME ANYMORE, MICHAEL... IT'S JUST A HOUSE.

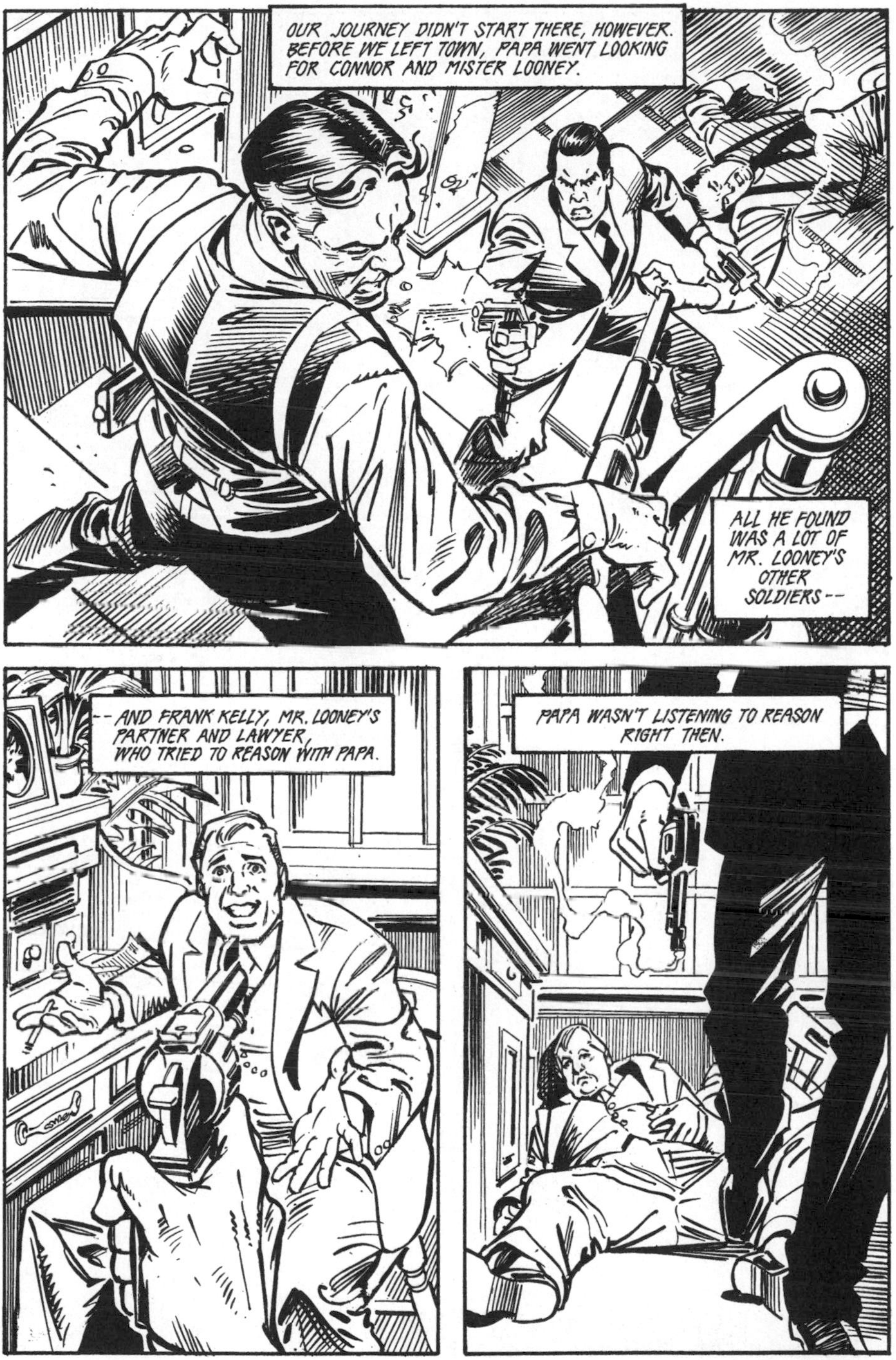
OUR JOURNEY DIDN'T START THERE, HOWEVER. BEFORE WE LEFT TOWN, PAPA WENT LOOKING FOR CONNOR AND MISTER LOONEY.
ALL HE FOUND WAS A LOT OF MR. LOONEY'S OTHER SOLDIERS--
--AND FRANK KELLY, MR. LOONEY'S PARTNER AND LAWYER, WHO TRIED TO REASON WITH PAPA.
PAPA WASN'T LISTENING TO REASON RIGHT THEN.

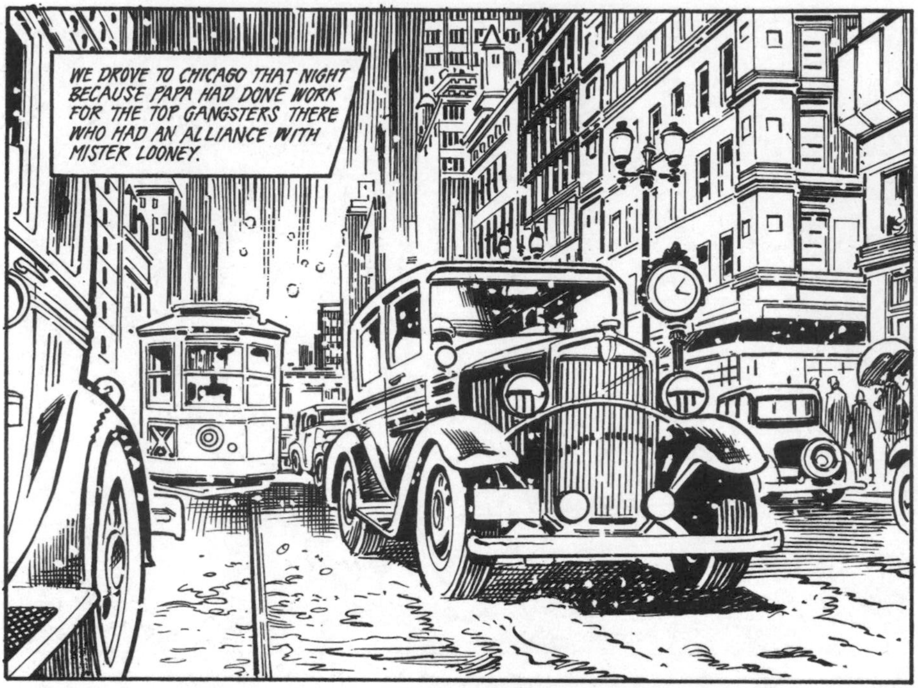
WE DROVE TO CHICAGO THAT NIGHT BECAUSE PAPA HAD DONE WORK FOR THE TOP GANGSTERS THERE WHO HAD AN ALLIANCE WITH MISTER LOONEY.

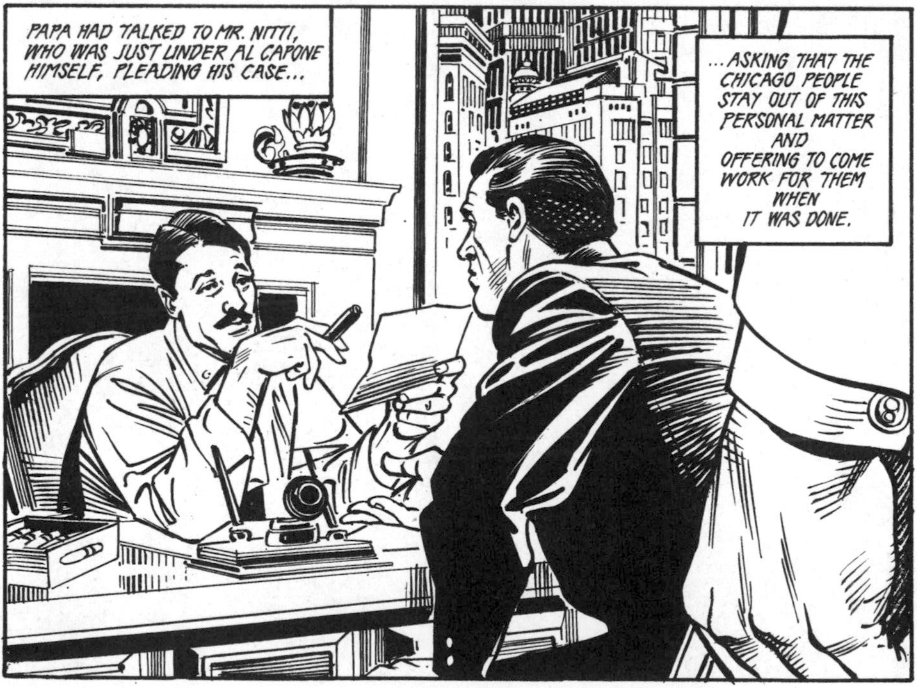
PAPA HAD TALKED TO MR. NITTI, WHO WAS JUST UNDER AL CAPONE HIMSELF, PLEADING HIS CASE...
...ASKING THAT THE CHICAGO PEOPLE STAY OUT OF THIS PERSONAL MATTER AND OFFERING TO COME WORK FOR THEM WHEN IT WAS DONE.

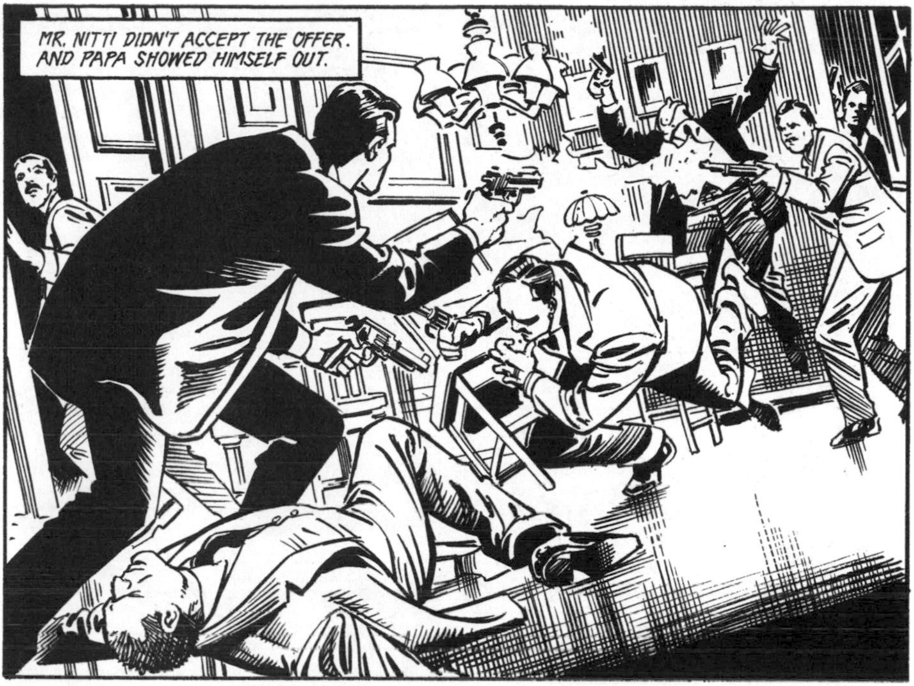
MR. NITTI DIDN'T ACCEPT THE OFFER. AND PAPA SHOWED HIMSELF OUT.

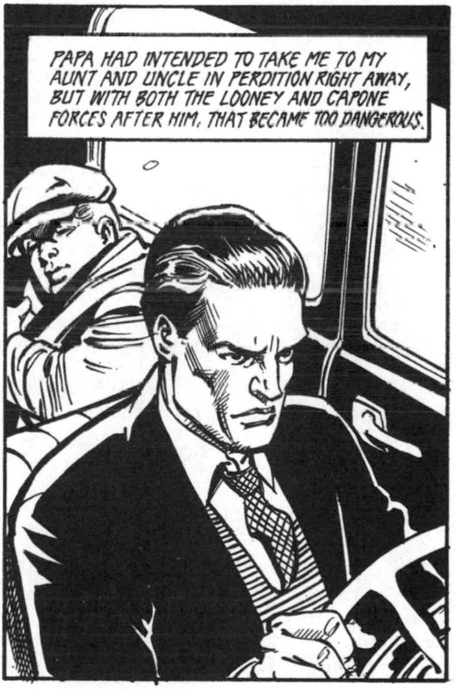
PAPA HAD INTENDED TO TAKE ME TO MY AUNT AND UNCLE IN PERDITION RIGHT AWAY, BUT WITH BOTH THE LOONEY AND CAPONE FORCES AFTER HIM, THAT BECAME TOO DANGEROUS.

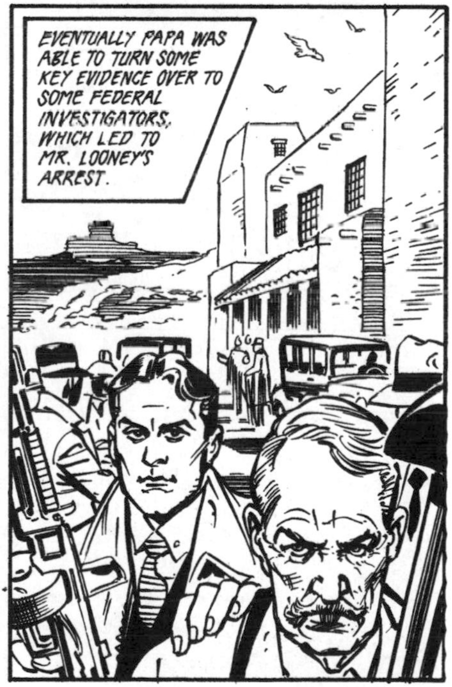
EVENTUALLY PAPA WAS ABLE TO TURN SOME KEY EVIDENCE OVER TO SOME FEDERAL INVESTIGATORS, WHICH LED TO MR. LOONEY'S ARREST.

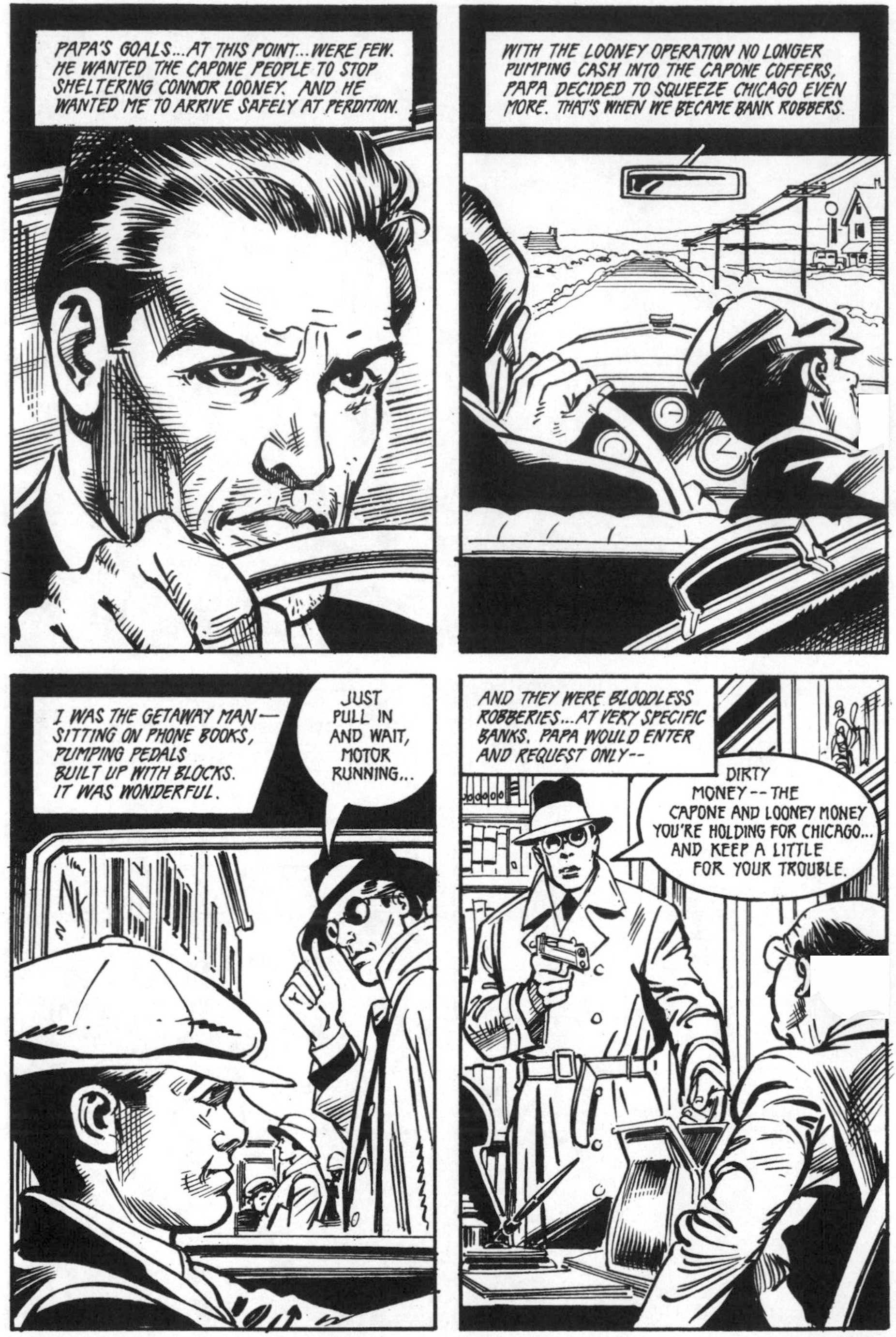
PAPA'S GOALS...AT THIS POINT...WERE FEW. HE WANTED THE CAPONE PEOPLE TO STOP SHELTERING CONNOR LOONEY. AND HE WANTED ME TO ARRIVE SAFELY AT PERDITION.
WITH THE LOONEY OPERATION NO LONGER PUMPING CASH INTO THE CAPONE COFFERS, PAPA DECIDED TO SQUEEZE CHICAGO EVEN MORE. THAT'S WHEN WE BECAME BANK ROBBERS.
I WAS THE GETAWAY MAN— SITTING ON PHONE BOOKS, PUMPING PEDALS BUILT UP WITH BLOCKS. IT WAS WONDERFUL.
JUST PULL IN AND WAIT, MOTOR RUNNING...
AND THEY WERE BLOODLESS ROBBERIES...AT VERY SPECIFIC BANKS. PAPA WOULD ENTER AND REQUEST ONLY--
DIRTY MONEY -- THE CAPONE AND LOONEY MONEY YOU'RE HOLDING FOR CHICAGO... AND KEEP A LITTLE FOR YOUR TROUBLE.

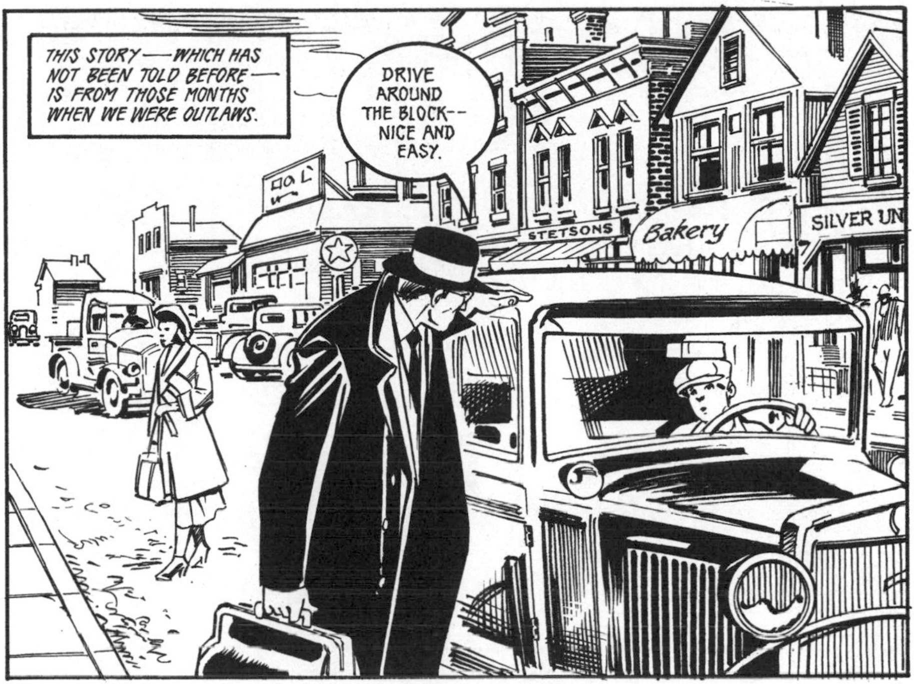
THIS STORY—WHICH HAS NOT BEEN TOLD BEFORE—IS FROM THOSE MONTHS WHEN WE WERE OUTLAWS.
DRIVE AROUND THE BLOCK--NICE AND EASY.
STETSONS
Bakery
SILVER UN
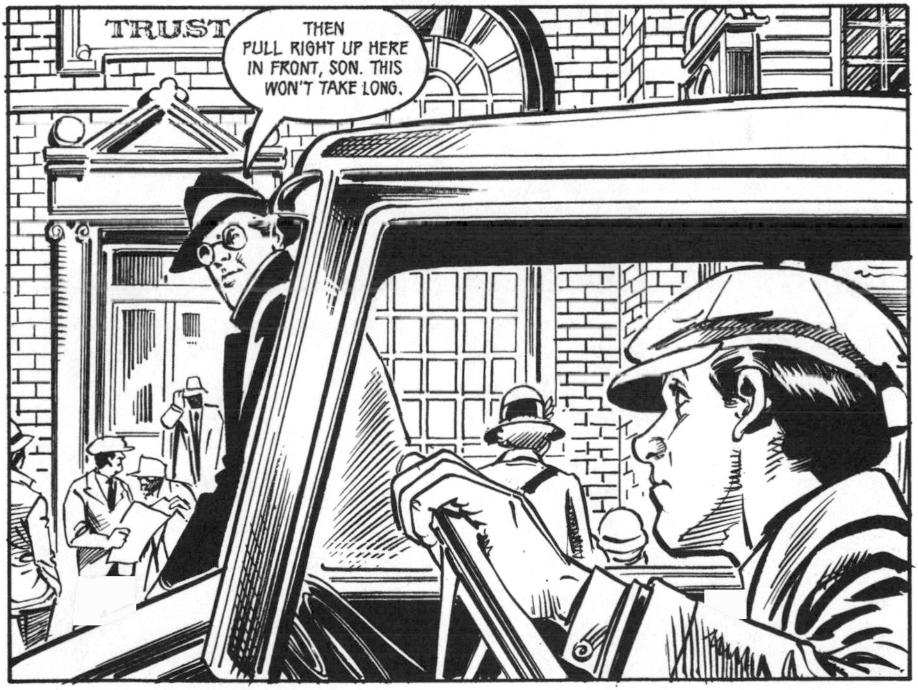
TRUST
THEN PULL RIGHT UP HERE IN FRONT, SON. THIS WON'T TAKE LONG.

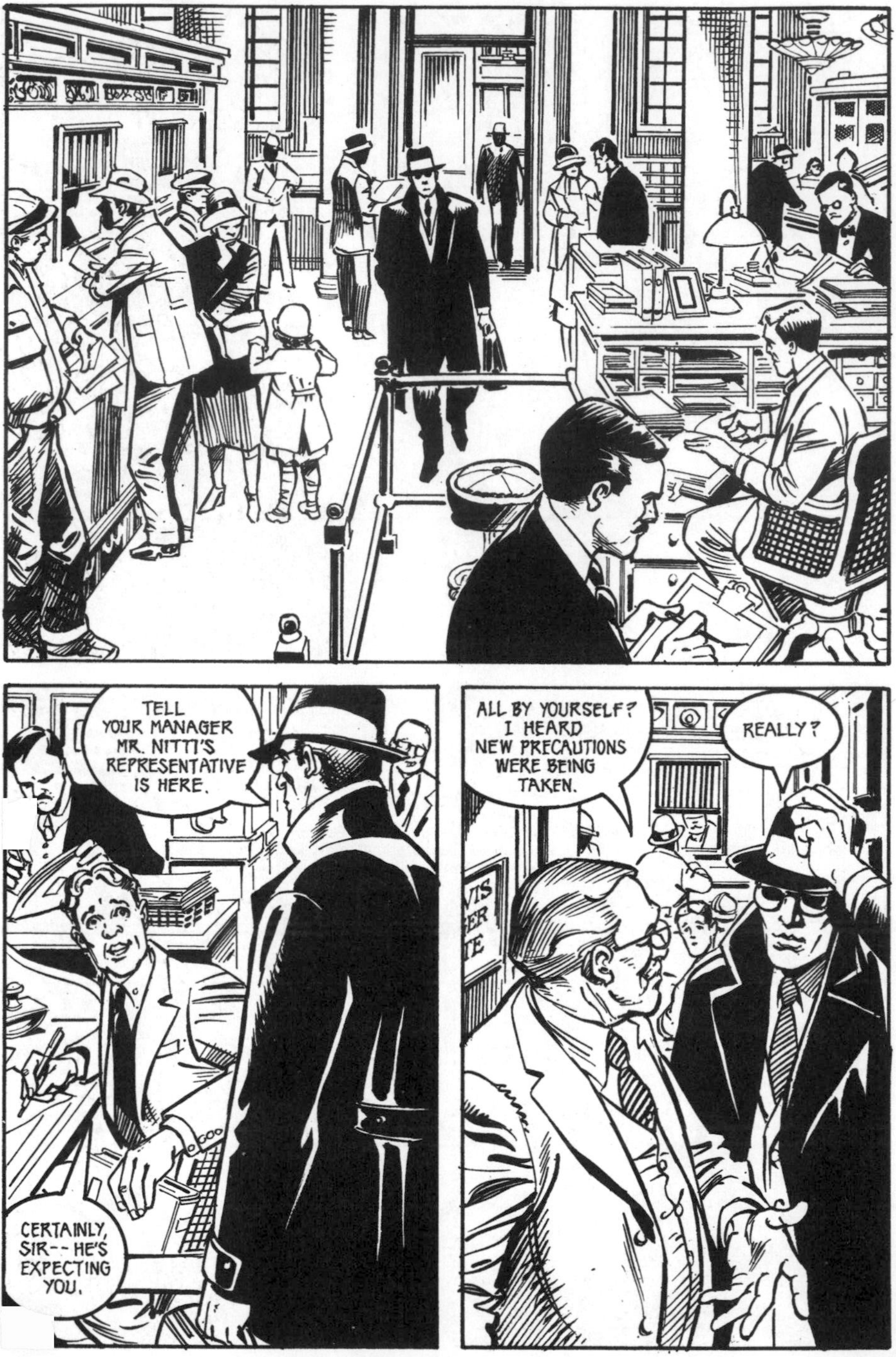
TELL YOUR MANAGER MR. NITTI'S REPRESENTATIVE IS HERE.
CERTAINLY, SIR-- HE'S EXPECTING YOU.
ALL BY YOURSELF? I HEARD NEW PRECAUTIONS WERE BEING TAKEN.
REALLY?

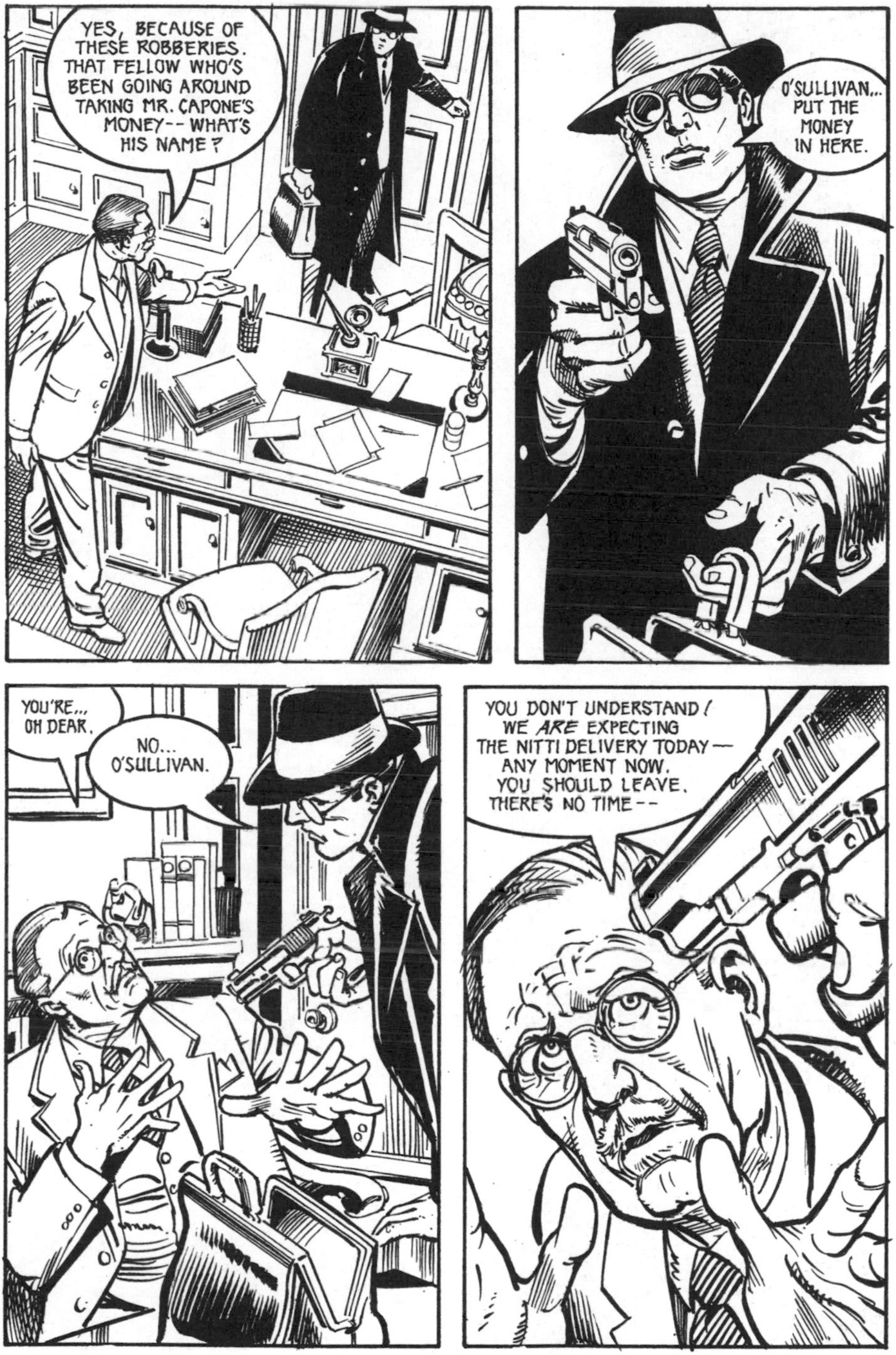
YES, BECAUSE OF THESE ROBBERIES. THAT FELLOW WHO'S BEEN GOING AROUND TAKING MR. CAPONE'S MONEY-- WHAT'S HIS NAME?
O'SULLIVAN... PUT THE MONEY IN HERE.
YOU'RE... OH DEAR.
NO... O'SULLIVAN.
YOU DON'T UNDERSTAND! WE *ARE* EXPECTING THE NITTI DELIVERY TODAY— ANY MOMENT NOW. YOU SHOULD LEAVE. THERE'S NO TIME--

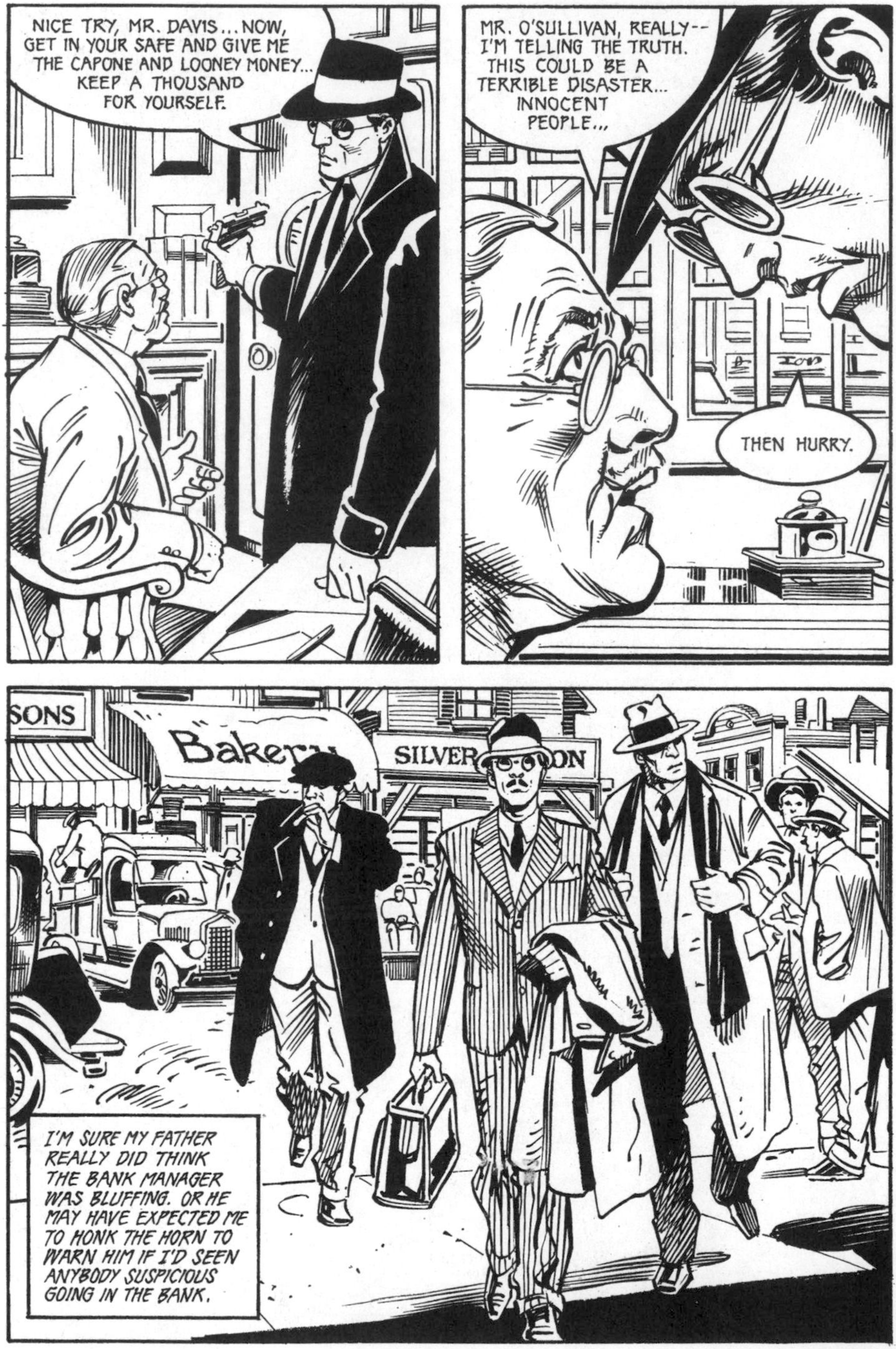
NICE TRY, MR. DAVIS... NOW, GET IN YOUR SAFE AND GIVE ME THE CAPONE AND LOONEY MONEY... KEEP A THOUSAND FOR YOURSELF.
MR. O'SULLIVAN, REALLY-- I'M TELLING THE TRUTH. THIS COULD BE A TERRIBLE DISASTER... INNOCENT PEOPLE...
THEN HURRY.
SONS
Bakery
SILVER
ON
I'M SURE MY FATHER REALLY DID THINK THE BANK MANAGER WAS BLUFFING. OR HE MAY HAVE EXPECTED ME TO HONK THE HORN TO WARN HIM IF I'D SEEN ANYBODY SUSPICIOUS GOING IN THE BANK.

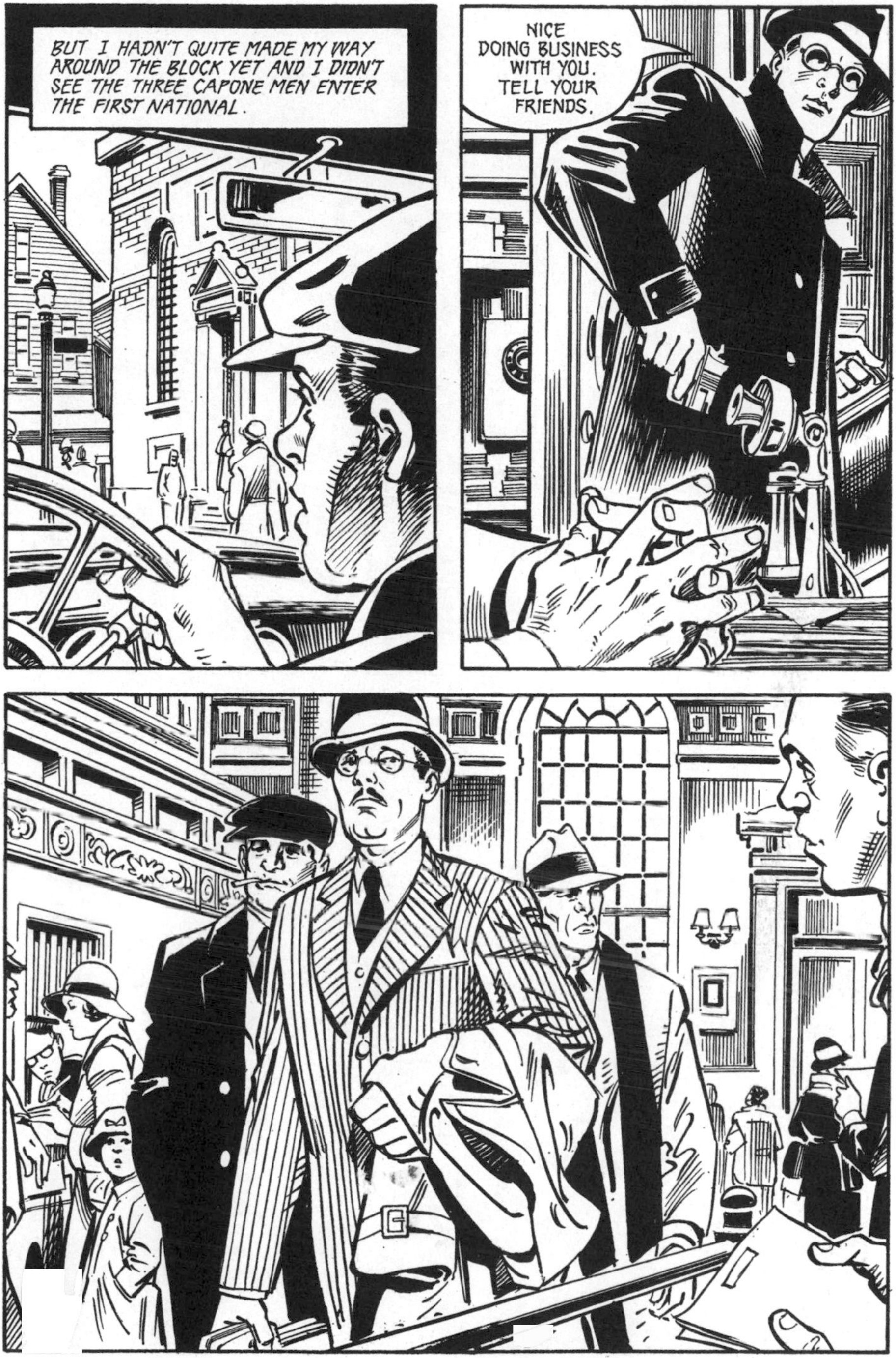
BUT I HADN'T QUITE MADE MY WAY AROUND THE BLOCK YET AND I DIDN'T SEE THE THREE CAPONE MEN ENTER THE FIRST NATIONAL.
NICE DOING BUSINESS WITH YOU. TELL YOUR FRIENDS.

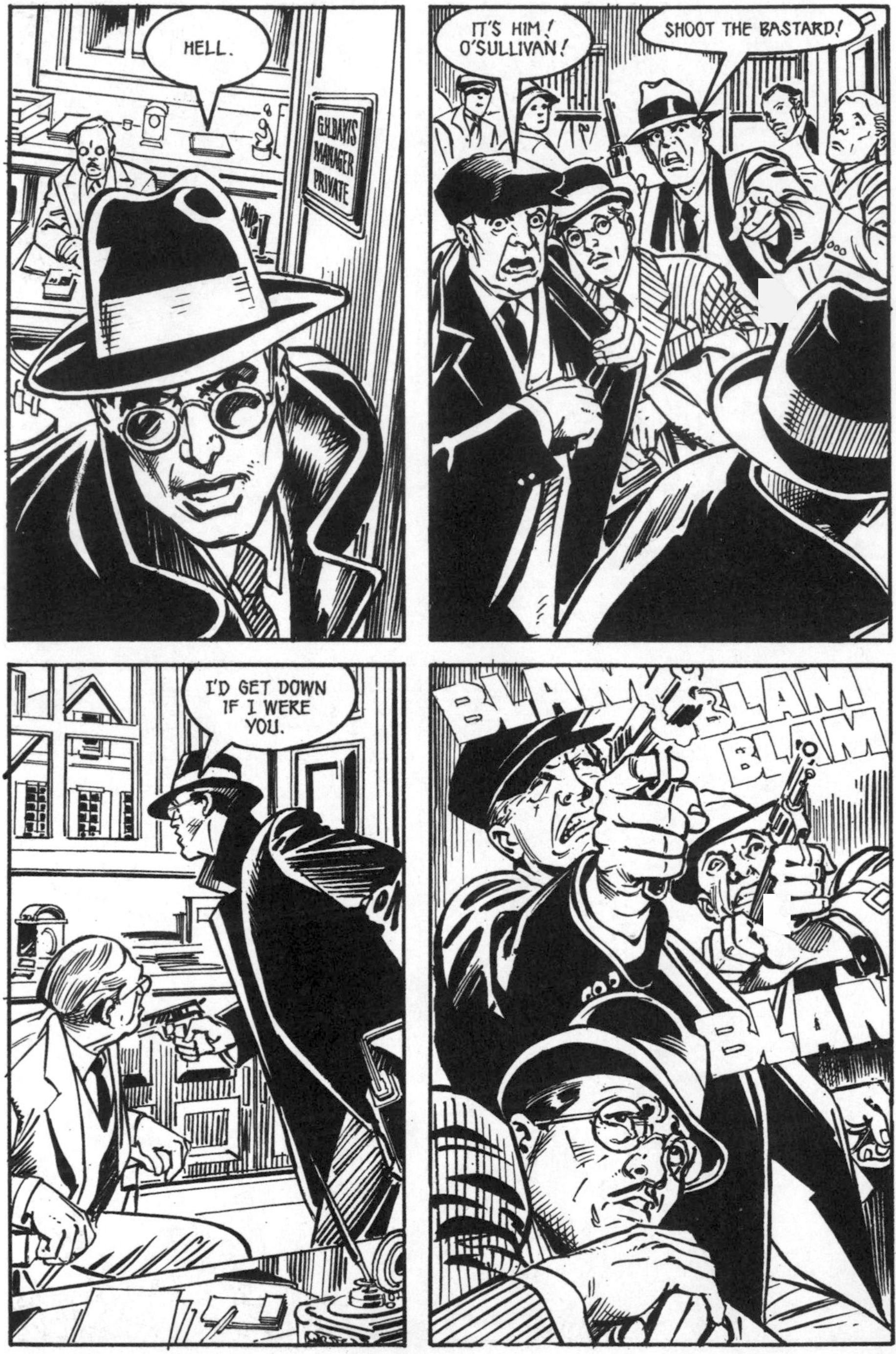
HELL.
G.H. DAVIS MANAGER PRIVATE
IT'S HIM! O'SULLIVAN!
SHOOT THE BASTARD!
I'D GET DOWN IF I WERE YOU.
BLAM
BLAM
BLAM

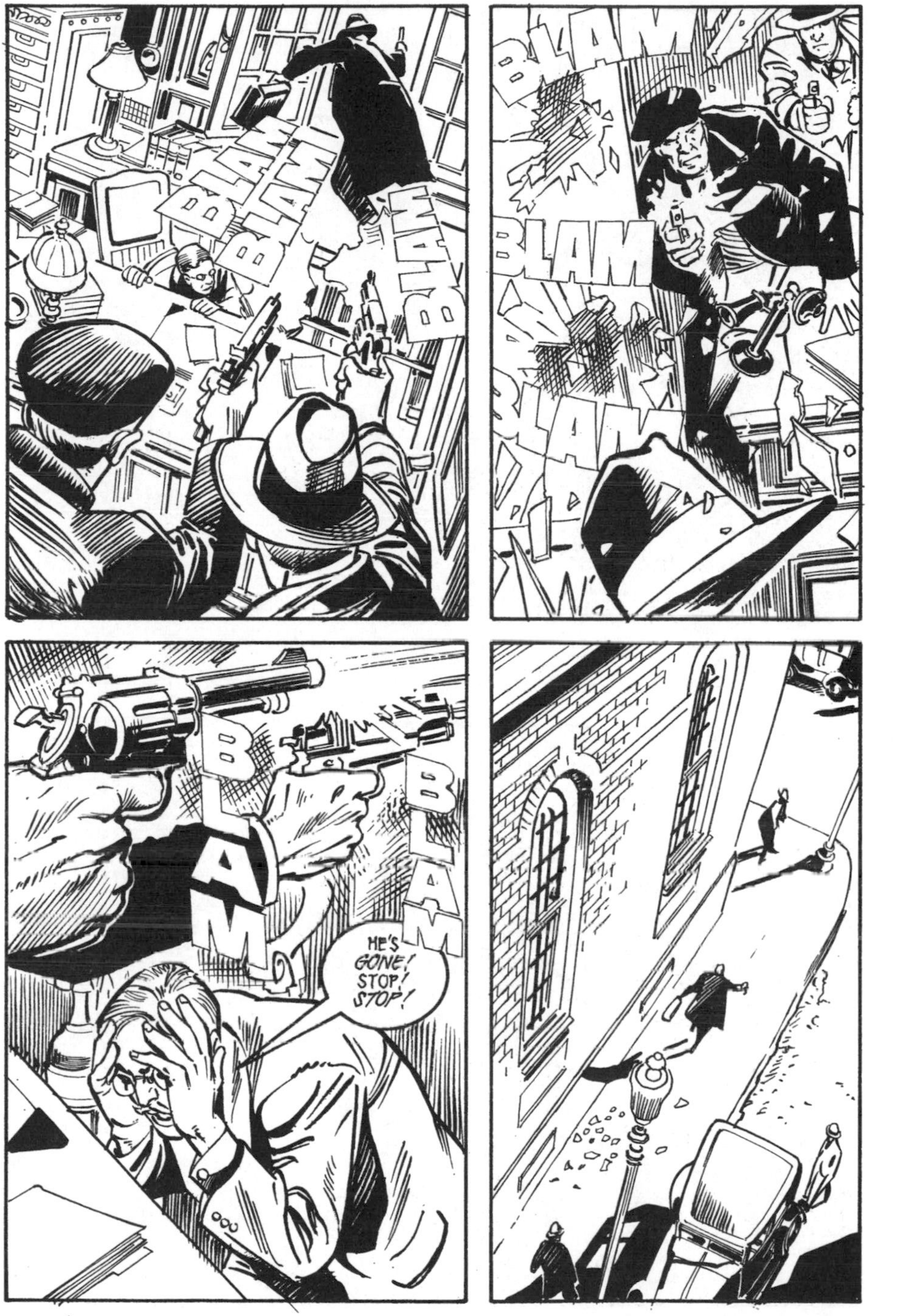
BLAM
BLAM
BLAM
BLAM
BLAM
BLAM
BLAM
BLAM
BLAM
HE'S *GONE!* STOP! STOP!

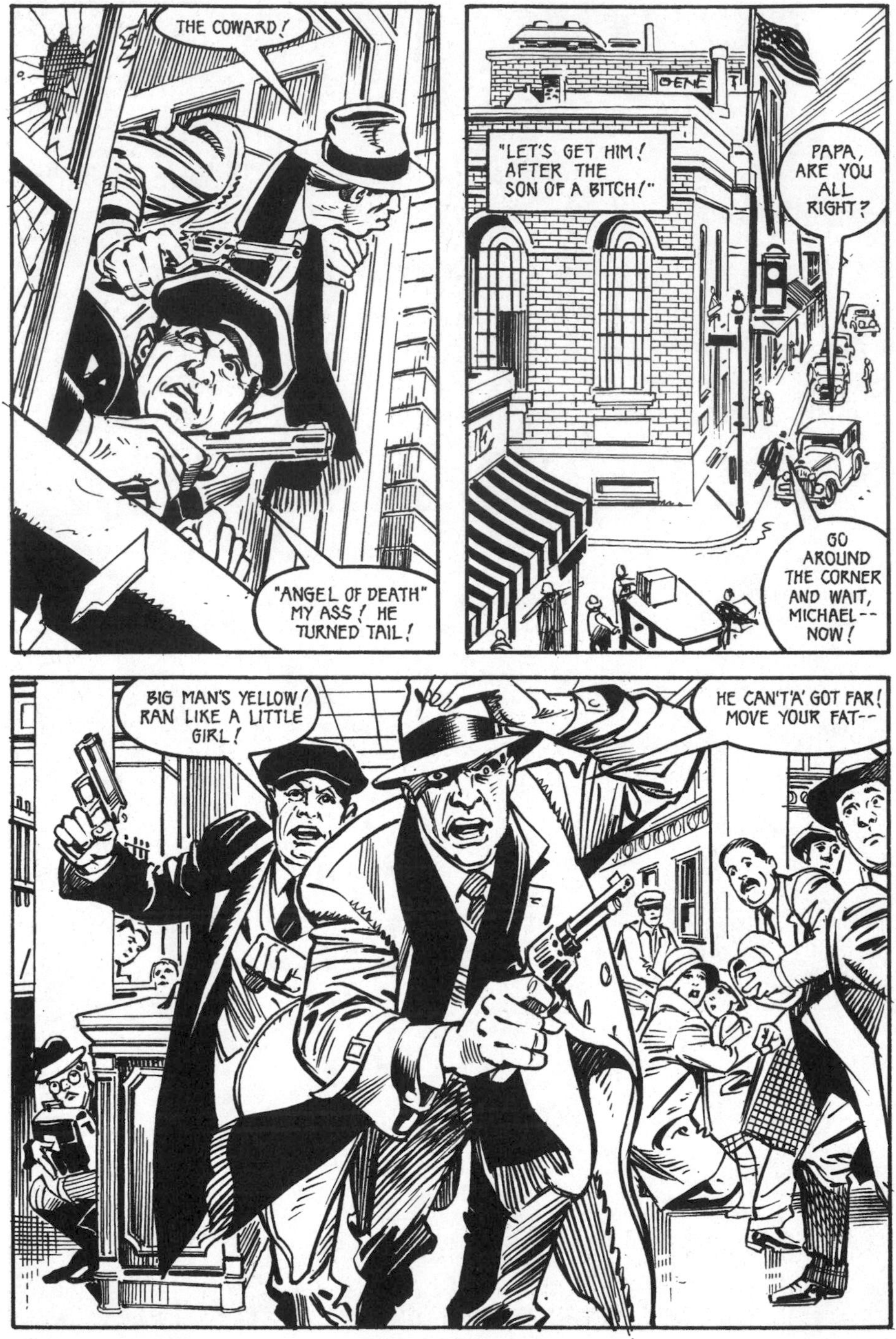
THE COWARD!
"ANGEL OF DEATH" MY ASS! HE TURNED TAIL!
"LET'S GET HIM! AFTER THE SON OF A BITCH!"
PAPA, ARE YOU ALL RIGHT?
GO AROUND THE CORNER AND WAIT, MICHAEL-- NOW!
BIG MAN'S YELLOW! RAN LIKE A LITTLE GIRL!
HE CAN'T'A' GOT FAR! MOVE YOUR FAT--

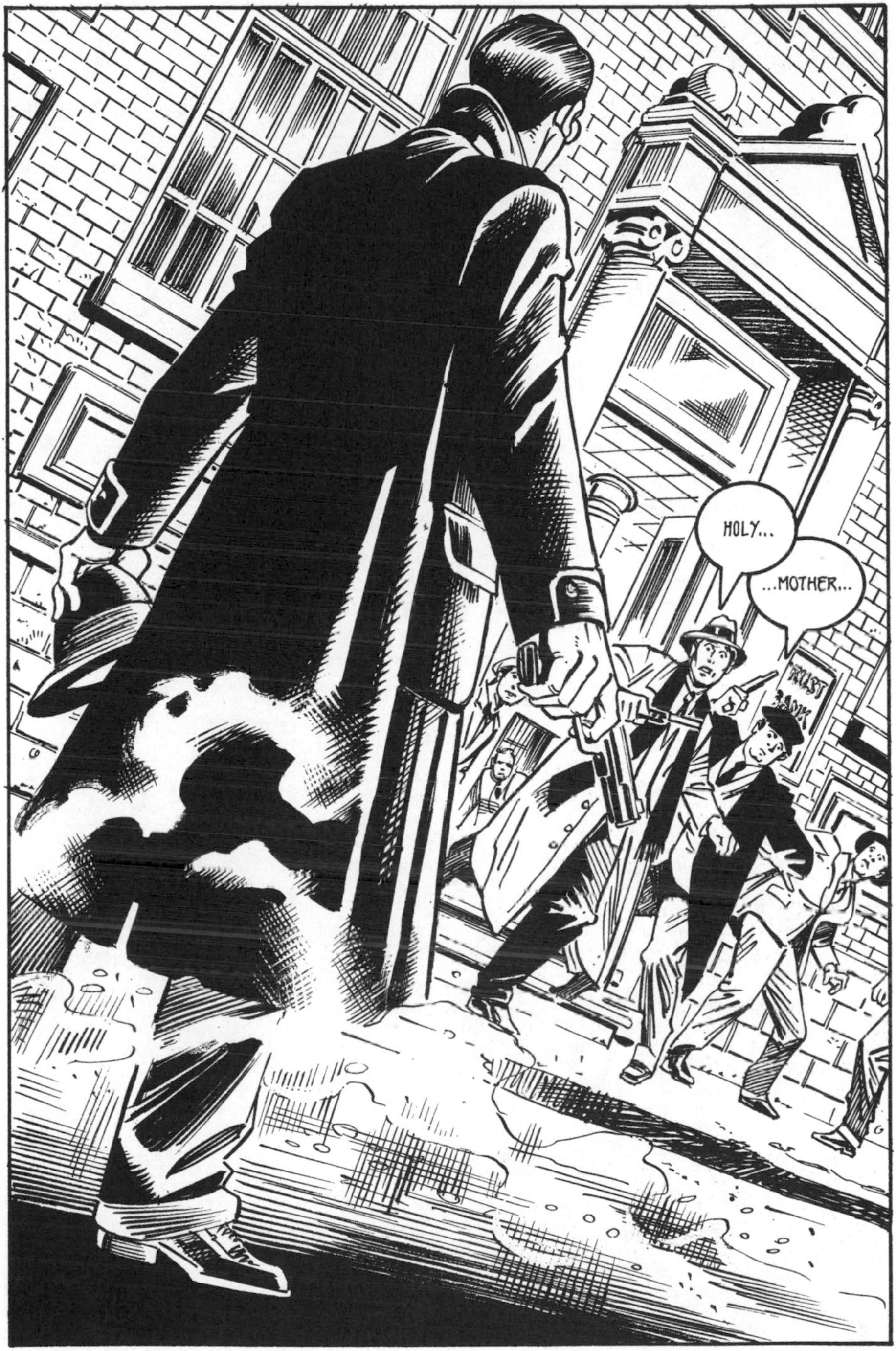
HOLY...
...MOTHER...

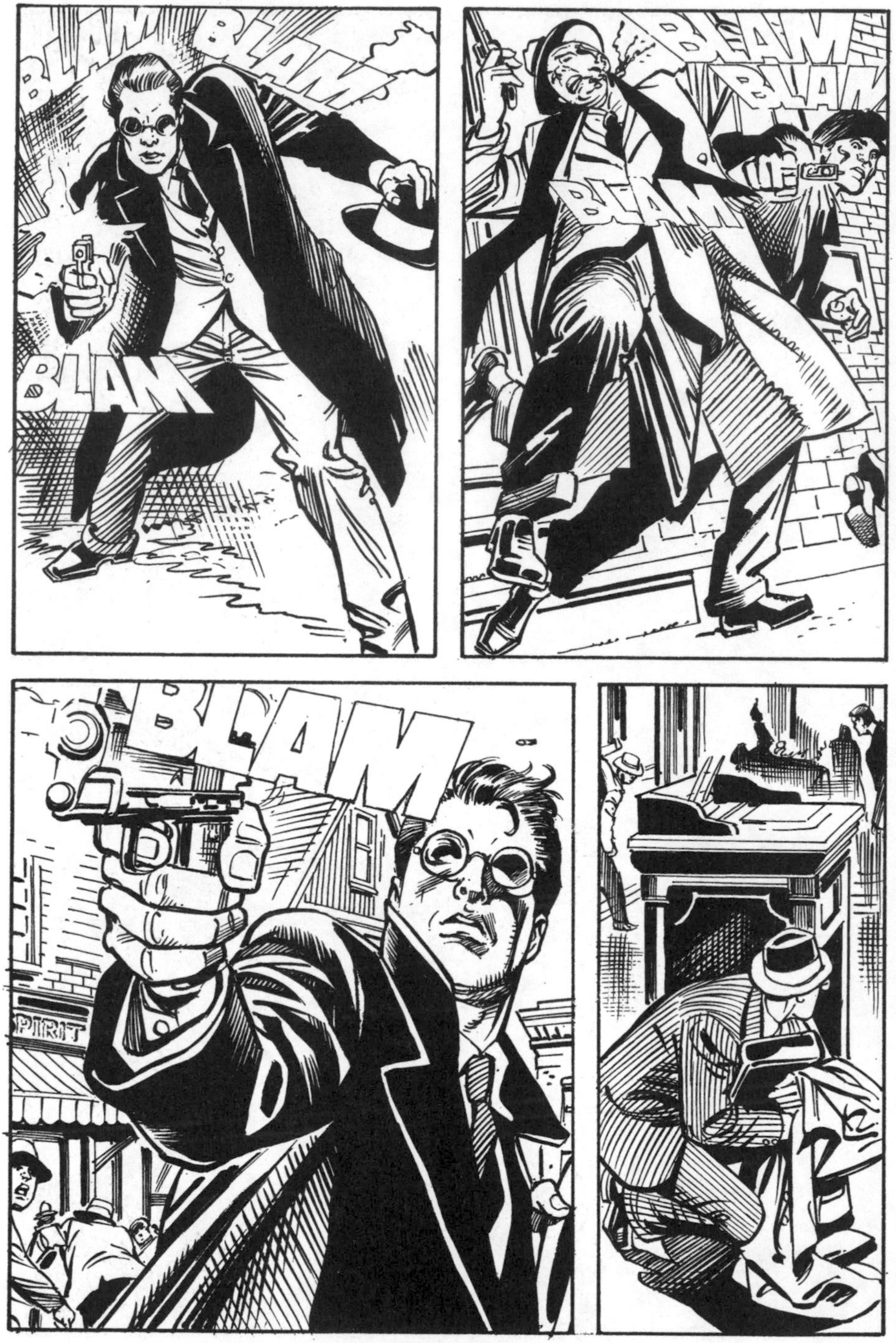
BLAM
BLAM
BLAM
BLAM
BLAM
BLAM
BLAM

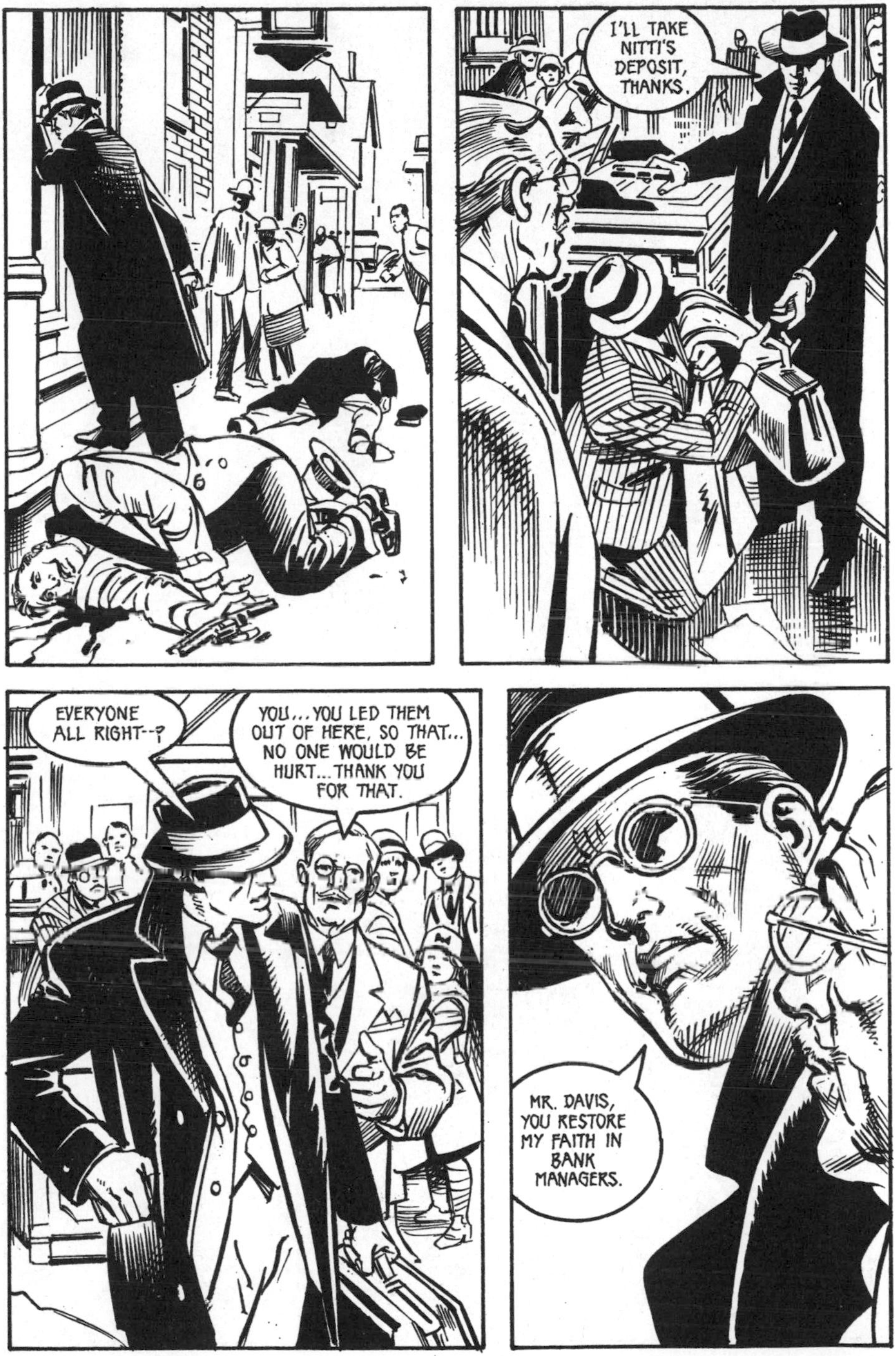
I'LL TAKE NITTI'S DEPOSIT, THANKS.
EVERYONE ALL RIGHT--?
YOU... YOU LED THEM OUT OF HERE, SO THAT... NO ONE WOULD BE HURT... THANK YOU FOR THAT.
MR. DAVIS, YOU RESTORE MY FAITH IN BANK MANAGERS.

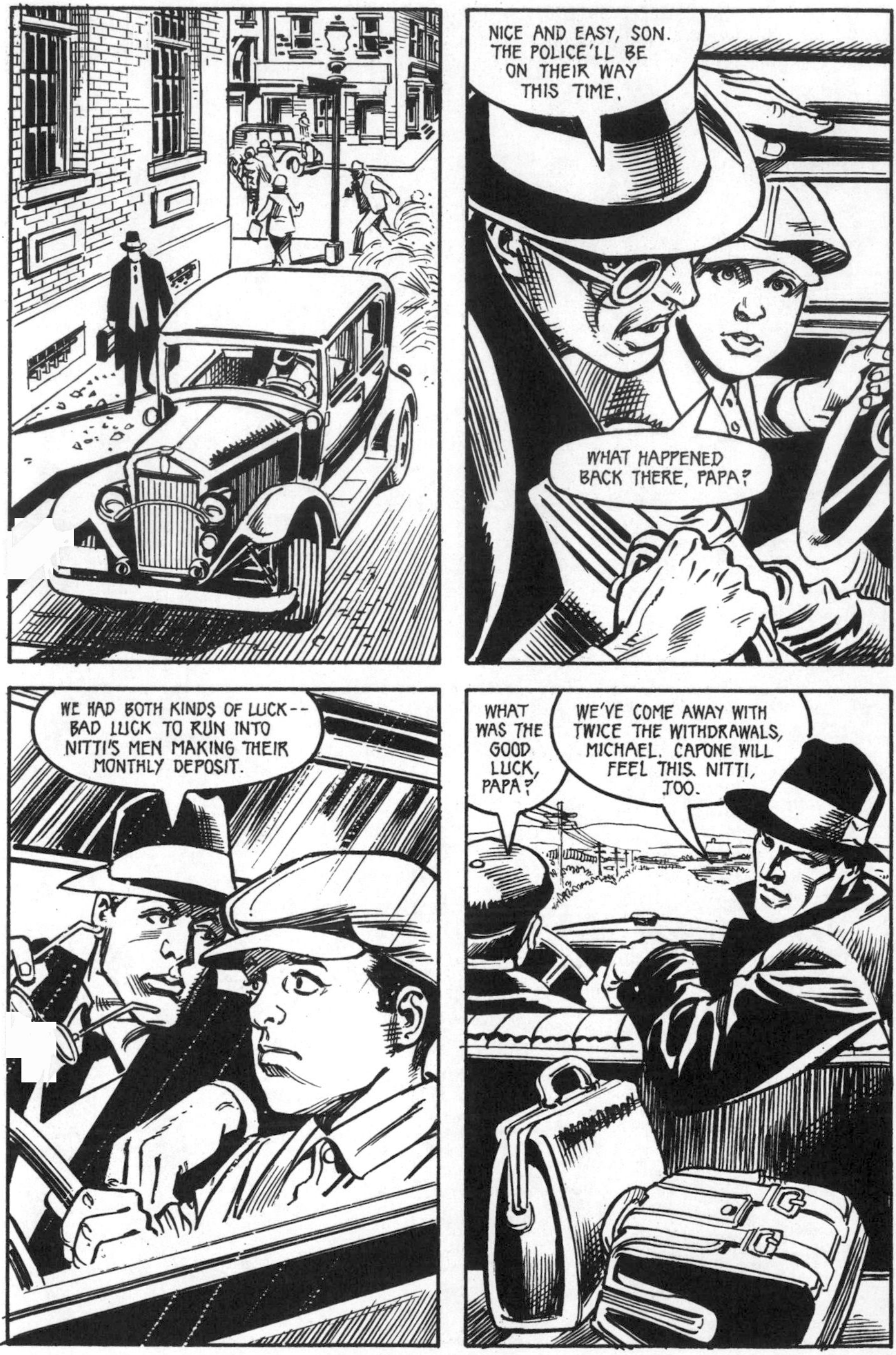
NICE AND EASY, SON. THE POLICE'LL BE ON THEIR WAY THIS TIME.
WHAT HAPPENED BACK THERE, PAPA?
WE HAD BOTH KINDS OF LUCK-- BAD LUCK TO RUN INTO NITTI'S MEN MAKING THEIR MONTHLY DEPOSIT.
WHAT WAS THE GOOD LUCK, PAPA?
WE'VE COME AWAY WITH TWICE THE WITHDRAWALS, MICHAEL. CAPONE WILL FEEL THIS. NITTI, TOO.

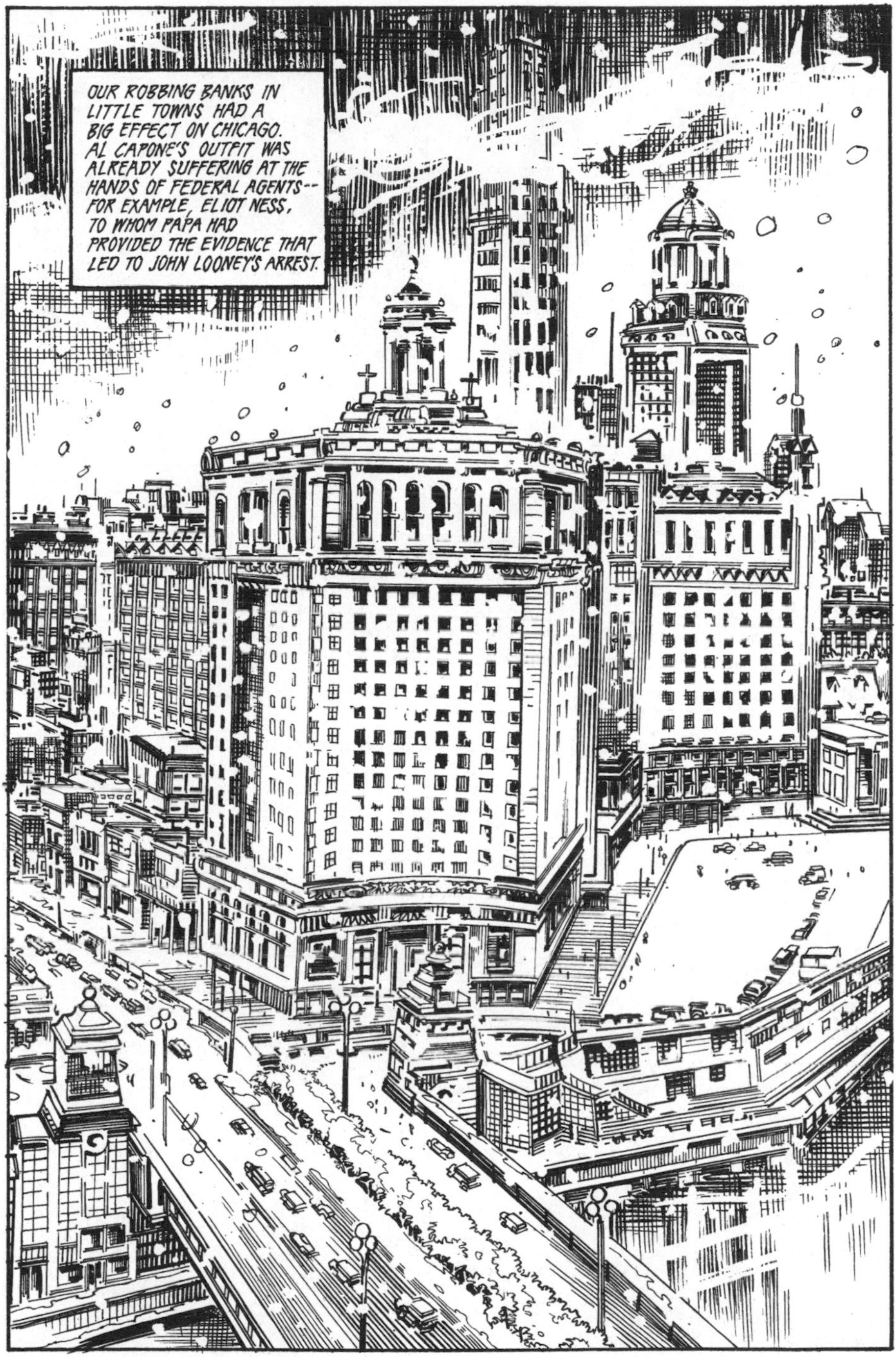
OUR ROBBING BANKS IN LITTLE TOWNS HAD A BIG EFFECT ON CHICAGO. AL CAPONE'S OUTFIT WAS ALREADY SUFFERING AT THE HANDS OF FEDERAL AGENTS-- FOR EXAMPLE, ELIOT NESS, TO WHOM PAPA HAD PROVIDED THE EVIDENCE THAT LED TO JOHN LOONEY'S ARREST.

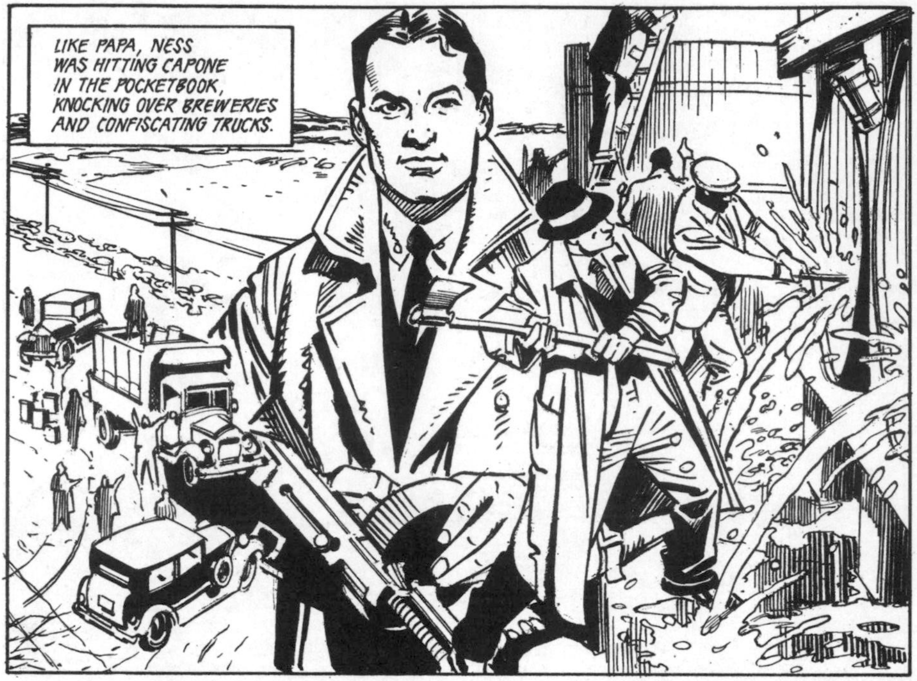
LIKE PAPA, NESS WAS HITTING CAPONE IN THE POCKETBOOK, KNOCKING OVER BREWERIES AND CONFISCATING TRUCKS.

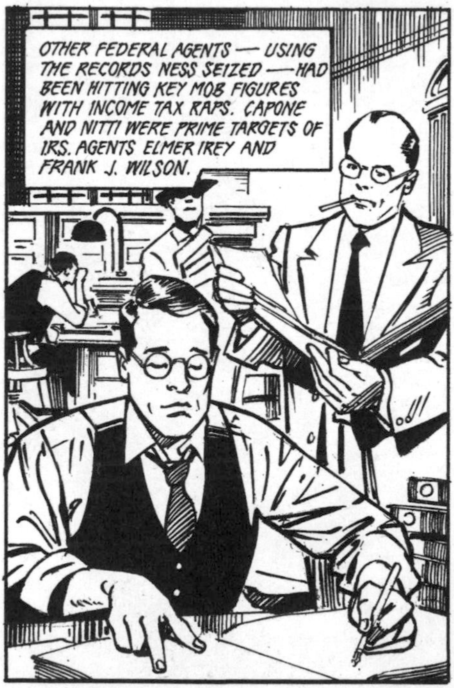
OTHER FEDERAL AGENTS — USING THE RECORDS NESS SEIZED — HAD BEEN HITTING KEY MOB FIGURES WITH INCOME TAX RAPS. CAPONE AND NITTI WERE PRIME TARGETS OF I.R.S. AGENTS ELMER IREY AND FRANK J. WILSON.

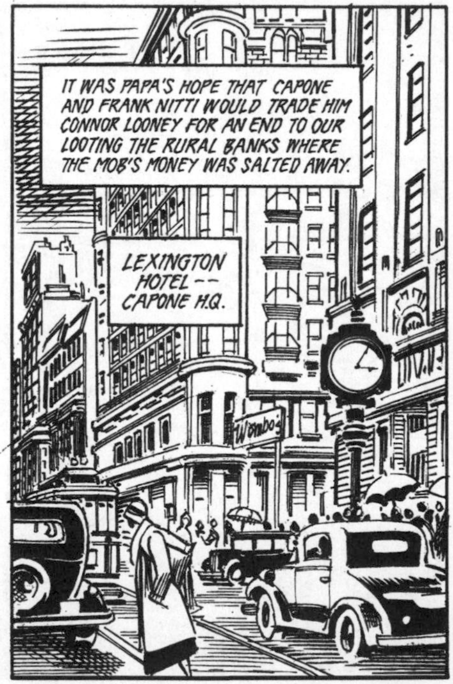
IT WAS PAPA'S HOPE THAT CAPONE AND FRANK NITTI WOULD TRADE HIM CONNOR LOONEY FOR AN END TO OUR LOOTING THE RURAL BANKS WHERE THE MOB'S MONEY WAS SALTED AWAY.
LEXINGTON HOTEL -- CAPONE H.Q.

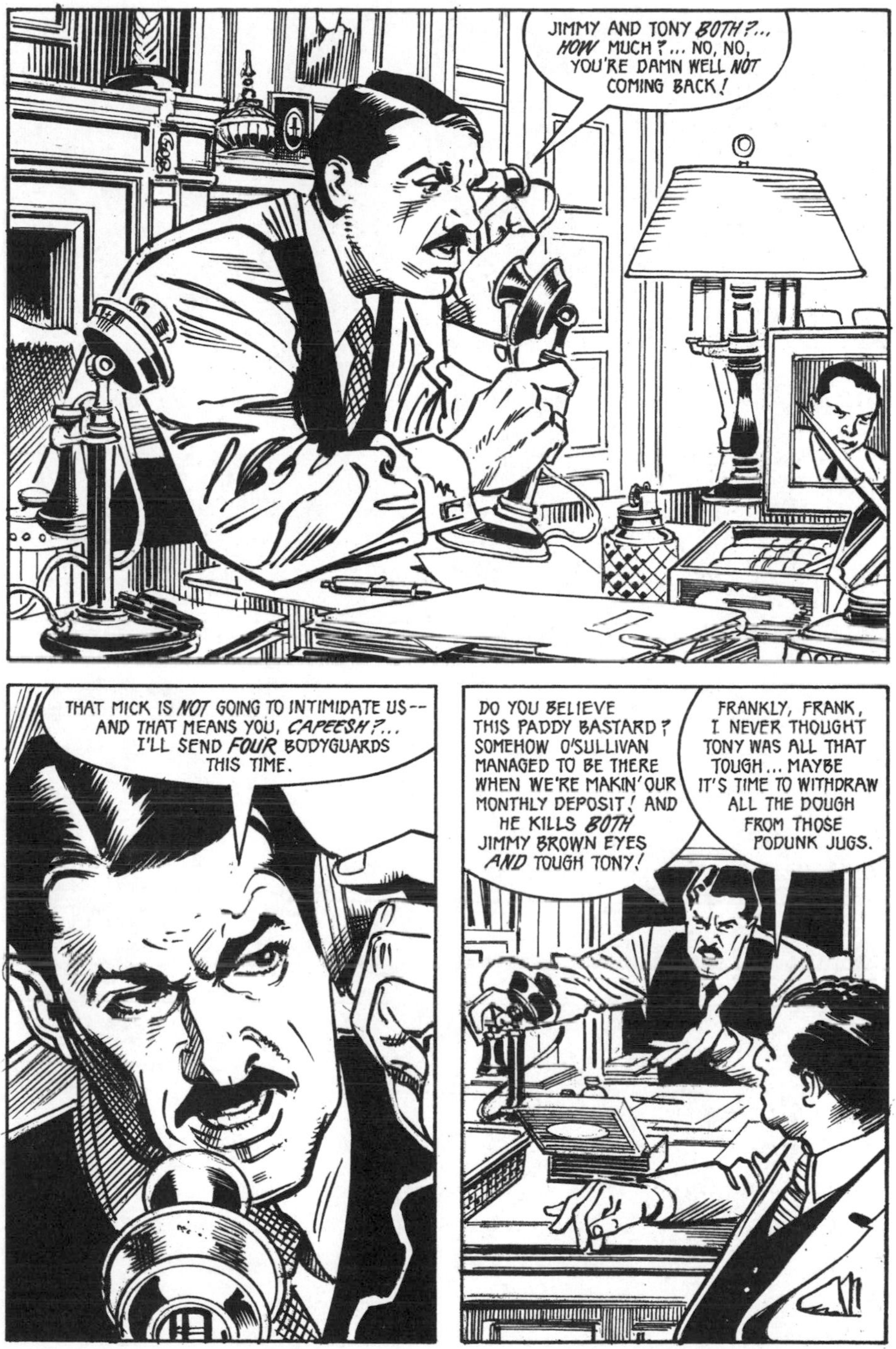
JIMMY AND TONY BOTH?.. HOW MUCH?... NO, NO, YOU'RE DAMN WELL NOT COMING BACK!
THAT MICK IS NOT GOING TO INTIMIDATE US-- AND THAT MEANS YOU, CAPEESH?... I'LL SEND FOUR BODYGUARDS THIS TIME.
DO YOU BELIEVE THIS PADDY BASTARD? SOMEHOW O'SULLIVAN MANAGED TO BE THERE WHEN WE'RE MAKIN' OUR MONTHLY DEPOSIT! AND HE KILLS BOTH JIMMY BROWN EYES AND TOUGH TONY!
FRANKLY, FRANK, I NEVER THOUGHT TONY WAS ALL THAT TOUGH... MAYBE IT'S TIME TO WITHDRAW ALL THE DOUGH FROM THOSE PODUNK JUGS.

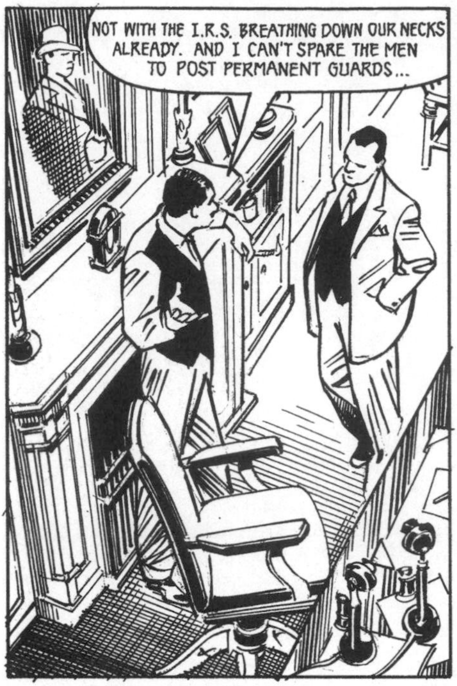
NOT WITH THE I.R.S. BREATHING DOWN OUR NECKS ALREADY. AND I CAN'T SPARE THE MEN TO POST PERMANENT GUARDS...

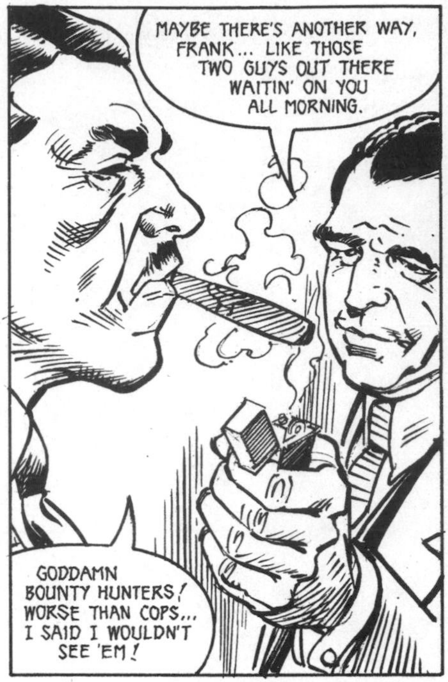
MAYBE THERE'S ANOTHER WAY, FRANK... LIKE THOSE TWO GUYS OUT THERE WAITIN' ON YOU ALL MORNING.
GODDAMN BOUNTY HUNTERS! WORSE THAN COPS... I SAID I WOULDN'T SEE 'EM!

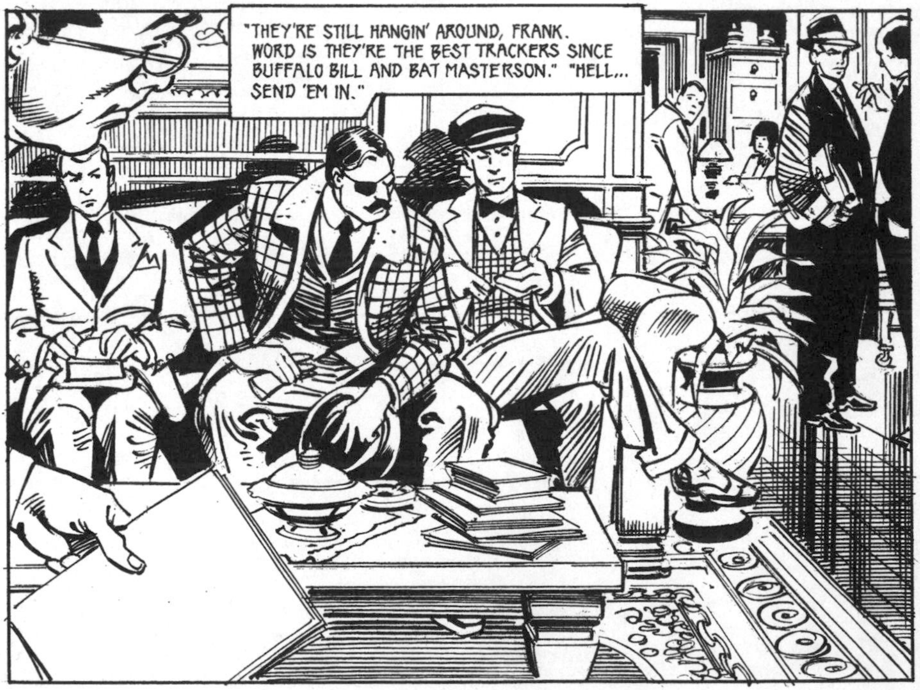
"THEY'RE STILL HANGIN' AROUND, FRANK. WORD IS THEY'RE THE BEST TRACKERS SINCE BUFFALO BILL AND BAT MASTERSON." "HELL... SEND 'EM IN."

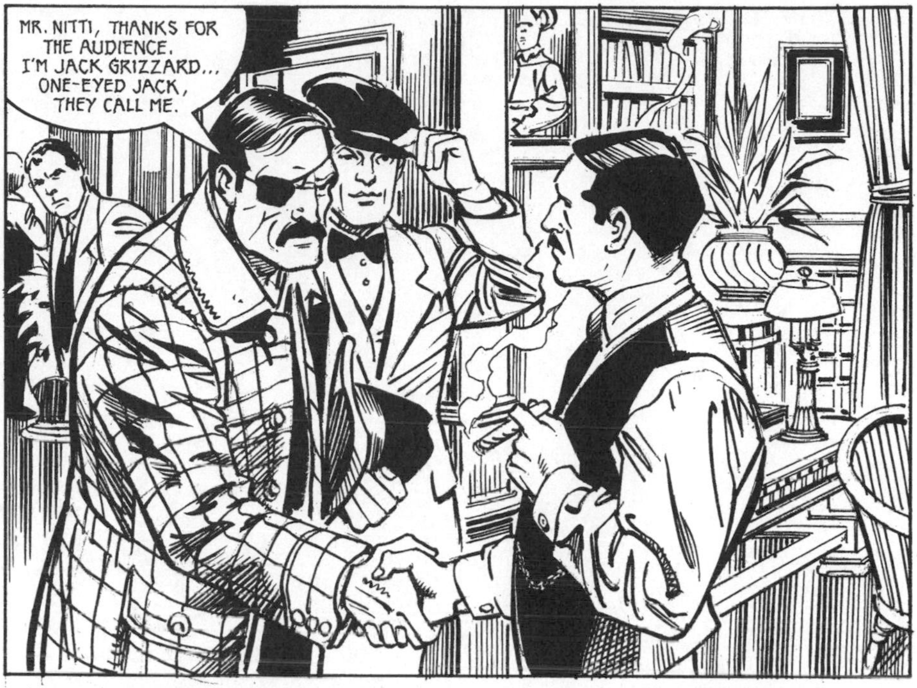
MR. NITTI, THANKS FOR THE AUDIENCE. I'M JACK GRIZZARD... ONE-EYED JACK, THEY CALL ME.

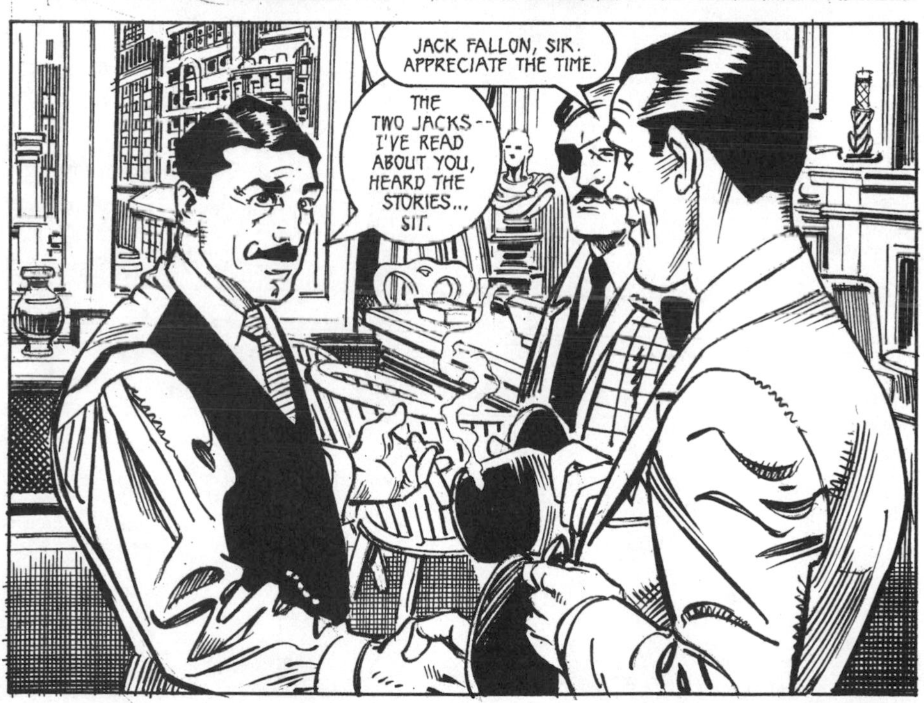
JACK FALLON, SIR. APPRECIATE THE TIME.
THE TWO JACKS-- I'VE READ ABOUT YOU, HEARD THE STORIES... SIT.

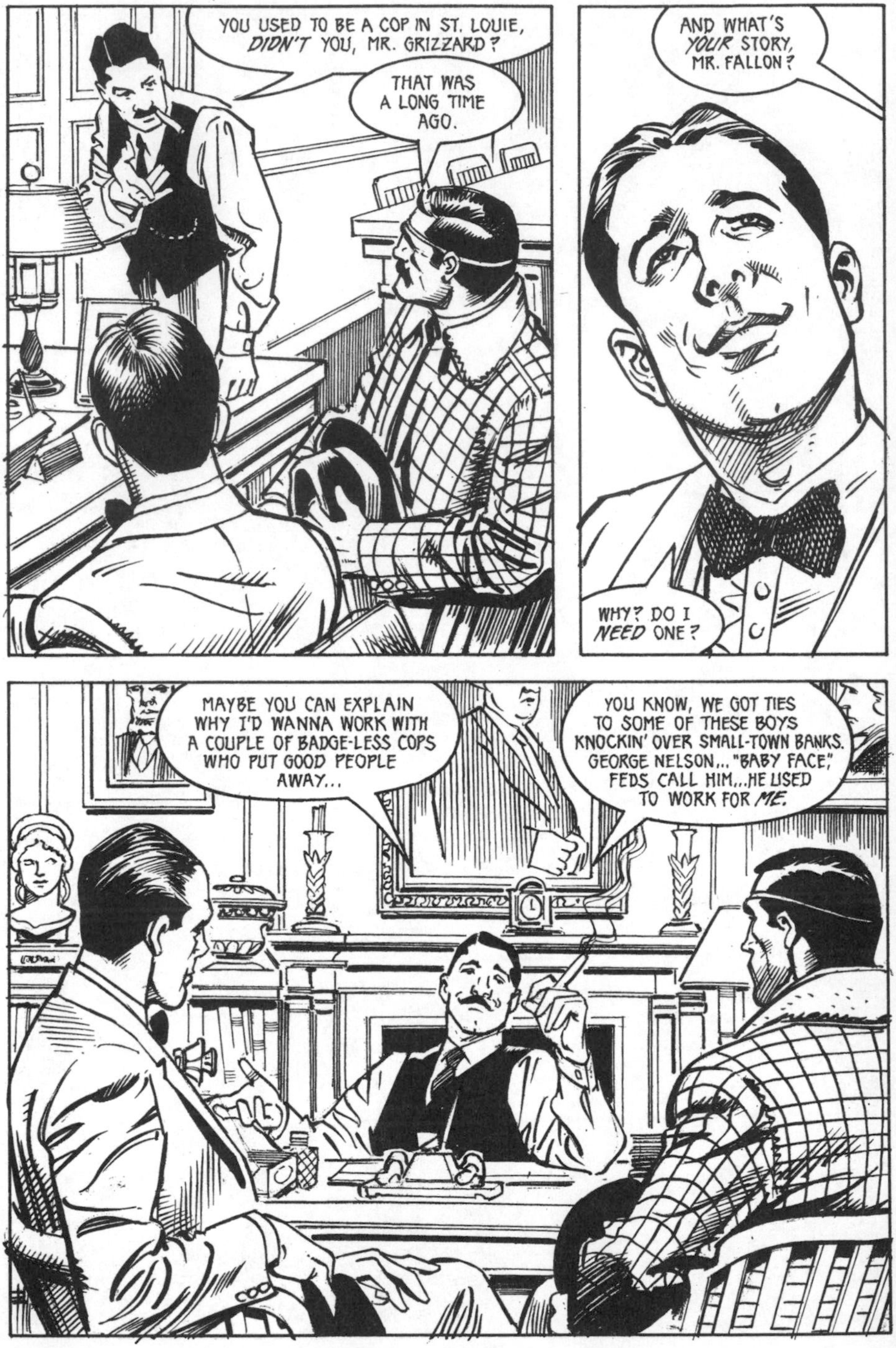

YOU USED TO BE A COP IN ST. LOUIE, *DIDN'T* YOU, MR. GRIZZARD?
THAT WAS A LONG TIME AGO.
AND WHAT'S *YOUR* STORY, MR. FALLON?
WHY? DO I *NEED* ONE?
MAYBE YOU CAN EXPLAIN WHY I'D WANNA WORK WITH A COUPLE OF BADGE-LESS COPS WHO PUT GOOD PEOPLE AWAY...
YOU KNOW, WE GOT TIES TO SOME OF THESE BOYS KNOCKIN' OVER SMALL-TOWN BANKS. GEORGE NELSON... "BABY FACE," FEDS CALL HIM... HE USED TO WORK FOR *ME*.

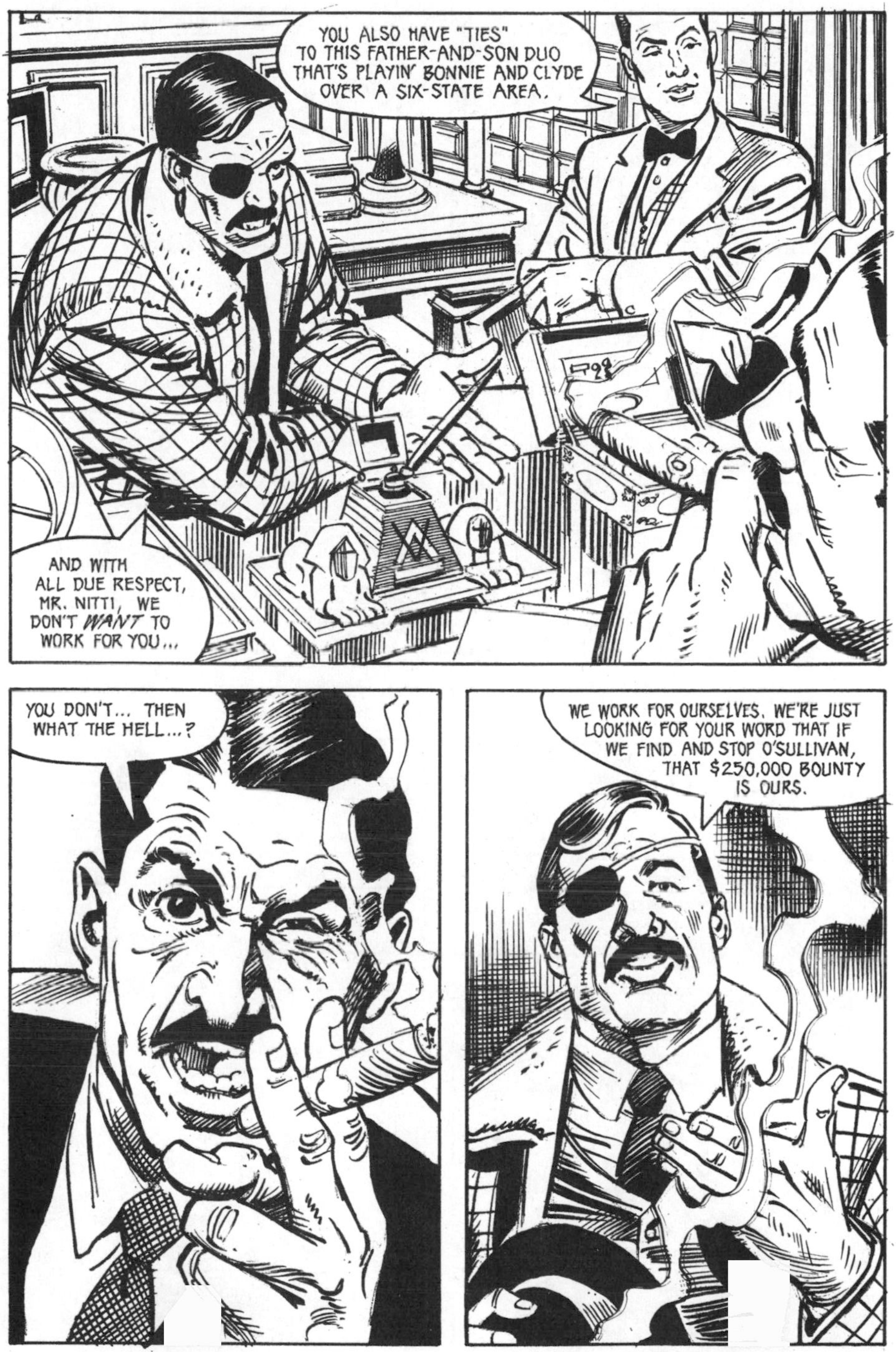
YOU ALSO HAVE "TIES" TO THIS FATHER-AND-SON DUO THAT'S PLAYIN' BONNIE AND CLYDE OVER A SIX-STATE AREA.
AND WITH ALL DUE RESPECT, MR. NITTI, WE DON'T *WANT* TO WORK FOR YOU...
YOU DON'T... THEN WHAT THE HELL...?
WE WORK FOR OURSELVES. WE'RE JUST LOOKING FOR YOUR WORD THAT IF WE FIND AND STOP O'SULLIVAN, THAT $250,000 BOUNTY IS OURS.

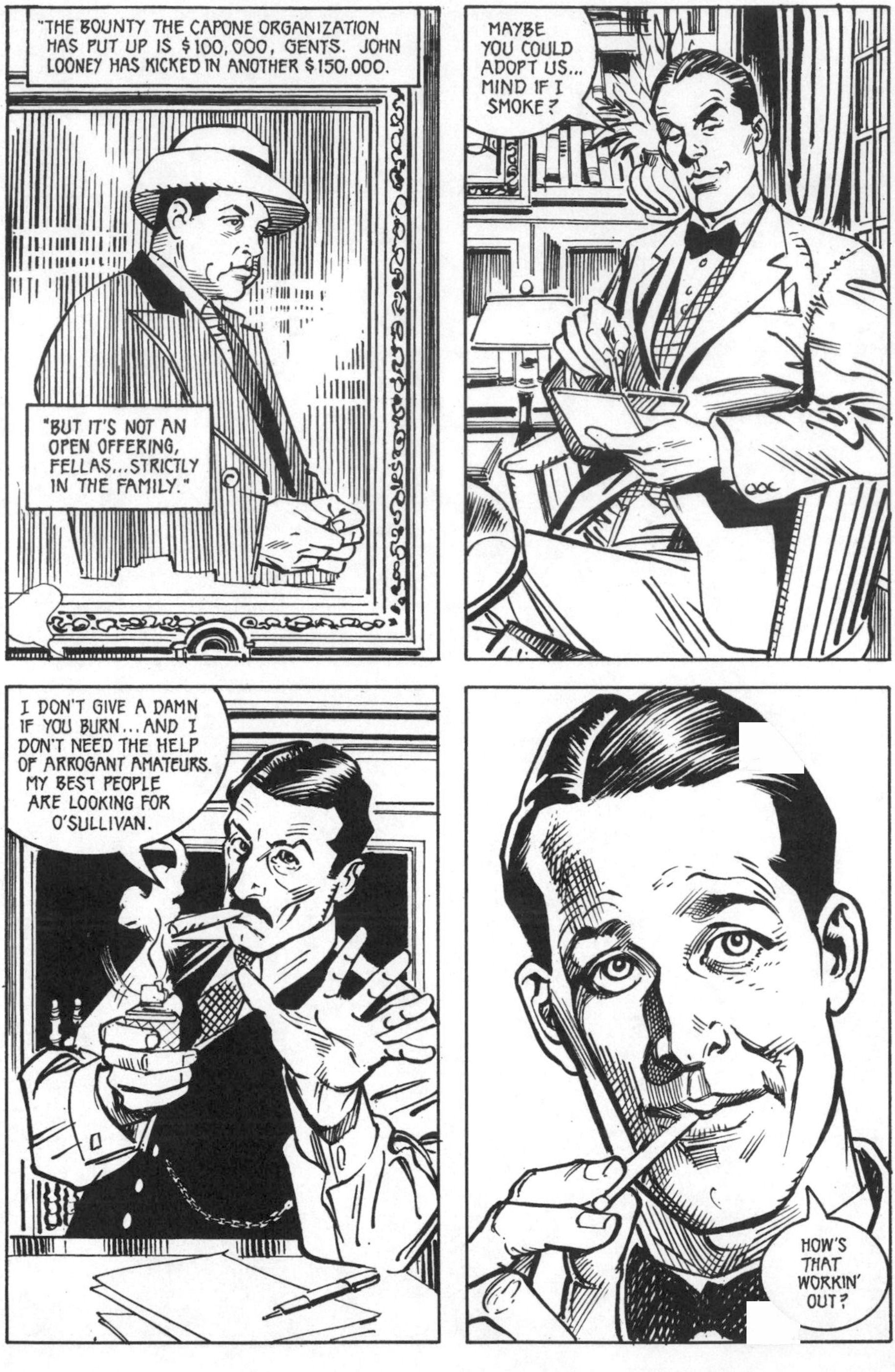
"THE BOUNTY THE CAPONE ORGANIZATION HAS PUT UP IS $100,000, GENTS. JOHN LOONEY HAS KICKED IN ANOTHER $150,000.
"BUT IT'S NOT AN OPEN OFFERING, FELLAS...STRICTLY IN THE FAMILY."
MAYBE YOU COULD ADOPT US... MIND IF I SMOKE?
I DON'T GIVE A DAMN IF YOU BURN... AND I DON'T NEED THE HELP OF ARROGANT AMATEURS. MY BEST PEOPLE ARE LOOKING FOR O'SULLIVAN.
HOW'S THAT WORKIN' OUT?

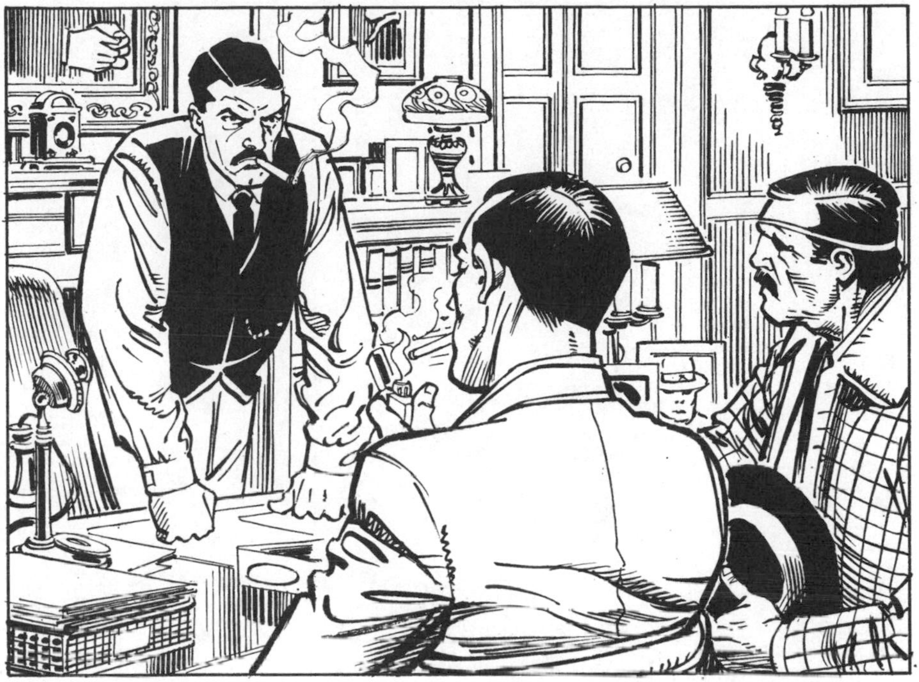

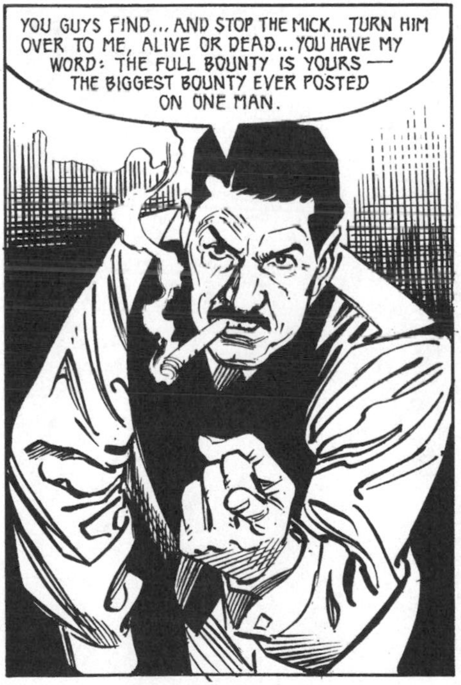
YOU GUYS FIND... AND STOP THE MICK... TURN HIM OVER TO ME, ALIVE OR DEAD... YOU HAVE MY WORD: THE FULL BOUNTY IS YOURS — THE BIGGEST BOUNTY EVER POSTED ON ONE MAN.

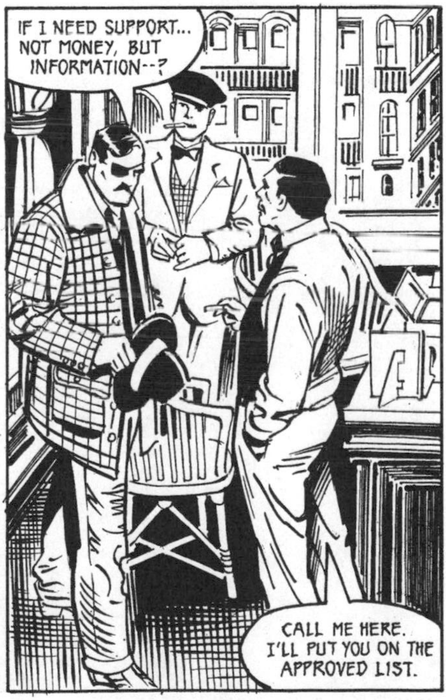
IF I NEED SUPPORT... NOT MONEY, BUT INFORMATION--?
CALL ME HERE. I'LL PUT YOU ON THE APPROVED LIST.

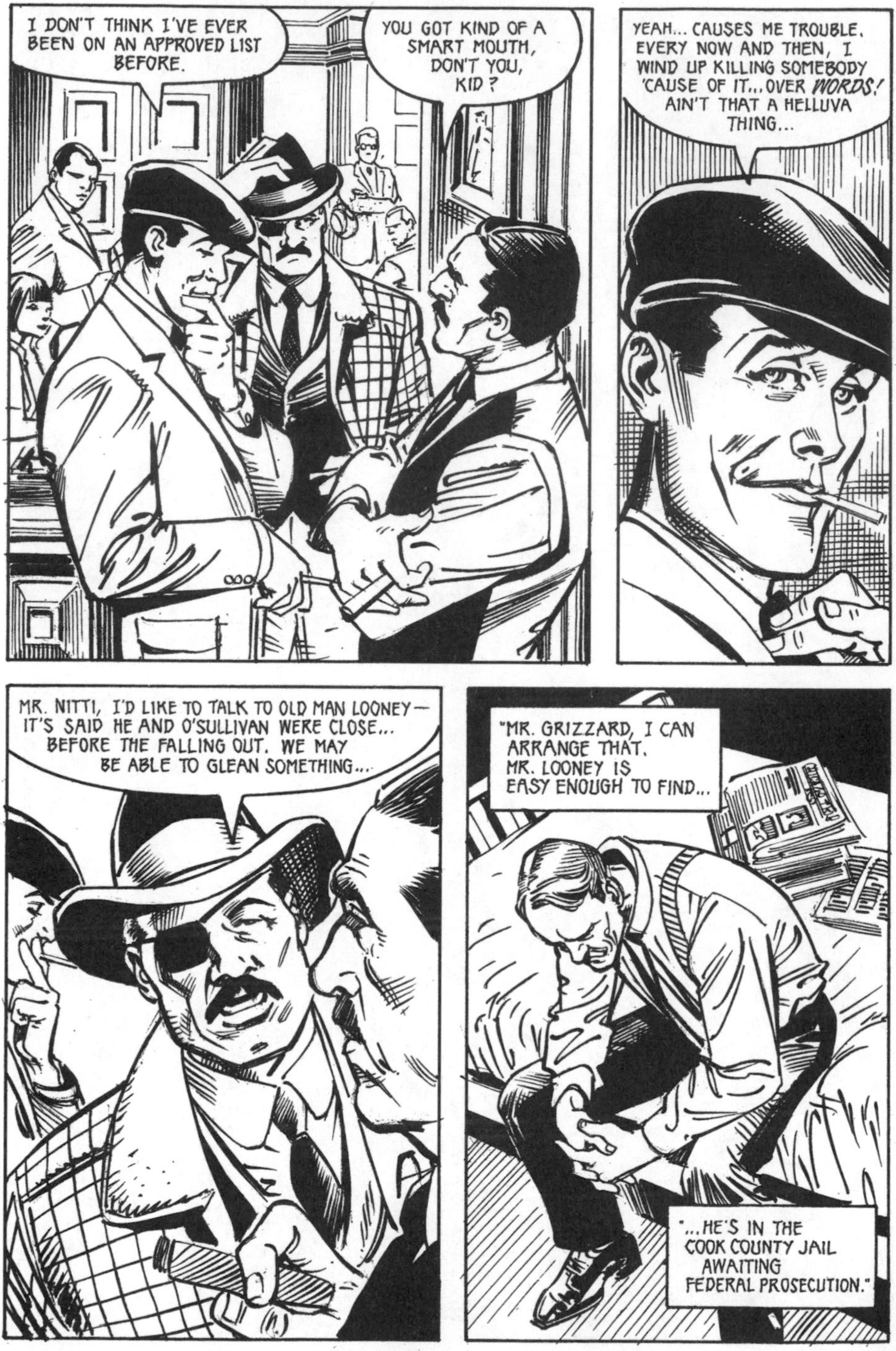
I DON'T THINK I'VE EVER BEEN ON AN APPROVED LIST BEFORE.
YOU GOT KIND OF A SMART MOUTH, DON'T YOU, KID?
YEAH... CAUSES ME TROUBLE. EVERY NOW AND THEN, I WIND UP KILLING SOMEBODY 'CAUSE OF IT... OVER *WORDS!* AIN'T THAT A HELLUVA THING...
MR. NITTI, I'D LIKE TO TALK TO OLD MAN LOONEY— IT'S SAID HE AND O'SULLIVAN WERE CLOSE... BEFORE THE FALLING OUT. WE MAY BE ABLE TO GLEAN SOMETHING...
"MR. GRIZZARD, I CAN ARRANGE THAT. MR. LOONEY IS EASY ENOUGH TO FIND...
"...HE'S IN THE COOK COUNTY JAIL AWAITING FEDERAL PROSECUTION."

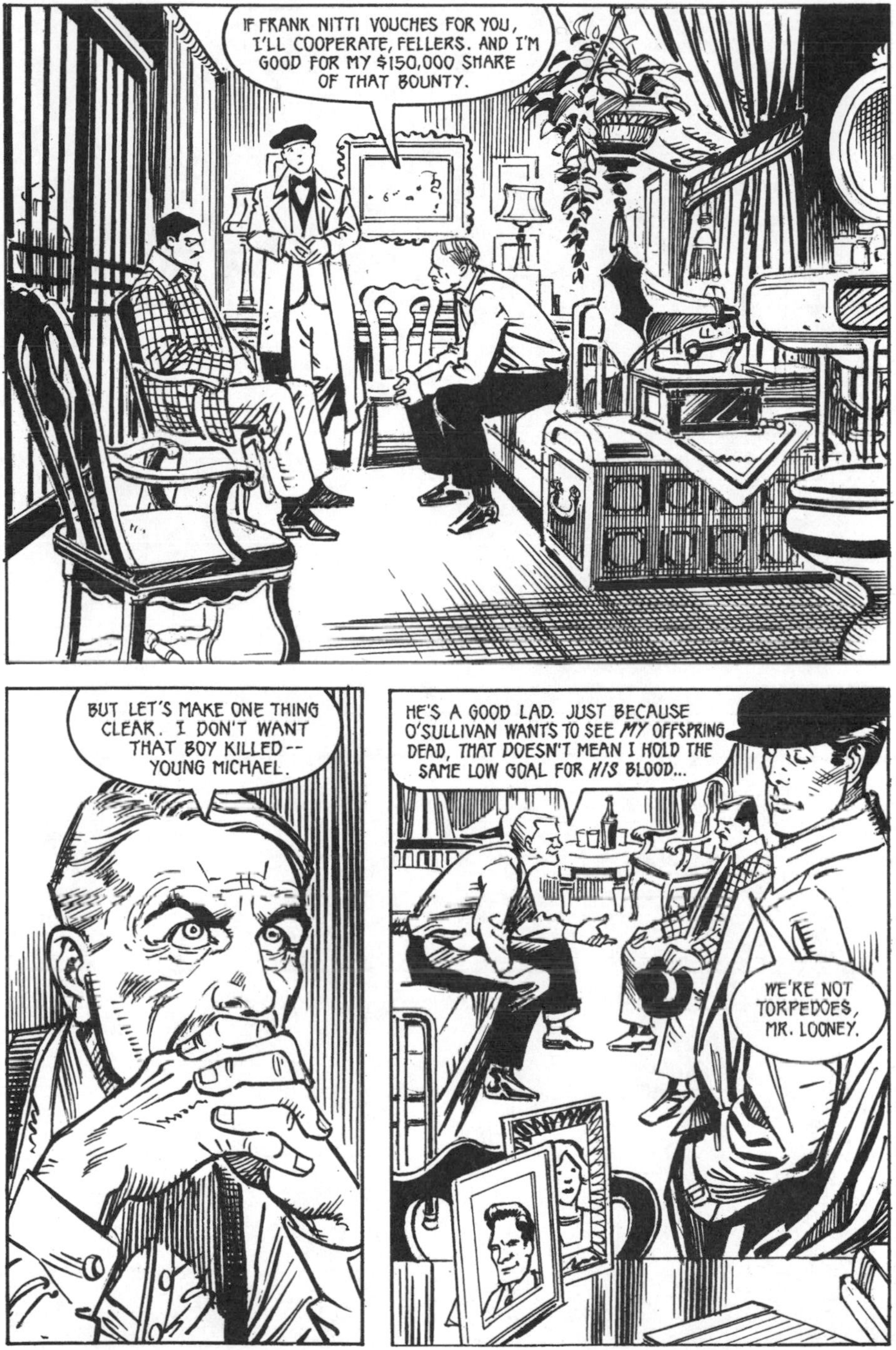
IF FRANK NITTI VOUCHES FOR YOU, I'LL COOPERATE, FELLERS. AND I'M GOOD FOR MY $150,000 SHARE OF THAT BOUNTY.
BUT LET'S MAKE ONE THING CLEAR. I DON'T WANT THAT BOY KILLED-- YOUNG MICHAEL.
HE'S A GOOD LAD. JUST BECAUSE O'SULLIVAN WANTS TO SEE *MY* OFFSPRING DEAD, THAT DOESN'T MEAN I HOLD THE SAME LOW GOAL FOR *HIS* BLOOD...
WE'RE NOT TORPEDOES, MR. LOONEY.

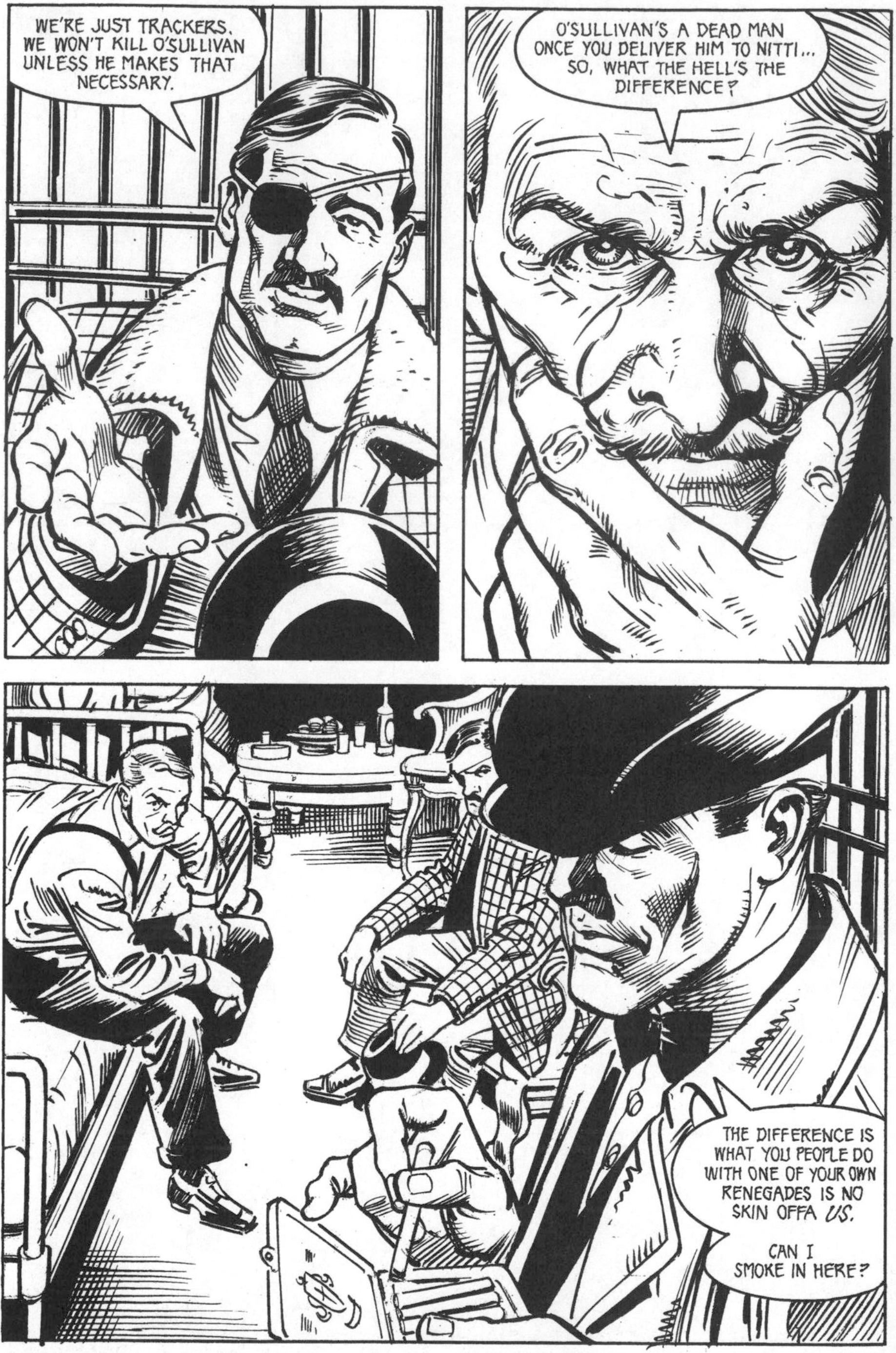

WE'RE JUST TRACKERS. WE WON'T KILL O'SULLIVAN UNLESS HE MAKES THAT NECESSARY.
O'SULLIVAN'S A DEAD MAN ONCE YOU DELIVER HIM TO NITTI... SO, WHAT THE HELL'S THE DIFFERENCE?
THE DIFFERENCE IS WHAT YOU PEOPLE DO WITH ONE OF YOUR OWN RENEGADES IS NO SKIN OFFA *US.*
CAN I SMOKE IN HERE?

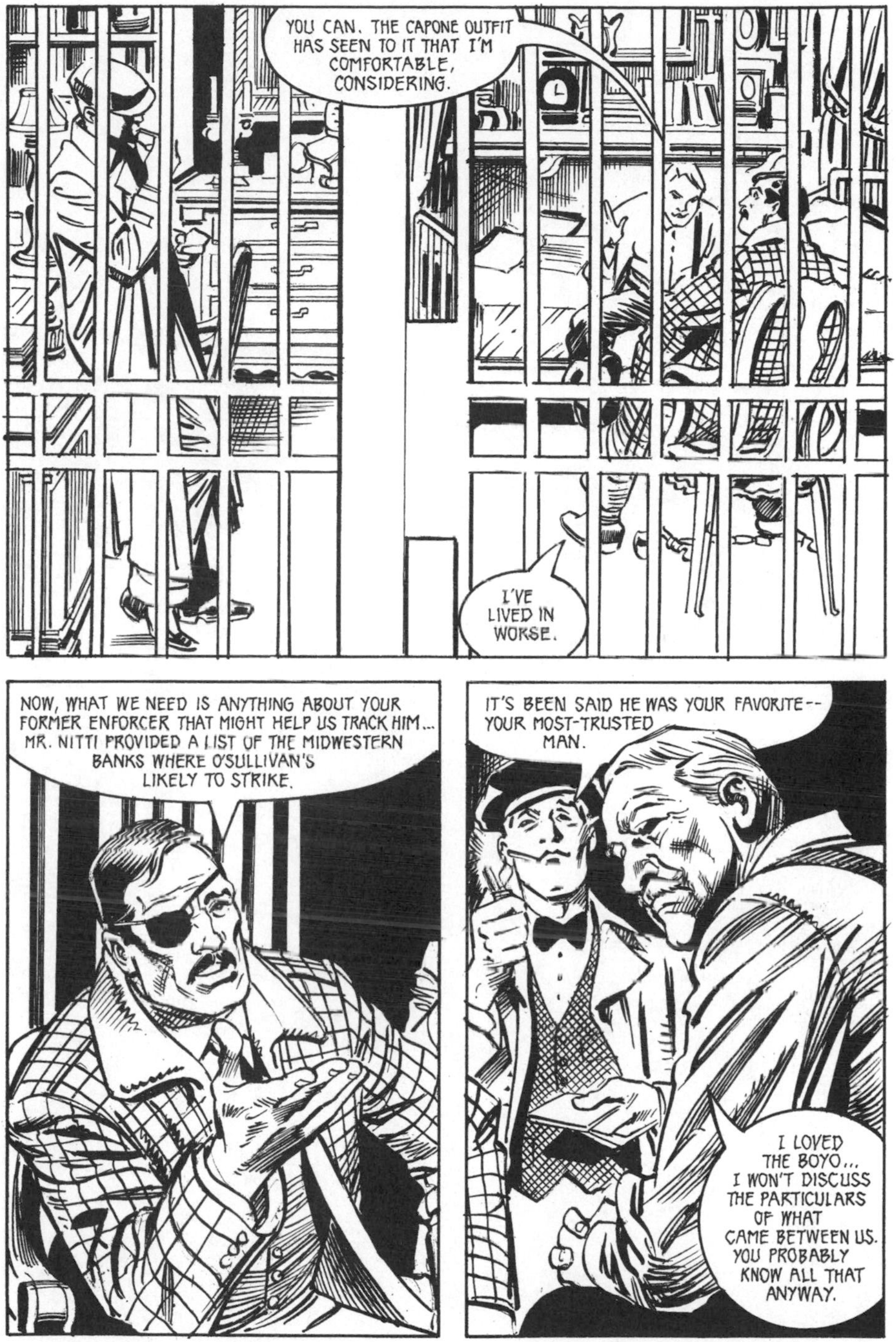
YOU CAN. THE CAPONE OUTFIT HAS SEEN TO IT THAT I'M COMFORTABLE, CONSIDERING.
I'VE LIVED IN WORSE.
NOW, WHAT WE NEED IS ANYTHING ABOUT YOUR FORMER ENFORCER THAT MIGHT HELP US TRACK HIM... MR. NITTI PROVIDED A LIST OF THE MIDWESTERN BANKS WHERE O'SULLIVAN'S LIKELY TO STRIKE.
IT'S BEEN SAID HE WAS YOUR FAVORITE-- YOUR MOST-TRUSTED MAN.
I LOVED THE BOYO... I WON'T DISCUSS THE PARTICULARS OF WHAT CAME BETWEEN US. YOU PROBABLY KNOW ALL THAT ANYWAY.

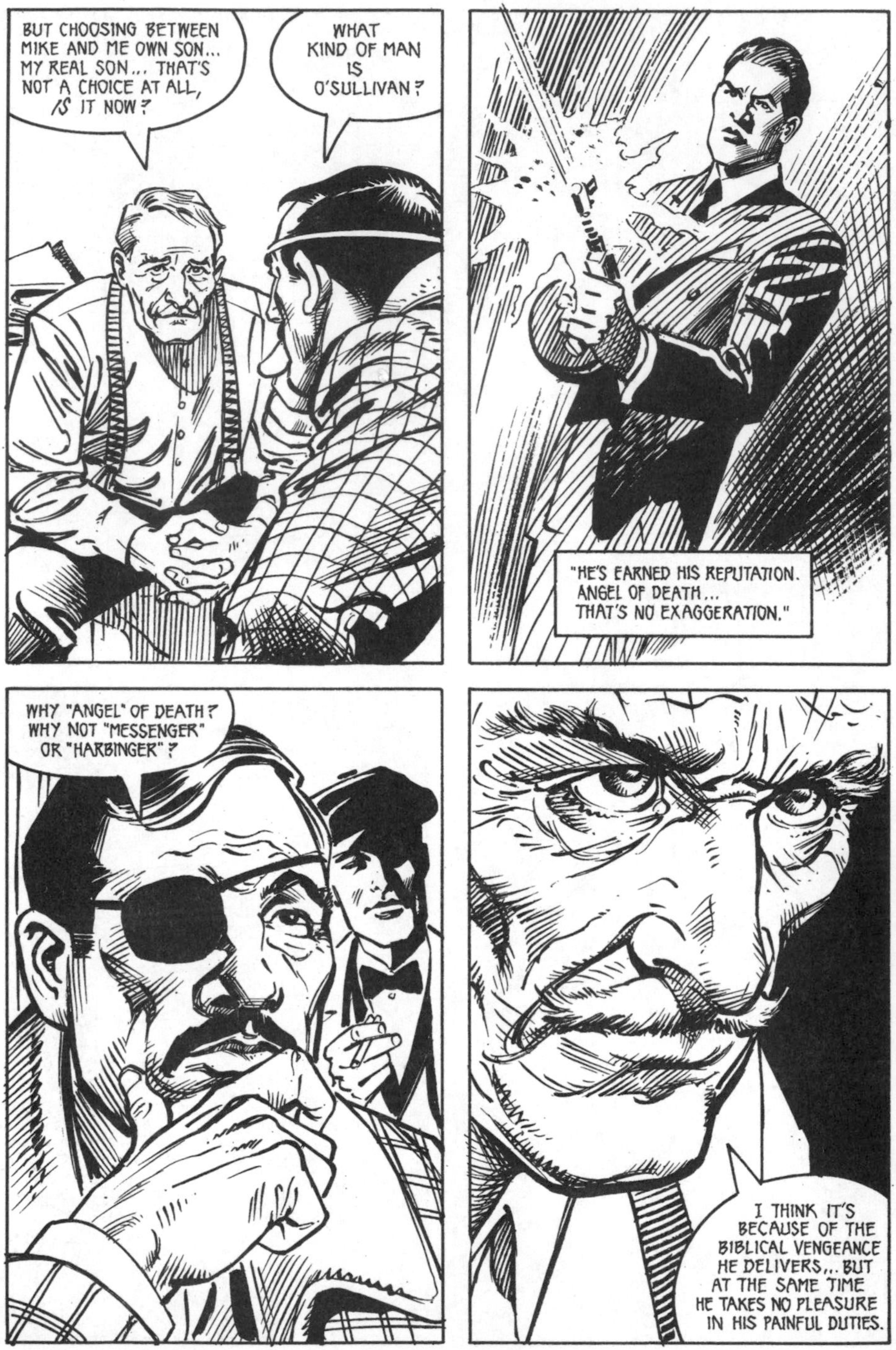
BUT CHOOSING BETWEEN MIKE AND ME OWN SON... MY REAL SON... THAT'S NOT A CHOICE AT ALL, IS IT NOW?
WHAT KIND OF MAN IS O'SULLIVAN?
"HE'S EARNED HIS REPUTATION. ANGEL OF DEATH... THAT'S NO EXAGGERATION."
WHY "ANGEL" OF DEATH? WHY NOT "MESSENGER" OR "HARBINGER"?
I THINK IT'S BECAUSE OF THE BIBLICAL VENGEANCE HE DELIVERS... BUT AT THE SAME TIME HE TAKES NO PLEASURE IN HIS PAINFUL DUTIES.

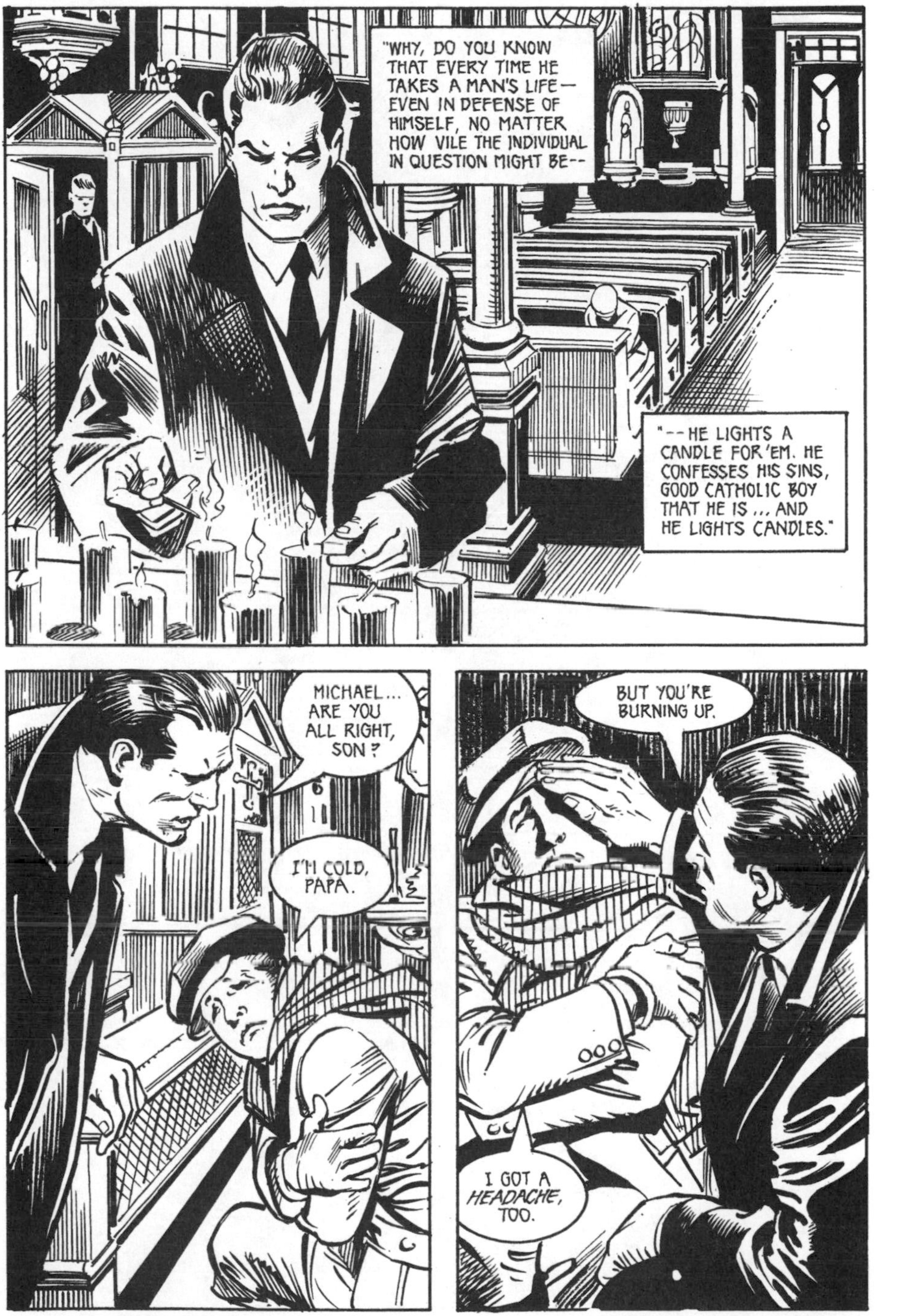
"WHY, DO YOU KNOW THAT EVERY TIME HE TAKES A MAN'S LIFE— EVEN IN DEFENSE OF HIMSELF, NO MATTER HOW VILE THE INDIVIDUAL IN QUESTION MIGHT BE--
"--HE LIGHTS A CANDLE FOR 'EM. HE CONFESSES HIS SINS, GOOD CATHOLIC BOY THAT HE IS ... AND HE LIGHTS CANDLES."
MICHAEL... ARE YOU ALL RIGHT, SON?
I'M COLD, PAPA.
BUT YOU'RE BURNING UP.
I GOT A *HEADACHE*, TOO.

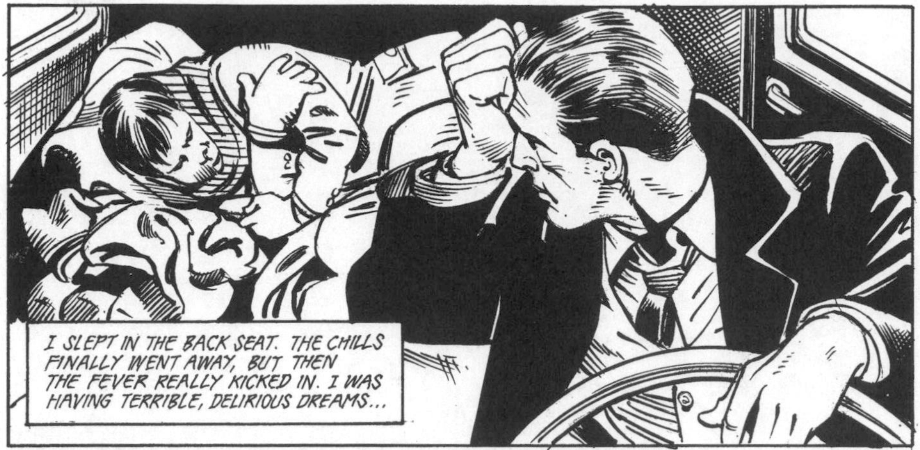
I SLEPT IN THE BACK SEAT. THE CHILLS FINALLY WENT AWAY, BUT THEN THE FEVER REALLY KICKED IN. I WAS HAVING TERRIBLE, DELIRIOUS DREAMS...

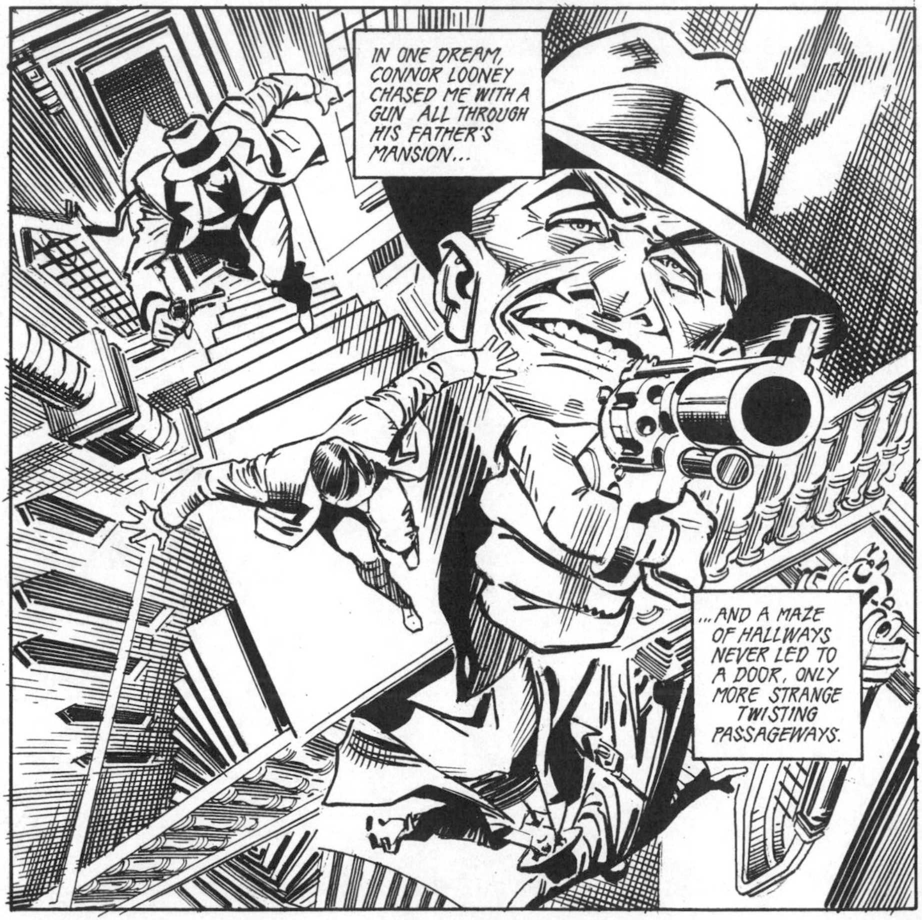
IN ONE DREAM, CONNOR LOONEY CHASED ME WITH A GUN ALL THROUGH HIS FATHER'S MANSION...
...AND A MAZE OF HALLWAYS NEVER LED TO A DOOR, ONLY MORE STRANGE TWISTING PASSAGEWAYS.

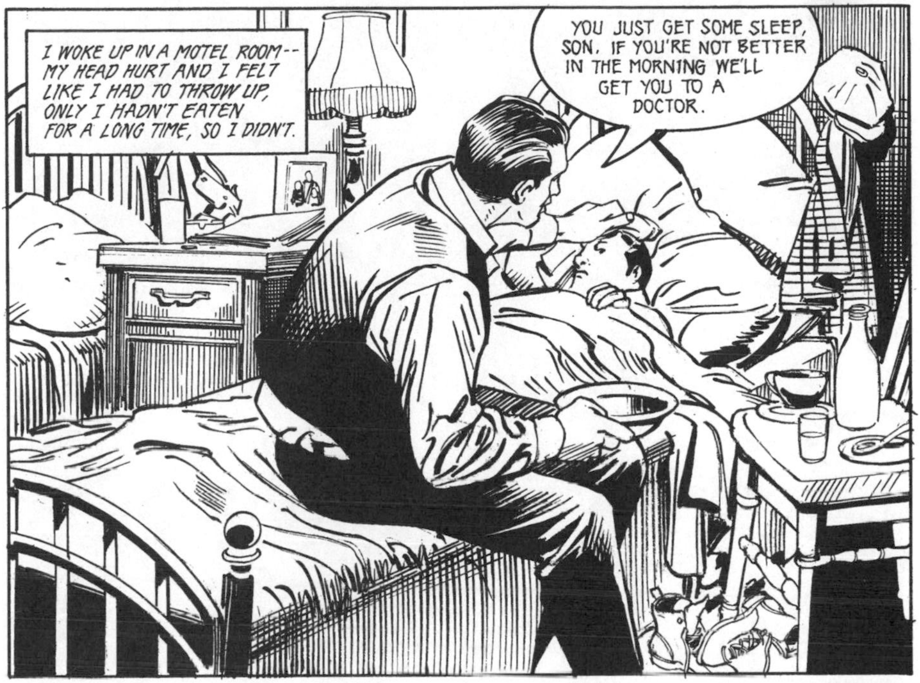
I WOKE UP IN A MOTEL ROOM-- MY HEAD HURT AND I FELT LIKE I HAD TO THROW UP, ONLY I HADN'T EATEN FOR A LONG TIME, SO I DIDN'T.
YOU JUST GET SOME SLEEP, SON. IF YOU'RE NOT BETTER IN THE MORNING WE'LL GET YOU TO A DOCTOR.

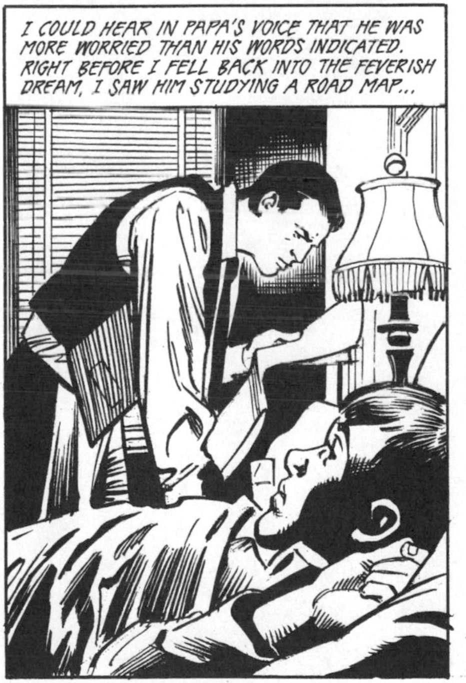
I COULD HEAR IN PAPA'S VOICE THAT HE WAS MORE WORRIED THAN HIS WORDS INDICATED. RIGHT BEFORE I FELL BACK INTO THE FEVERISH DREAM, I SAW HIM STUDYING A ROAD MAP...

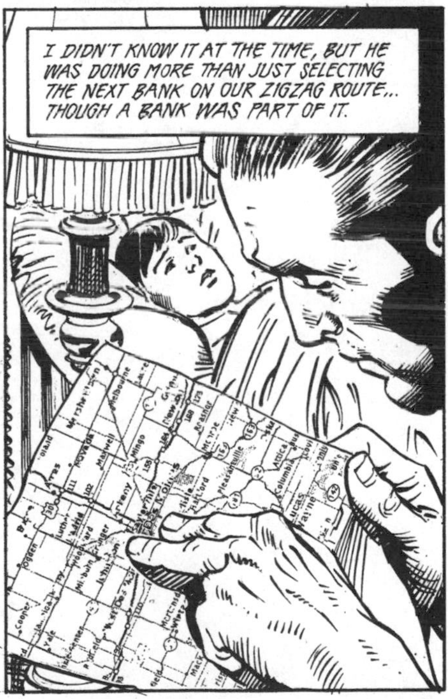
I DIDN'T KNOW IT AT THE TIME, BUT HE WAS DOING MORE THAN JUST SELECTING THE NEXT BANK ON OUR ZIGZAG ROUTE... THOUGH A BANK WAS PART OF IT.

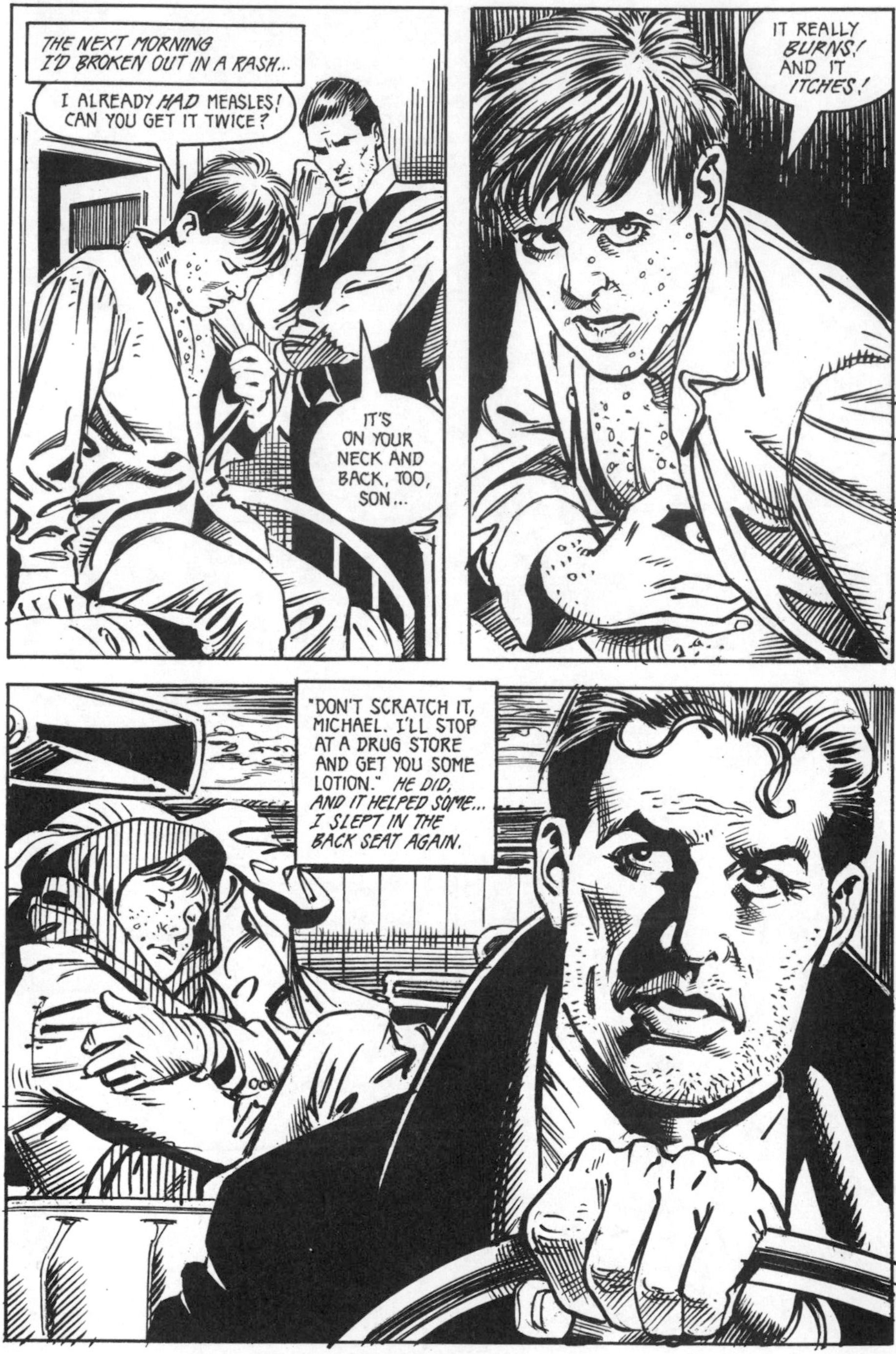
THE NEXT MORNING I'D BROKEN OUT IN A RASH...
I ALREADY HAD MEASLES! CAN YOU GET IT TWICE?
IT'S ON YOUR NECK AND BACK, TOO, SON...
IT REALLY BURNS! AND IT ITCHES!
"DON'T SCRATCH IT, MICHAEL. I'LL STOP AT A DRUG STORE AND GET YOU SOME LOTION." HE DID, AND IT HELPED SOME... I SLEPT IN THE BACK SEAT AGAIN.

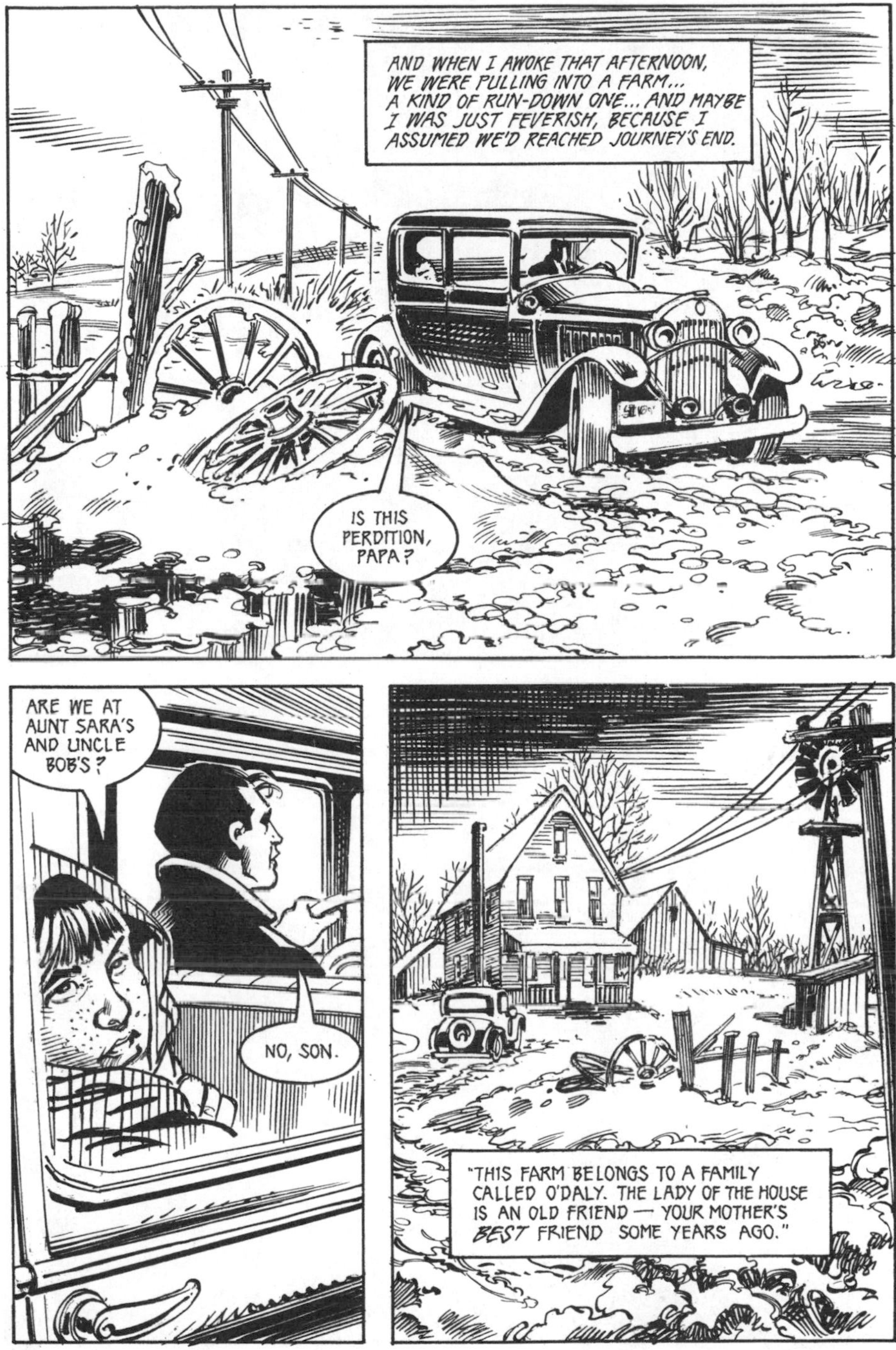

AND WHEN I AWOKE THAT AFTERNOON, WE WERE PULLING INTO A FARM... A KIND OF RUN-DOWN ONE... AND MAYBE I WAS JUST FEVERISH, BECAUSE I ASSUMED WE'D REACHED JOURNEY'S END.
IS THIS PERDITION, PAPA?
ARE WE AT AUNT SARA'S AND UNCLE BOB'S?
NO, SON.
"THIS FARM BELONGS TO A FAMILY CALLED O'DALY. THE LADY OF THE HOUSE IS AN OLD FRIEND — YOUR MOTHER'S BEST FRIEND SOME YEARS AGO."

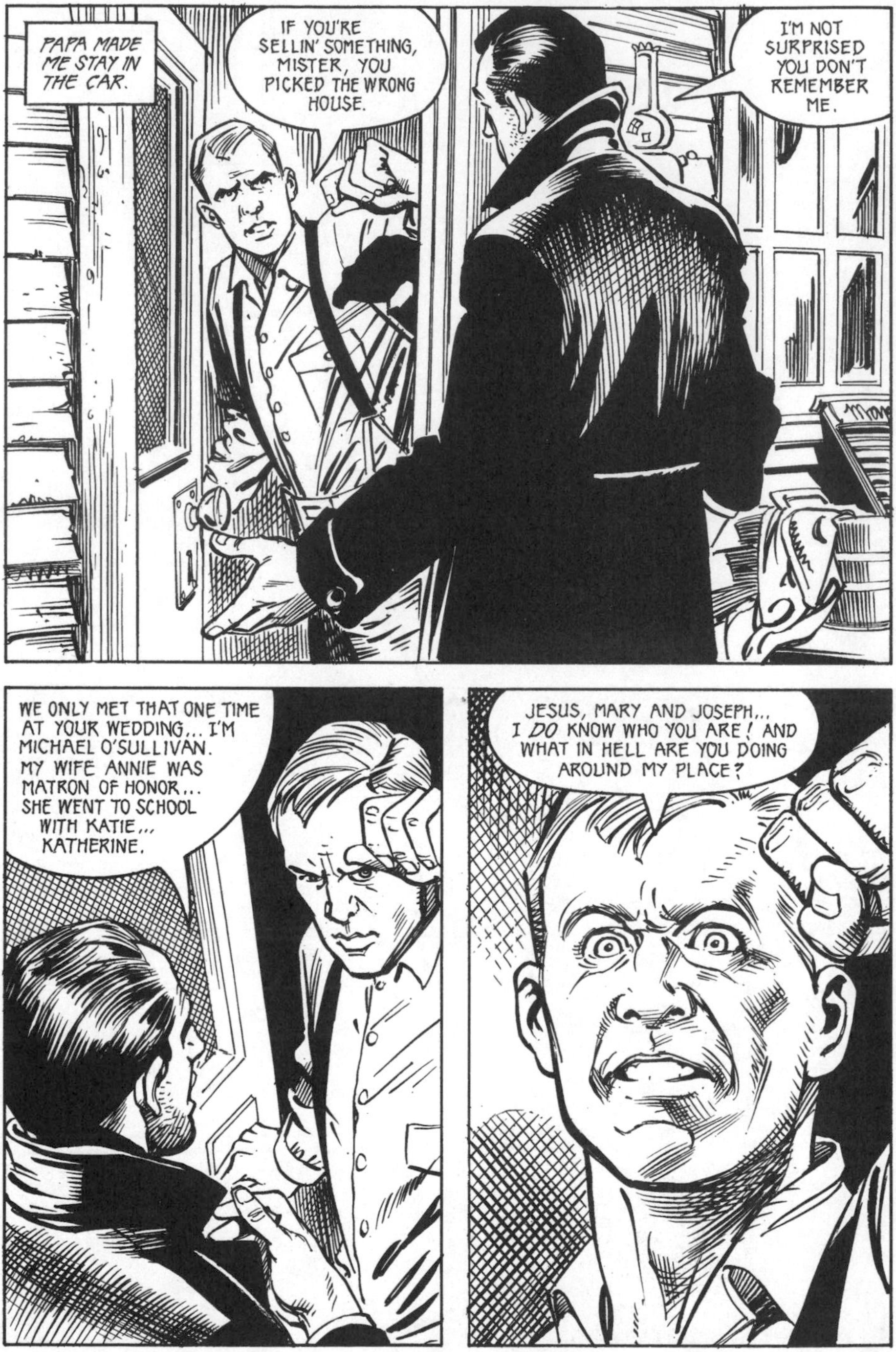
PAPA MADE ME STAY IN THE CAR.
IF YOU'RE SELLIN' SOMETHING, MISTER, YOU PICKED THE WRONG HOUSE.
I'M NOT SURPRISED YOU DON'T REMEMBER ME.
WE ONLY MET THAT ONE TIME AT YOUR WEDDING... I'M MICHAEL O'SULLIVAN. MY WIFE ANNIE WAS MATRON OF HONOR... SHE WENT TO SCHOOL WITH KATIE... KATHERINE.
JESUS, MARY AND JOSEPH... I *DO* KNOW WHO YOU ARE! AND WHAT IN HELL ARE YOU DOING AROUND MY PLACE?

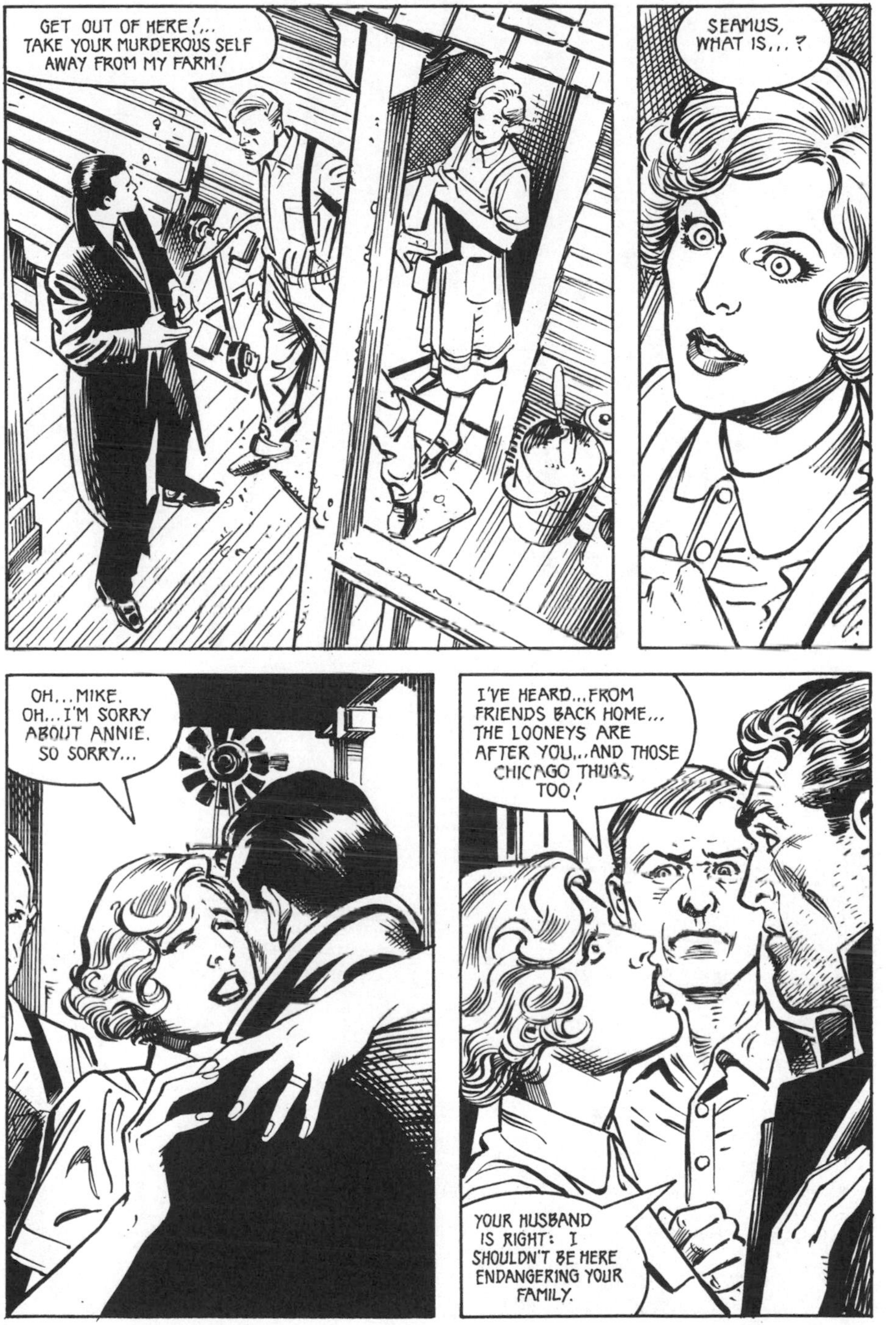
GET OUT OF HERE!... TAKE YOUR MURDEROUS SELF AWAY FROM MY FARM!
SEAMUS, WHAT IS... ?
OH... MIKE. OH... I'M SORRY ABOUT ANNIE. SO SORRY...
I'VE HEARD... FROM FRIENDS BACK HOME... THE LOONEYS ARE AFTER YOU... AND THOSE CHICAGO THUGS, TOO!
YOUR HUSBAND IS RIGHT: I SHOULDN'T BE HERE ENDANGERING YOUR FAMILY.

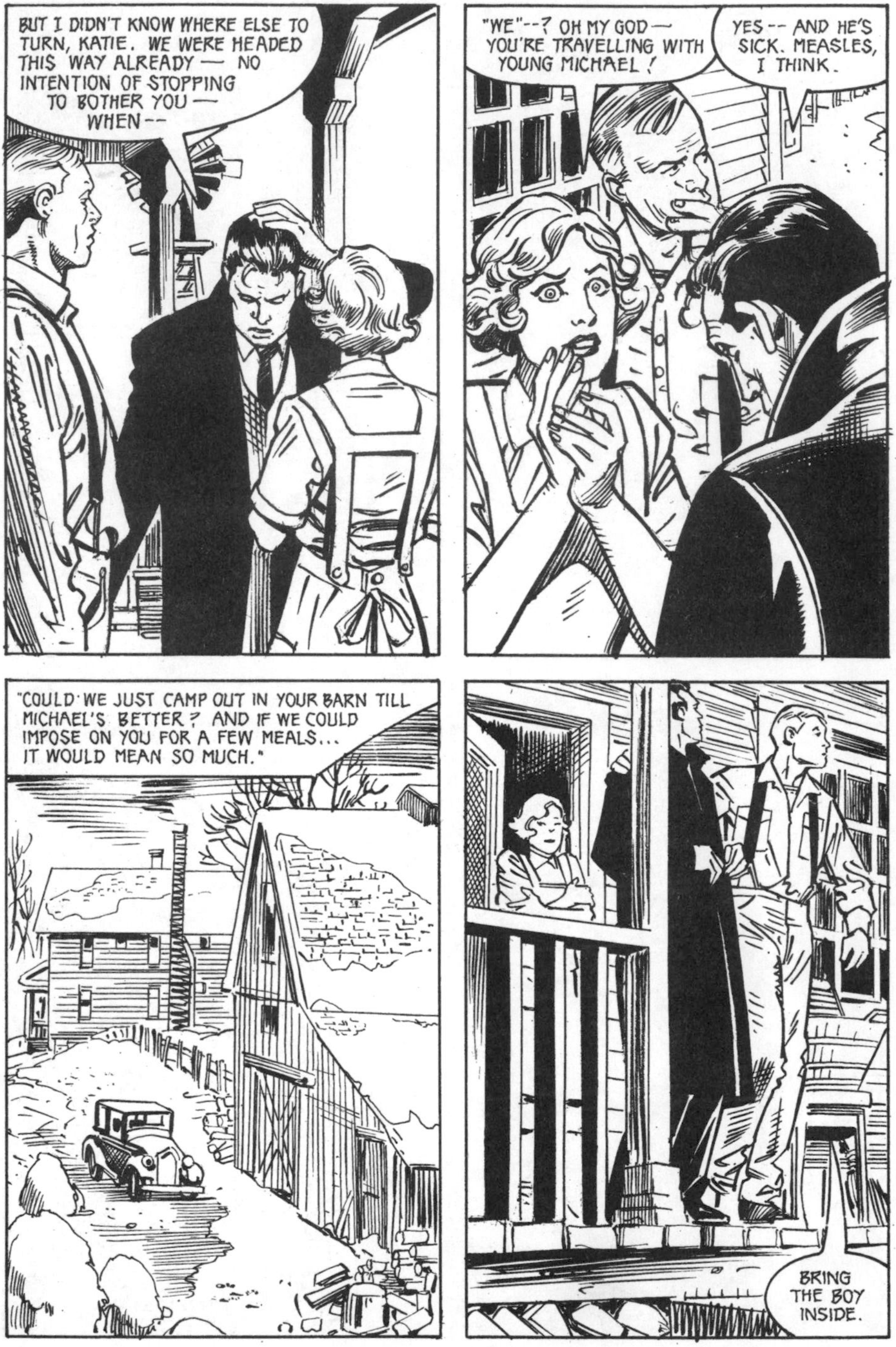

BUT I DIDN'T KNOW WHERE ELSE TO TURN, KATIE. WE WERE HEADED THIS WAY ALREADY — NO INTENTION OF STOPPING TO BOTHER YOU — WHEN --
"WE"--? OH MY GOD — YOU'RE TRAVELLING WITH YOUNG MICHAEL!
YES -- AND HE'S SICK. MEASLES, I THINK.
"COULD WE JUST CAMP OUT IN YOUR BARN TILL MICHAEL'S BETTER? AND IF WE COULD IMPOSE ON YOU FOR A FEW MEALS... IT WOULD MEAN SO MUCH."
BRING THE BOY INSIDE.

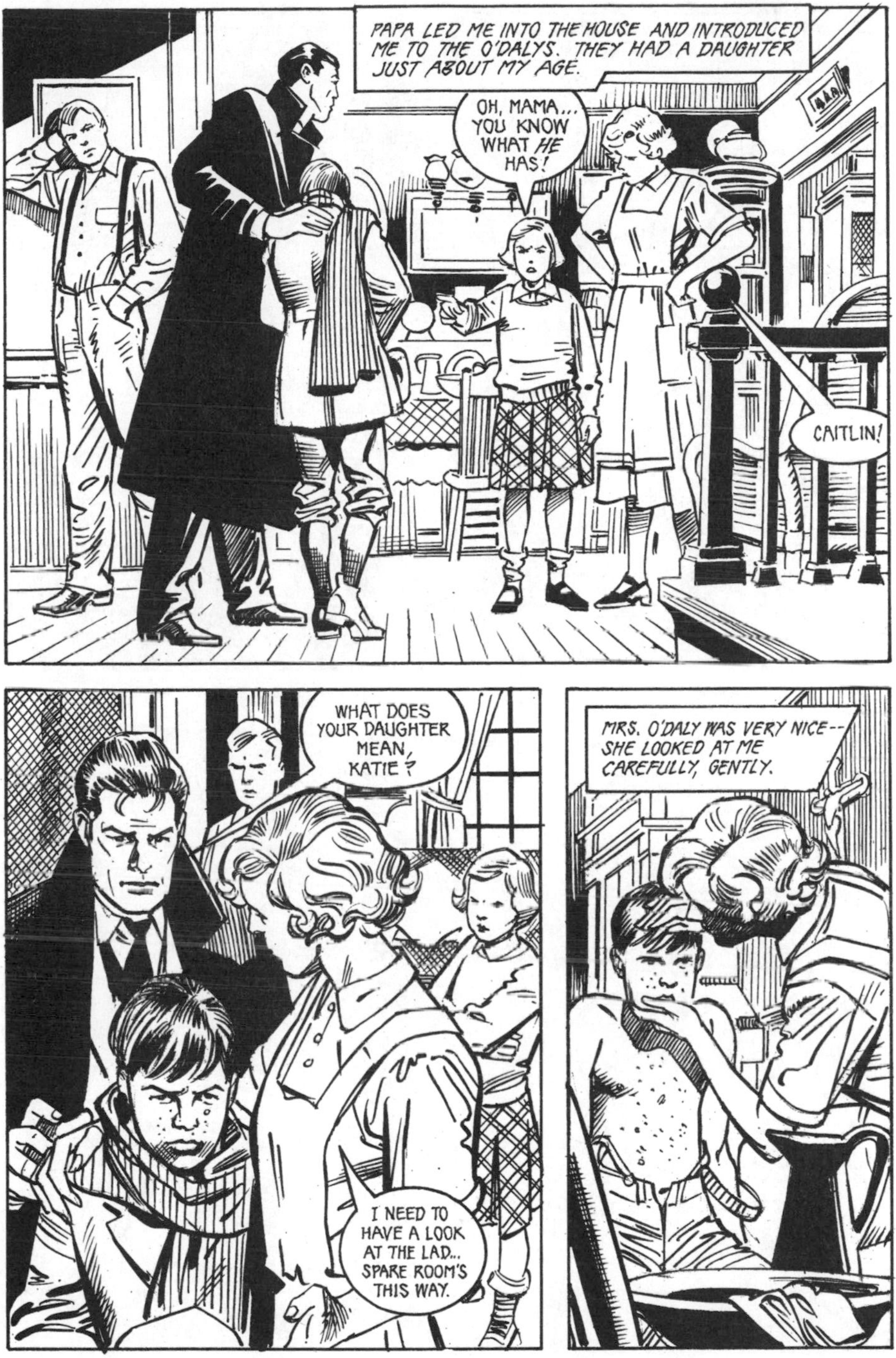
PAPA LED ME INTO THE HOUSE AND INTRODUCED ME TO THE O'DALYS. THEY HAD A DAUGHTER JUST ABOUT MY AGE.
OH, MAMA... YOU KNOW WHAT HE HAS!
CAITLIN!
WHAT DOES YOUR DAUGHTER MEAN, KATIE?
I NEED TO HAVE A LOOK AT THE LAD... SPARE ROOM'S THIS WAY.
MRS. O'DALY WAS VERY NICE-- SHE LOOKED AT ME CAREFULLY, GENTLY.

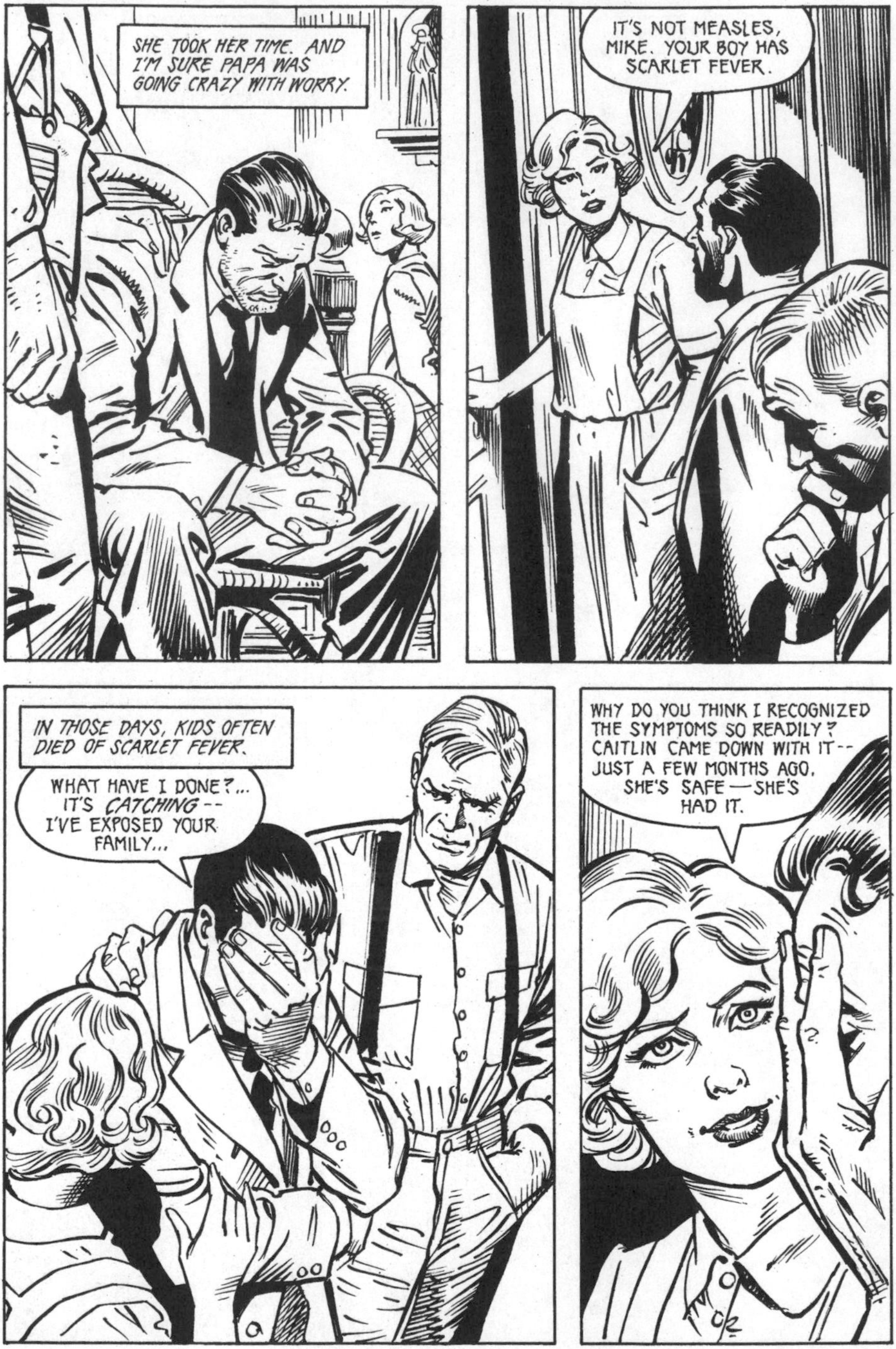
SHE TOOK HER TIME. AND I'M SURE PAPA WAS GOING CRAZY WITH WORRY.
IT'S NOT MEASLES, MIKE. YOUR BOY HAS SCARLET FEVER.
IN THOSE DAYS, KIDS OFTEN DIED OF SCARLET FEVER.
WHAT HAVE I DONE?... IT'S *CATCHING* -- I'VE EXPOSED YOUR FAMILY...
WHY DO YOU THINK I RECOGNIZED THE SYMPTOMS SO READILY? CAITLIN CAME DOWN WITH IT -- JUST A FEW MONTHS AGO. SHE'S SAFE — SHE'S HAD IT.

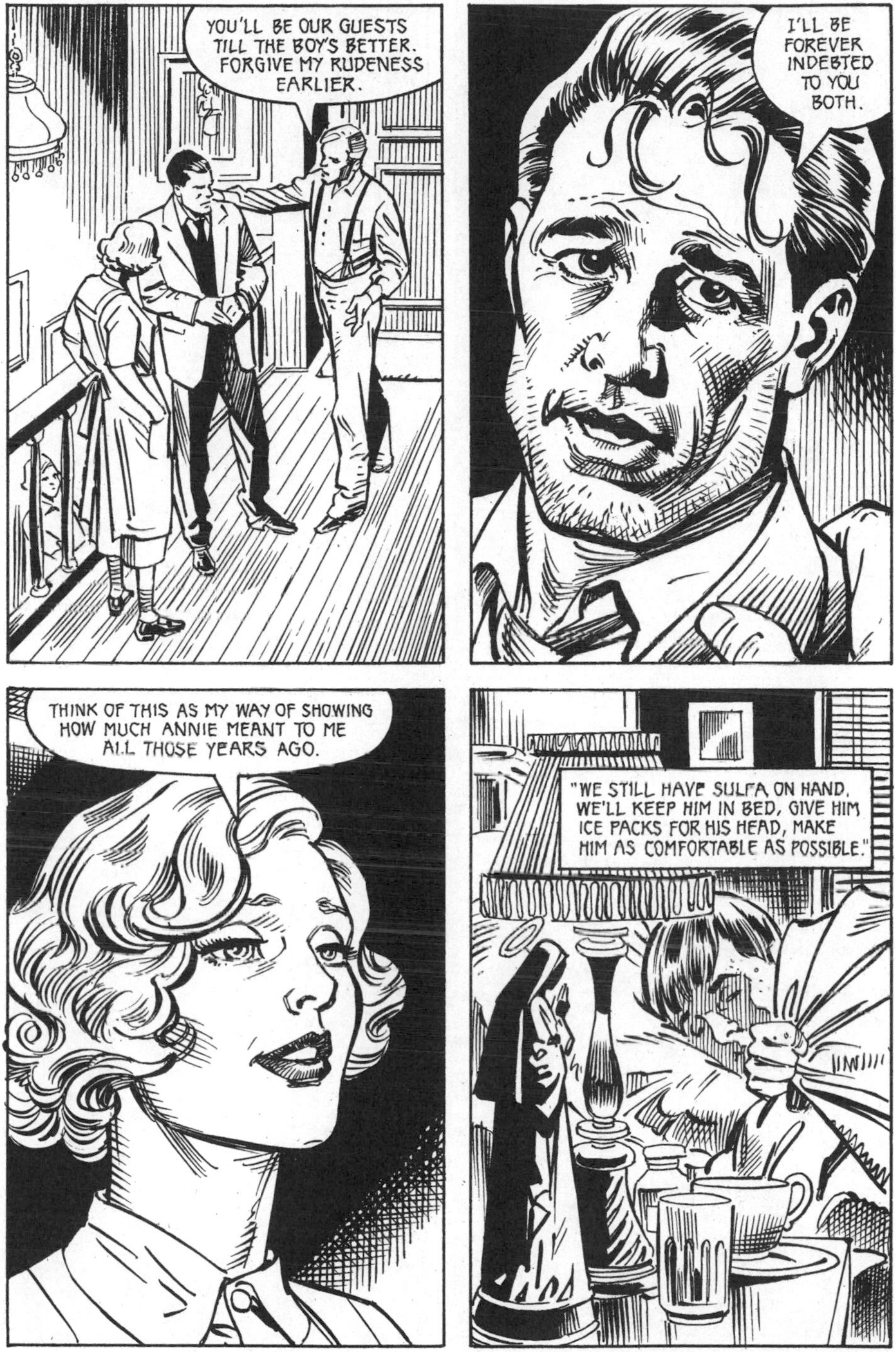
YOU'LL BE OUR GUESTS TILL THE BOY'S BETTER. FORGIVE MY RUDENESS EARLIER.
I'LL BE FOREVER INDEBTED TO YOU BOTH.
THINK OF THIS AS MY WAY OF SHOWING HOW MUCH ANNIE MEANT TO ME ALL THOSE YEARS AGO.
"WE STILL HAVE SULFA ON HAND. WE'LL KEEP HIM IN BED, GIVE HIM ICE PACKS FOR HIS HEAD, MAKE HIM AS COMFORTABLE AS POSSIBLE."

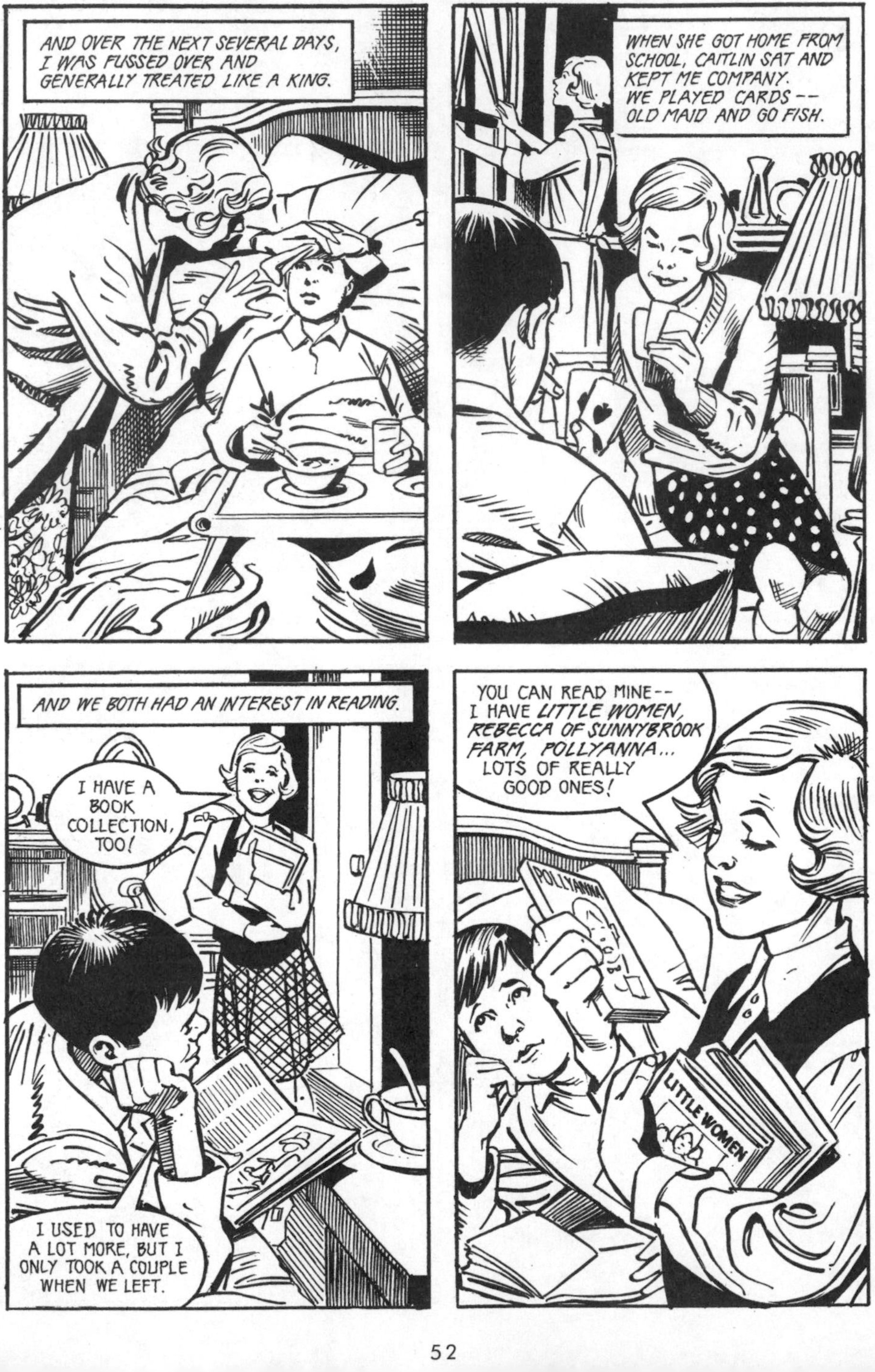
AND OVER THE NEXT SEVERAL DAYS, I WAS FUSSED OVER AND GENERALLY TREATED LIKE A KING.
WHEN SHE GOT HOME FROM SCHOOL, CAITLIN SAT AND KEPT ME COMPANY. WE PLAYED CARDS -- OLD MAID AND GO FISH.
AND WE BOTH HAD AN INTEREST IN READING.
I HAVE A BOOK COLLECTION, TOO!
I USED TO HAVE A LOT MORE, BUT I ONLY TOOK A COUPLE WHEN WE LEFT.
YOU CAN READ MINE-- I HAVE *LITTLE WOMEN*, *REBECCA OF SUNNYBROOK FARM*, *POLLYANNA*... LOTS OF REALLY GOOD ONES!
POLLYANNA
LITTLE WOMEN

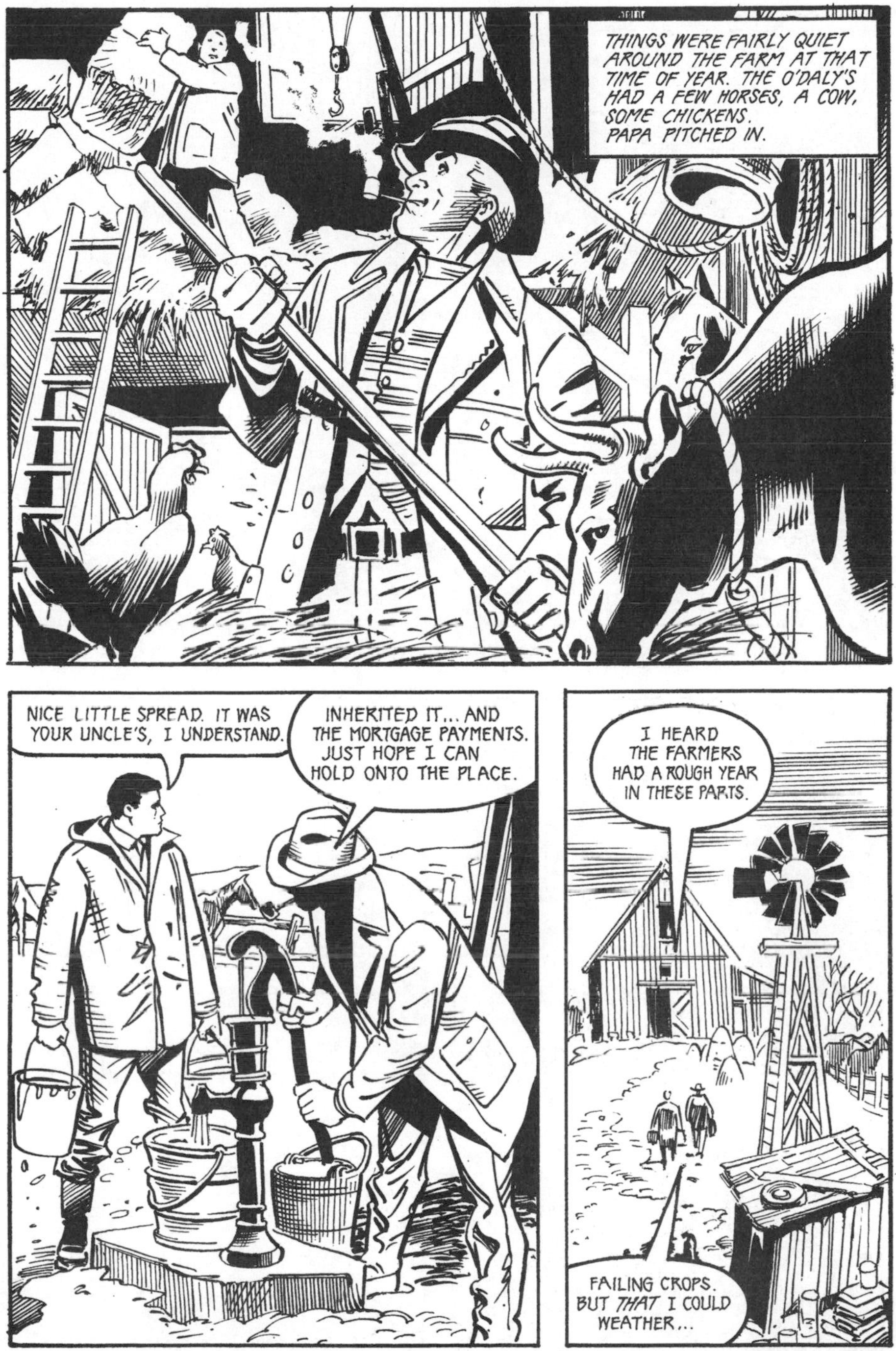
THINGS WERE FAIRLY QUIET AROUND THE FARM AT THAT TIME OF YEAR. THE O'DALY'S HAD A FEW HORSES, A COW, SOME CHICKENS. PAPA PITCHED IN.
NICE LITTLE SPREAD. IT WAS YOUR UNCLE'S, I UNDERSTAND.
INHERITED IT... AND THE MORTGAGE PAYMENTS. JUST HOPE I CAN HOLD ONTO THE PLACE.
I HEARD THE FARMERS HAD A ROUGH YEAR IN THESE PARTS.
FAILING CROPS. BUT *THAT* I COULD WEATHER...

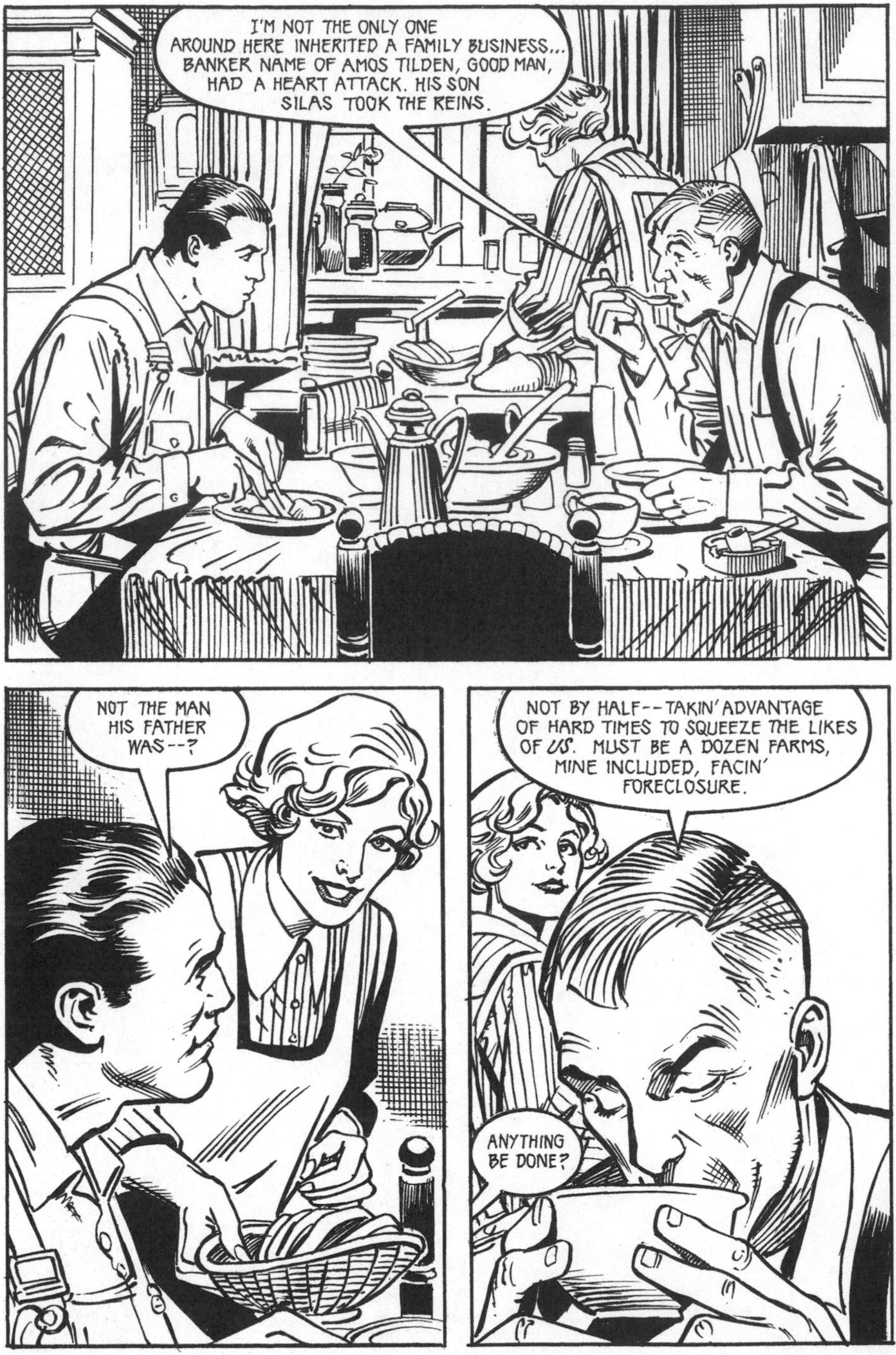
I'M NOT THE ONLY ONE AROUND HERE INHERITED A FAMILY BUSINESS... BANKER NAME OF AMOS TILDEN, GOOD MAN, HAD A HEART ATTACK. HIS SON SILAS TOOK THE REINS.
NOT THE MAN HIS FATHER WAS--?
NOT BY HALF--TAKIN' ADVANTAGE OF HARD TIMES TO SQUEEZE THE LIKES OF *US*. MUST BE A DOZEN FARMS, MINE INCLUDED, FACIN' FORECLOSURE.
ANYTHING BE DONE?

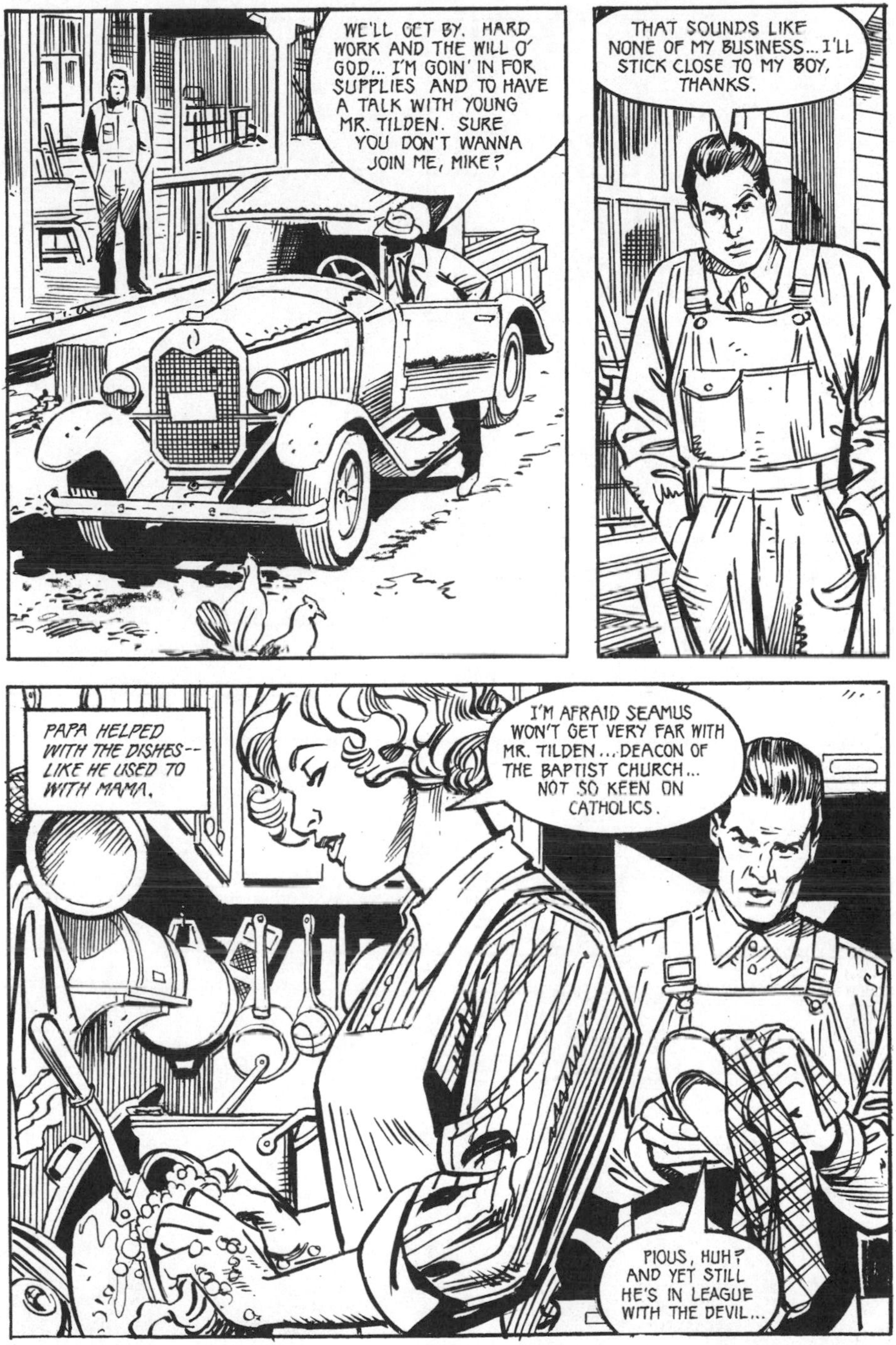
WE'LL GET BY. HARD WORK AND THE WILL O' GOD... I'M GOIN' IN FOR SUPPLIES AND TO HAVE A TALK WITH YOUNG MR. TILDEN. SURE YOU DON'T WANNA JOIN ME, MIKE?
THAT SOUNDS LIKE NONE OF MY BUSINESS... I'LL STICK CLOSE TO MY BOY, THANKS.
PAPA HELPED WITH THE DISHES-- LIKE HE USED TO WITH MAMA.
I'M AFRAID SEAMUS WON'T GET VERY FAR WITH MR. TILDEN... DEACON OF THE BAPTIST CHURCH... NOT SO KEEN ON CATHOLICS.
PIOUS, HUH? AND YET STILL HE'S IN LEAGUE WITH THE DEVIL...

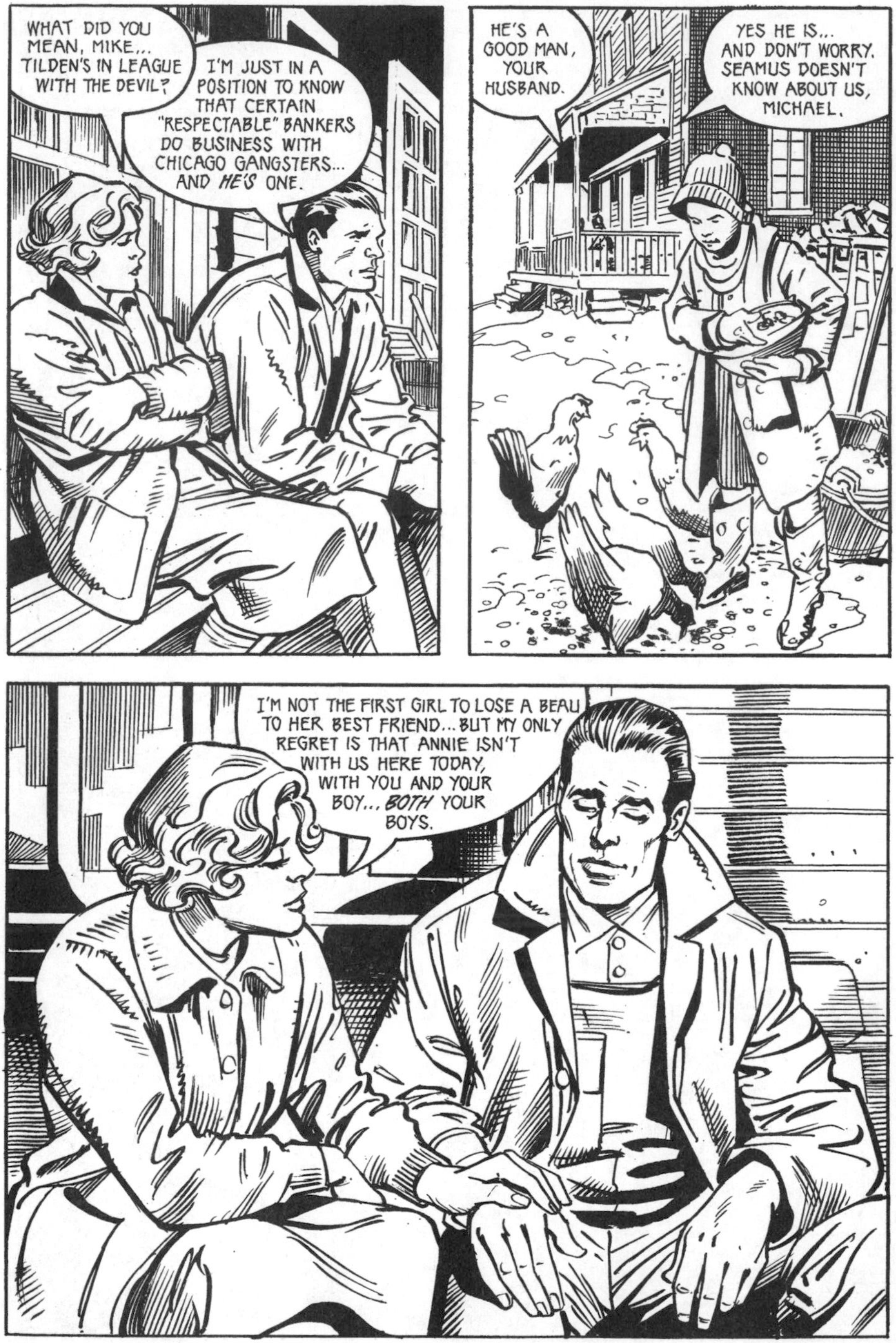
WHAT DID YOU MEAN, MIKE... TILDEN'S IN LEAGUE WITH THE DEVIL?
I'M JUST IN A POSITION TO KNOW THAT CERTAIN "RESPECTABLE" BANKERS DO BUSINESS WITH CHICAGO GANGSTERS... AND *HE'S* ONE.
HE'S A GOOD MAN, YOUR HUSBAND.
YES HE IS... AND DON'T WORRY. SEAMUS DOESN'T KNOW ABOUT US, MICHAEL.
I'M NOT THE FIRST GIRL TO LOSE A BEAU TO HER BEST FRIEND... BUT MY ONLY REGRET IS THAT ANNIE ISN'T WITH US HERE TODAY, WITH YOU AND YOUR BOY... *BOTH* YOUR BOYS.

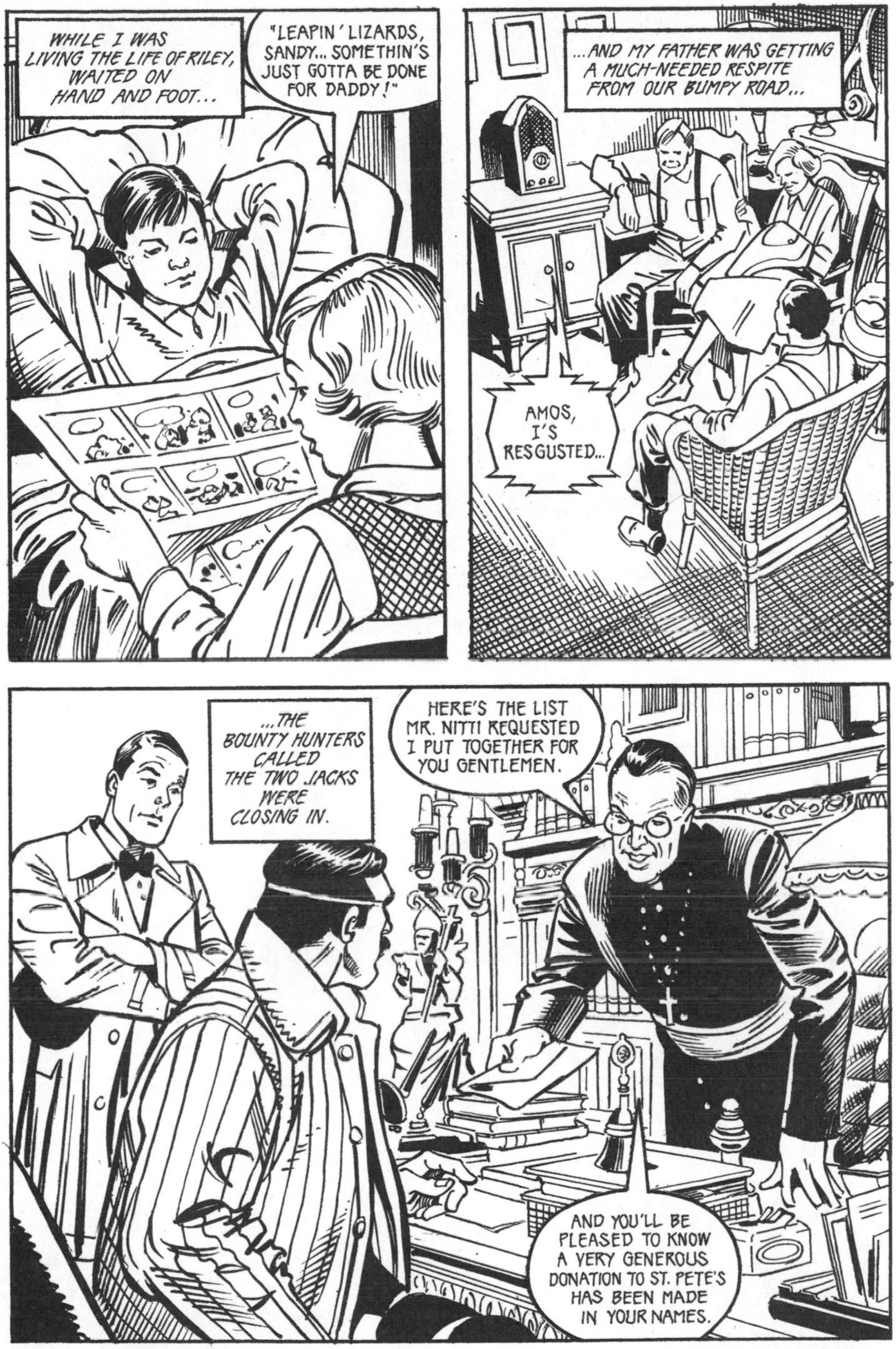
WHILE I WAS LIVING THE LIFE OF RILEY, WAITED ON HAND AND FOOT...
"LEAPIN' LIZARDS, SANDY... SOMETHIN'S JUST GOTTA BE DONE FOR DADDY!"
...AND MY FATHER WAS GETTING A MUCH-NEEDED RESPITE FROM OUR BUMPY ROAD...
AMOS, I'S RESGUSTED...
...THE BOUNTY HUNTERS CALLED THE TWO JACKS WERE CLOSING IN.
HERE'S THE LIST MR. NITTI REQUESTED I PUT TOGETHER FOR YOU GENTLEMEN.
AND YOU'LL BE PLEASED TO KNOW A VERY GENEROUS DONATION TO ST. PETE'S HAS BEEN MADE IN YOUR NAMES.

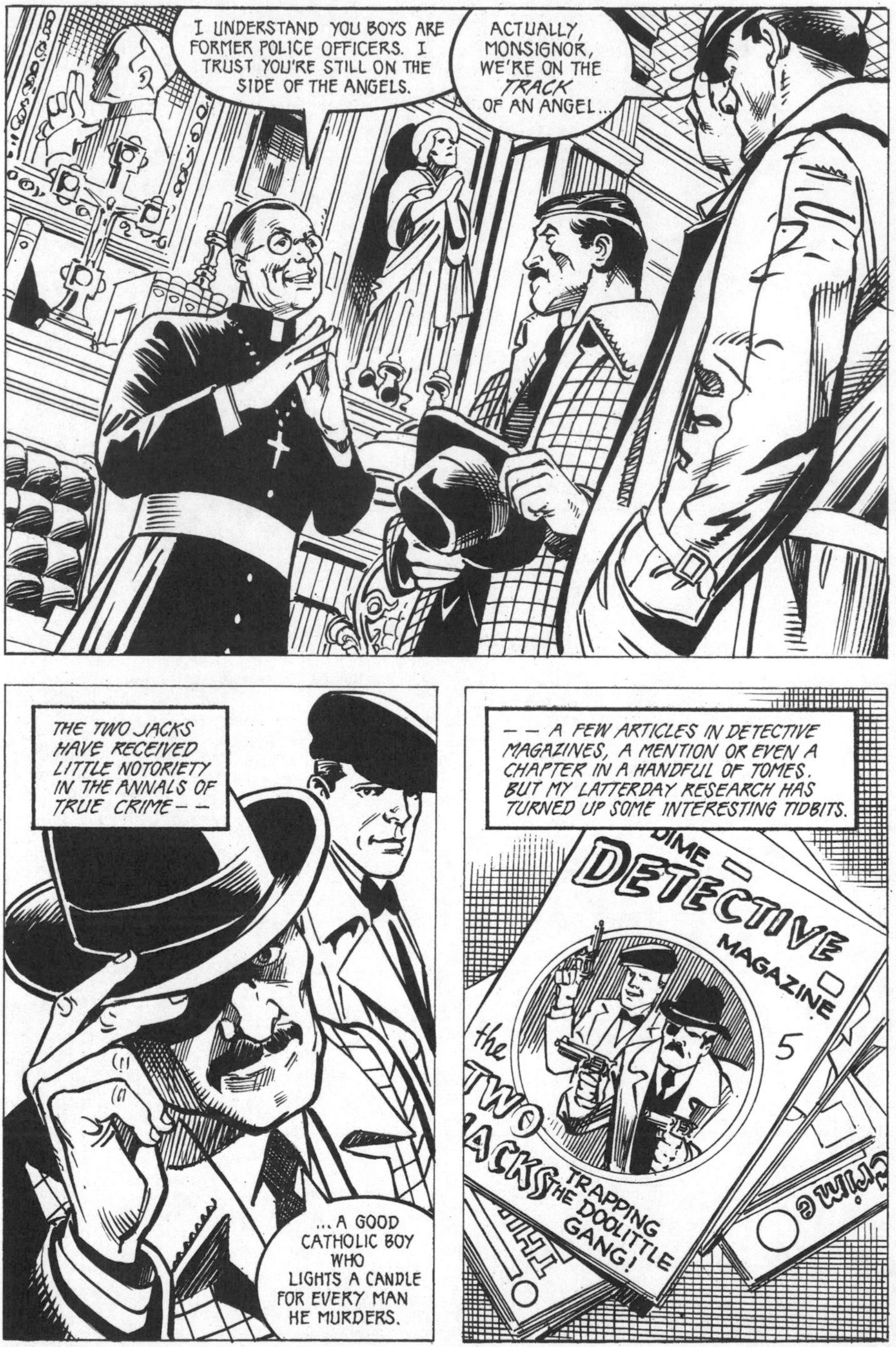
I UNDERSTAND YOU BOYS ARE FORMER POLICE OFFICERS. I TRUST YOU'RE STILL ON THE SIDE OF THE ANGELS.
ACTUALLY, MONSIGNOR, WE'RE ON THE *TRACK* OF AN ANGEL...
THE TWO JACKS HAVE RECEIVED LITTLE NOTORIETY IN THE ANNALS OF TRUE CRIME--
...A GOOD CATHOLIC BOY WHO LIGHTS A CANDLE FOR EVERY MAN HE MURDERS.
--A FEW ARTICLES IN DETECTIVE MAGAZINES, A MENTION OR EVEN A CHAPTER IN A HANDFUL OF TOMES. BUT MY LATTERDAY RESEARCH HAS TURNED UP SOME INTERESTING TIDBITS.
DIME
DETECTIVE
MAGAZINE
5
the
TWO
TRAPPING THE DOOLITTLE GANG!

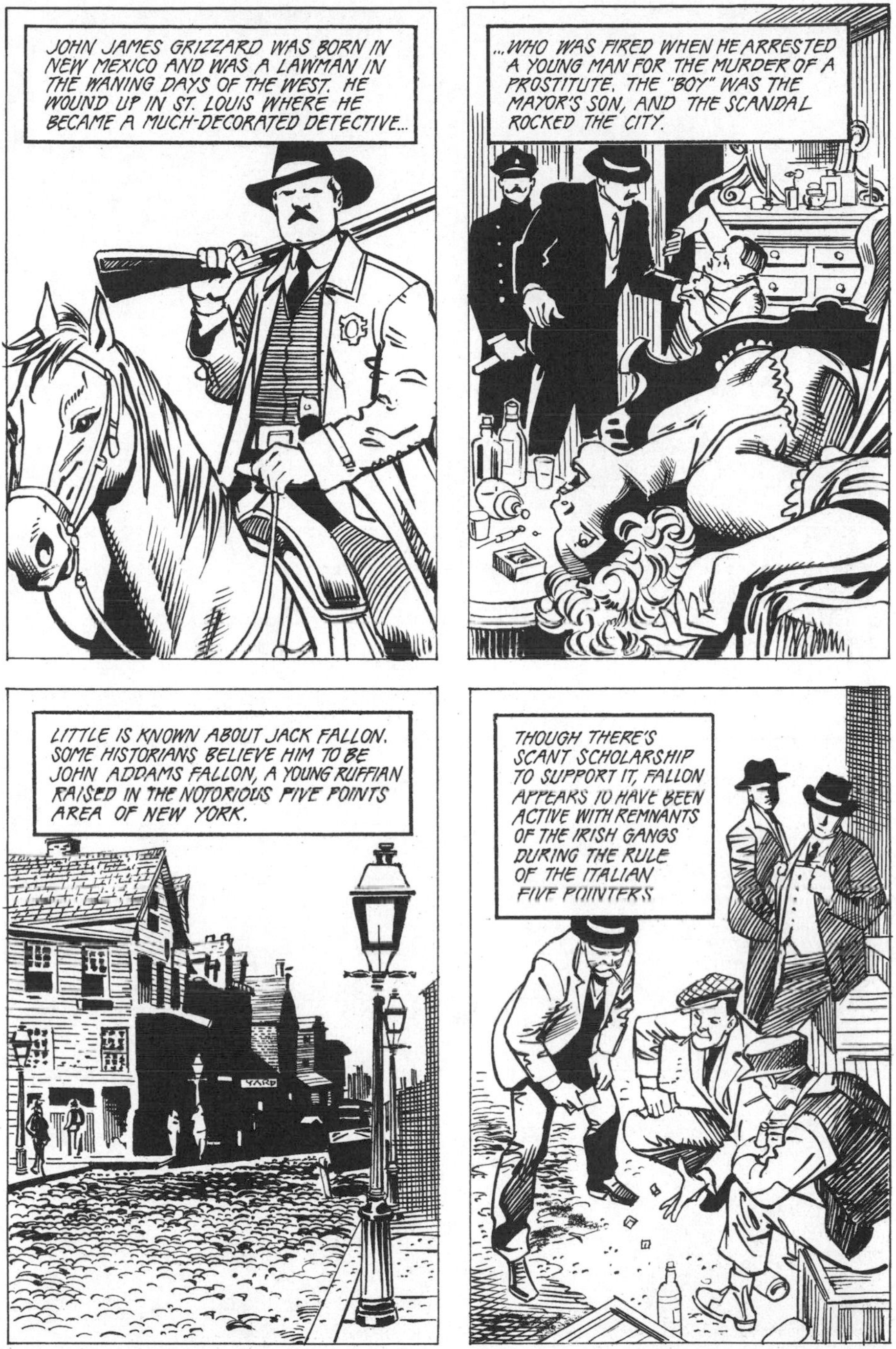
JOHN JAMES GRIZZARD WAS BORN IN NEW MEXICO AND WAS A LAWMAN IN THE WANING DAYS OF THE WEST. HE WOUND UP IN ST. LOUIS WHERE HE BECAME A MUCH-DECORATED DETECTIVE...
...WHO WAS FIRED WHEN HE ARRESTED A YOUNG MAN FOR THE MURDER OF A PROSTITUTE. THE "BOY" WAS THE MAYOR'S SON, AND THE SCANDAL ROCKED THE CITY.
LITTLE IS KNOWN ABOUT JACK FALLON. SOME HISTORIANS BELIEVE HIM TO BE JOHN ADDAMS FALLON, A YOUNG RUFFIAN RAISED IN THE NOTORIOUS FIVE POINTS AREA OF NEW YORK.
YARD
THOUGH THERE'S SCANT SCHOLARSHIP TO SUPPORT IT, FALLON APPEARS TO HAVE BEEN ACTIVE WITH REMNANTS OF THE IRISH GANGS DURING THE RULE OF THE ITALIAN FIVE POINTERS.

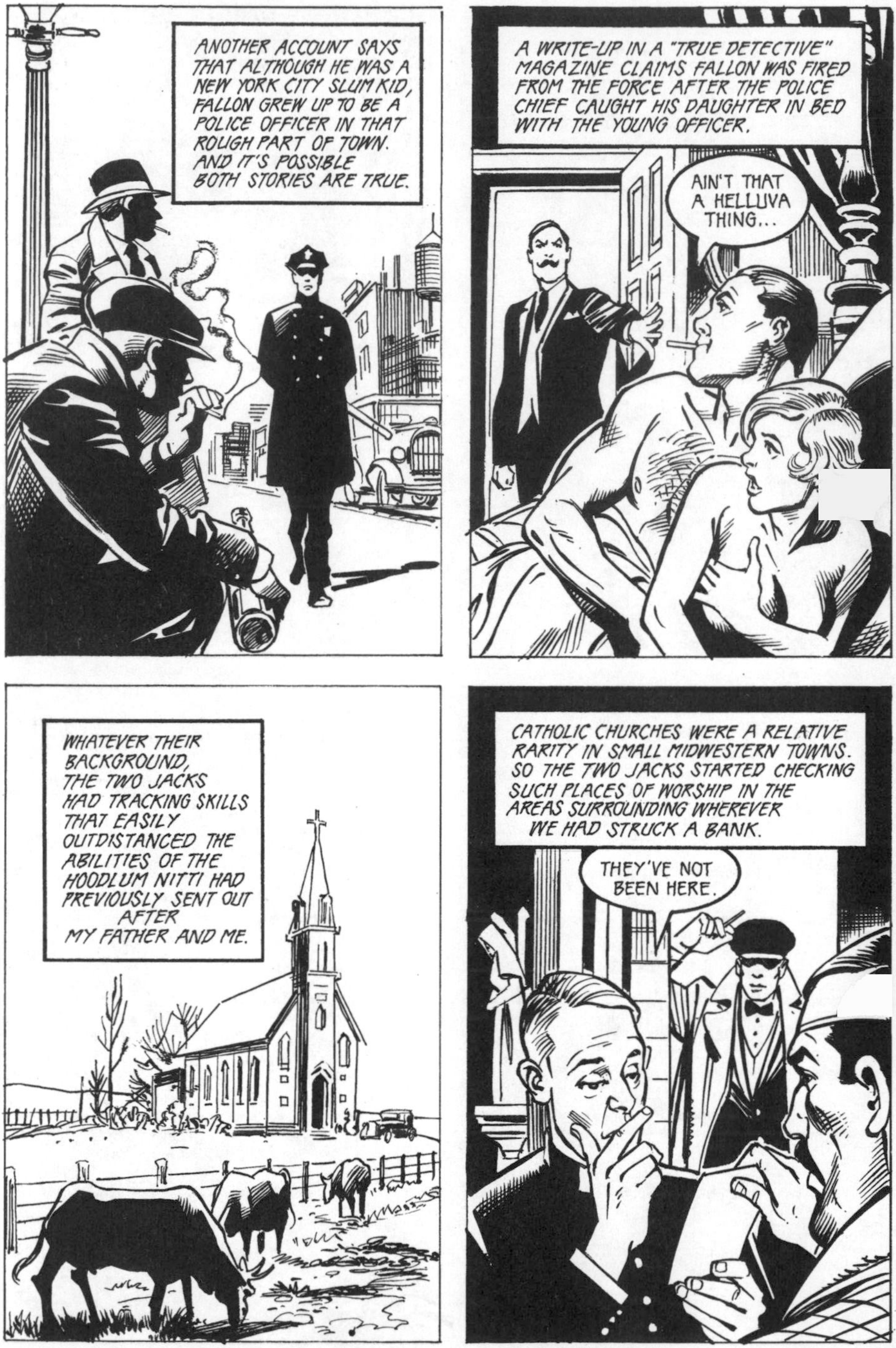
ANOTHER ACCOUNT SAYS THAT ALTHOUGH HE WAS A NEW YORK CITY SLUM KID, FALLON GREW UP TO BE A POLICE OFFICER IN THAT ROUGH PART OF TOWN. AND IT'S POSSIBLE BOTH STORIES ARE TRUE.
A WRITE-UP IN A "TRUE DETECTIVE" MAGAZINE CLAIMS FALLON WAS FIRED FROM THE FORCE AFTER THE POLICE CHIEF CAUGHT HIS DAUGHTER IN BED WITH THE YOUNG OFFICER.
AIN'T THAT A HELLUVA THING...
WHATEVER THEIR BACKGROUND, THE TWO JACKS HAD TRACKING SKILLS THAT EASILY OUTDISTANCED THE ABILITIES OF THE HOODLUM NITTI HAD PREVIOUSLY SENT OUT AFTER MY FATHER AND ME.
CATHOLIC CHURCHES WERE A RELATIVE RARITY IN SMALL MIDWESTERN TOWNS. SO THE TWO JACKS STARTED CHECKING SUCH PLACES OF WORSHIP IN THE AREAS SURROUNDING WHEREVER WE HAD STRUCK A BANK.
THEY'VE NOT BEEN HERE.

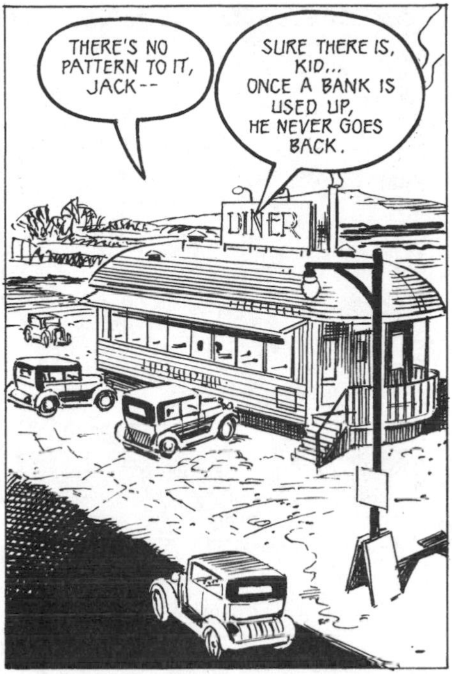
THERE'S NO PATTERN TO IT, JACK--
SURE THERE IS, KID... ONCE A BANK IS USED UP, HE NEVER GOES BACK.
DINER

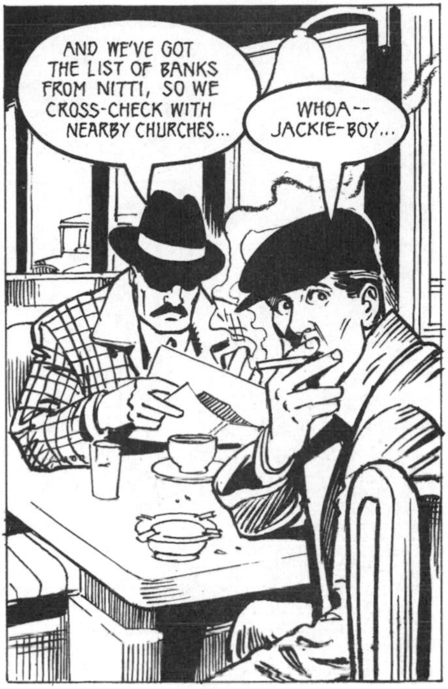
AND WE'VE GOT THE LIST OF BANKS FROM NITTI, SO WE CROSS-CHECK WITH NEARBY CHURCHES...
WHOA-- JACKIE-BOY...

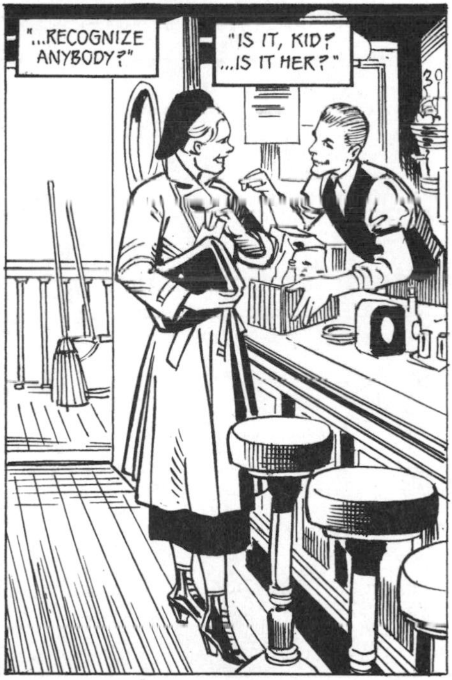
"...RECOGNIZE ANYBODY?"
"IS IT, KID? ...IS IT HER?"

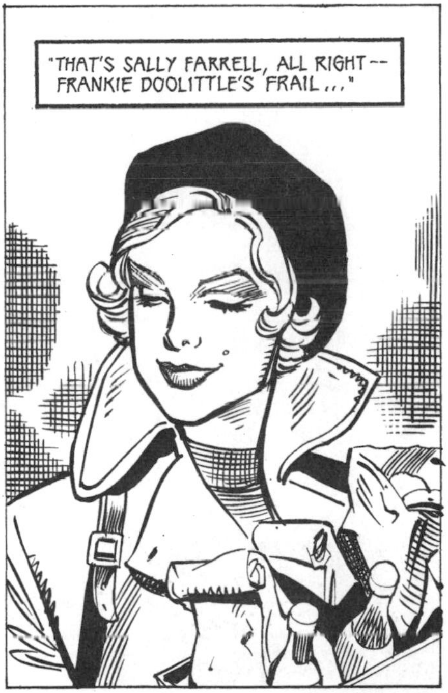
"THAT'S SALLY FARRELL, ALL RIGHT-- FRANKIE DOOLITTLE'S FRAIL..."

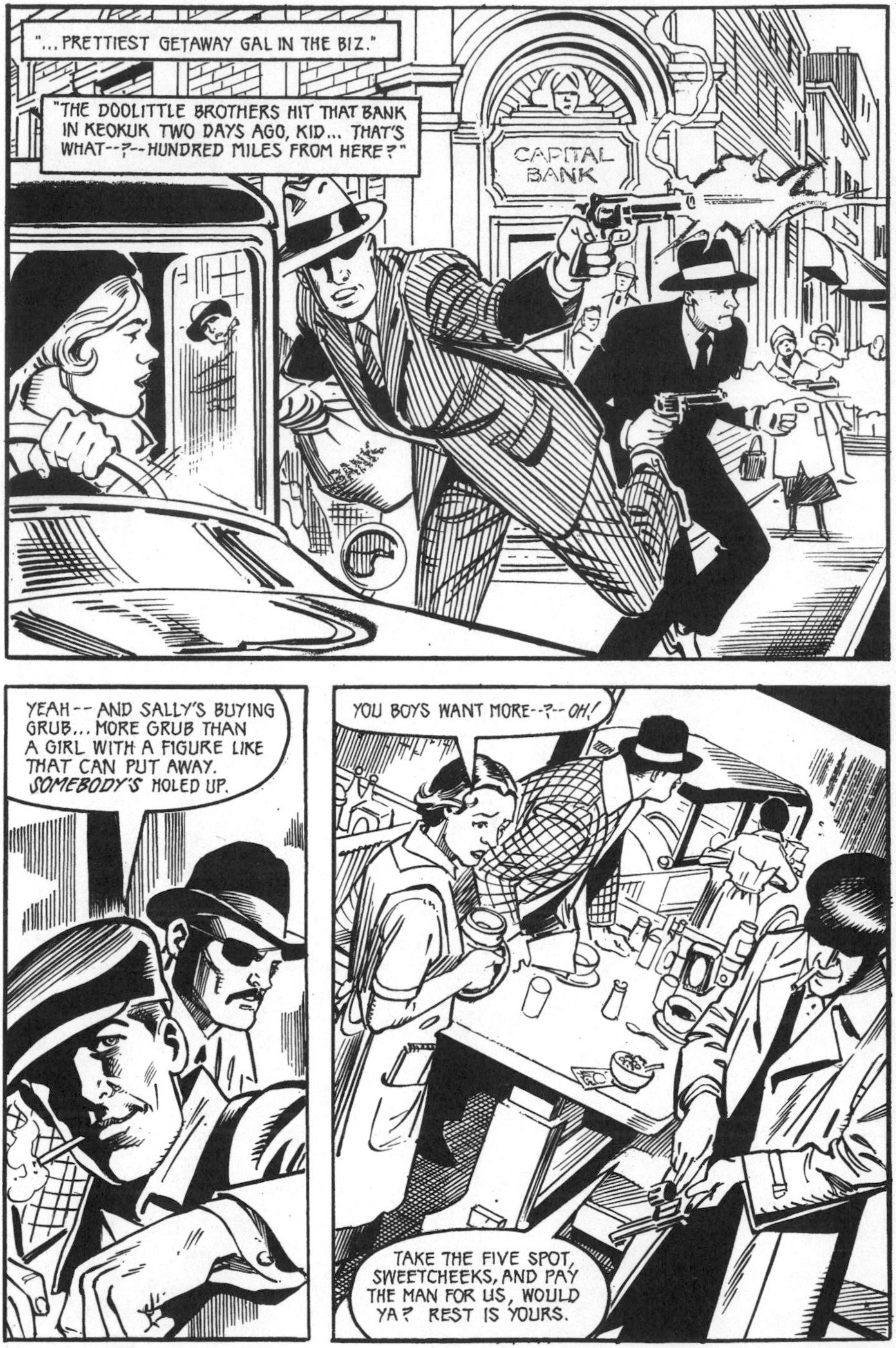
"...PRETTIEST GETAWAY GAL IN THE BIZ."
"THE DOOLITTLE BROTHERS HIT THAT BANK IN KEOKUK TWO DAYS AGO, KID... THAT'S WHAT--?--HUNDRED MILES FROM HERE?"
CAPITAL BANK
BANK
YEAH-- AND SALLY'S BUYING GRUB... MORE GRUB THAN A GIRL WITH A FIGURE LIKE THAT CAN PUT AWAY. SOMEBODY'S HOLED UP.
YOU BOYS WANT MORE--?-- OH!
TAKE THE FIVE SPOT, SWEETCHEEKS, AND PAY THE MAN FOR US, WOULD YA? REST IS YOURS.

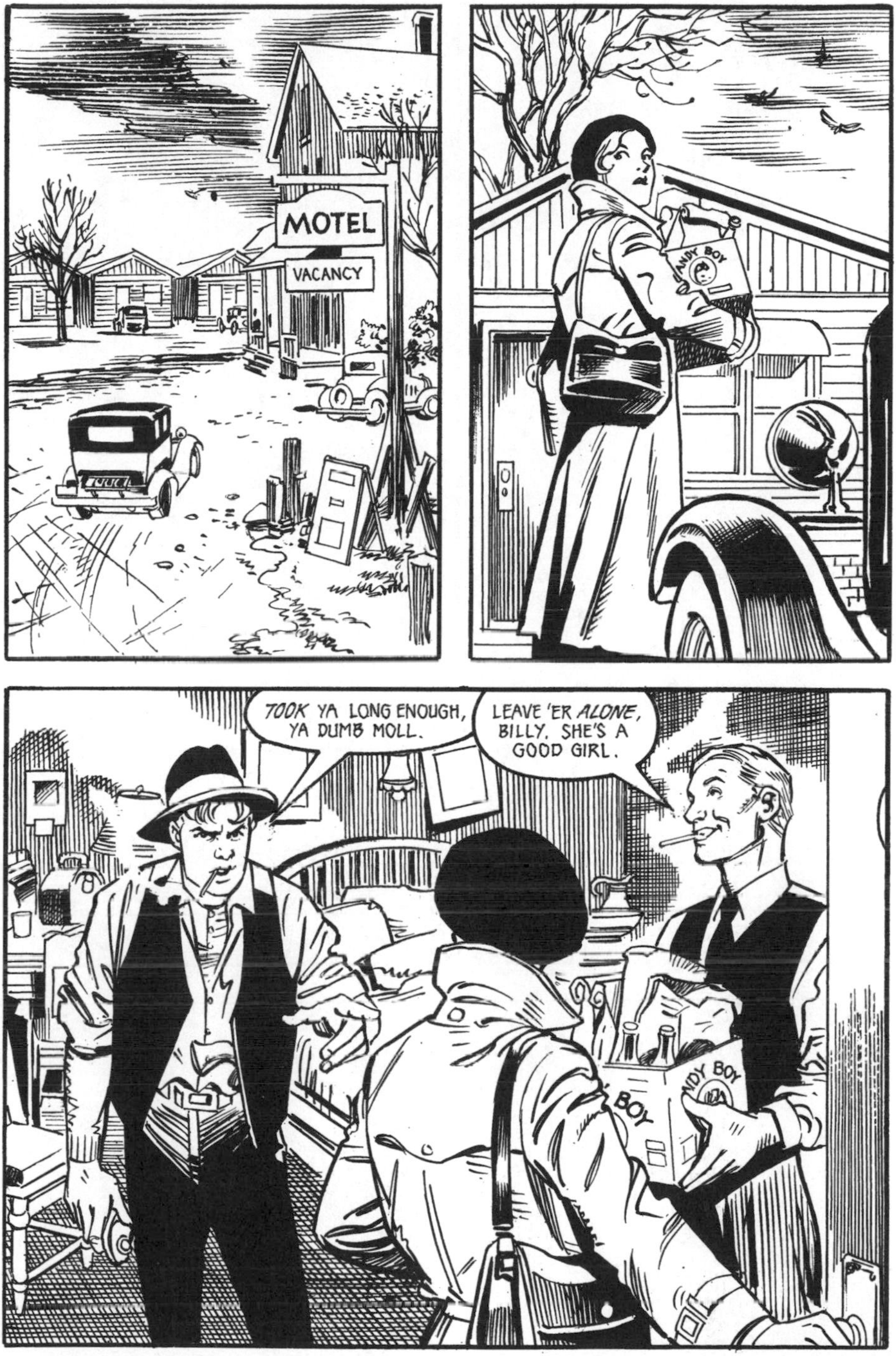
MOTEL
VACANCY
TOOK YA LONG ENOUGH, YA DUMB MOLL.
LEAVE 'ER *ALONE*, BILLY. SHE'S A GOOD GIRL.

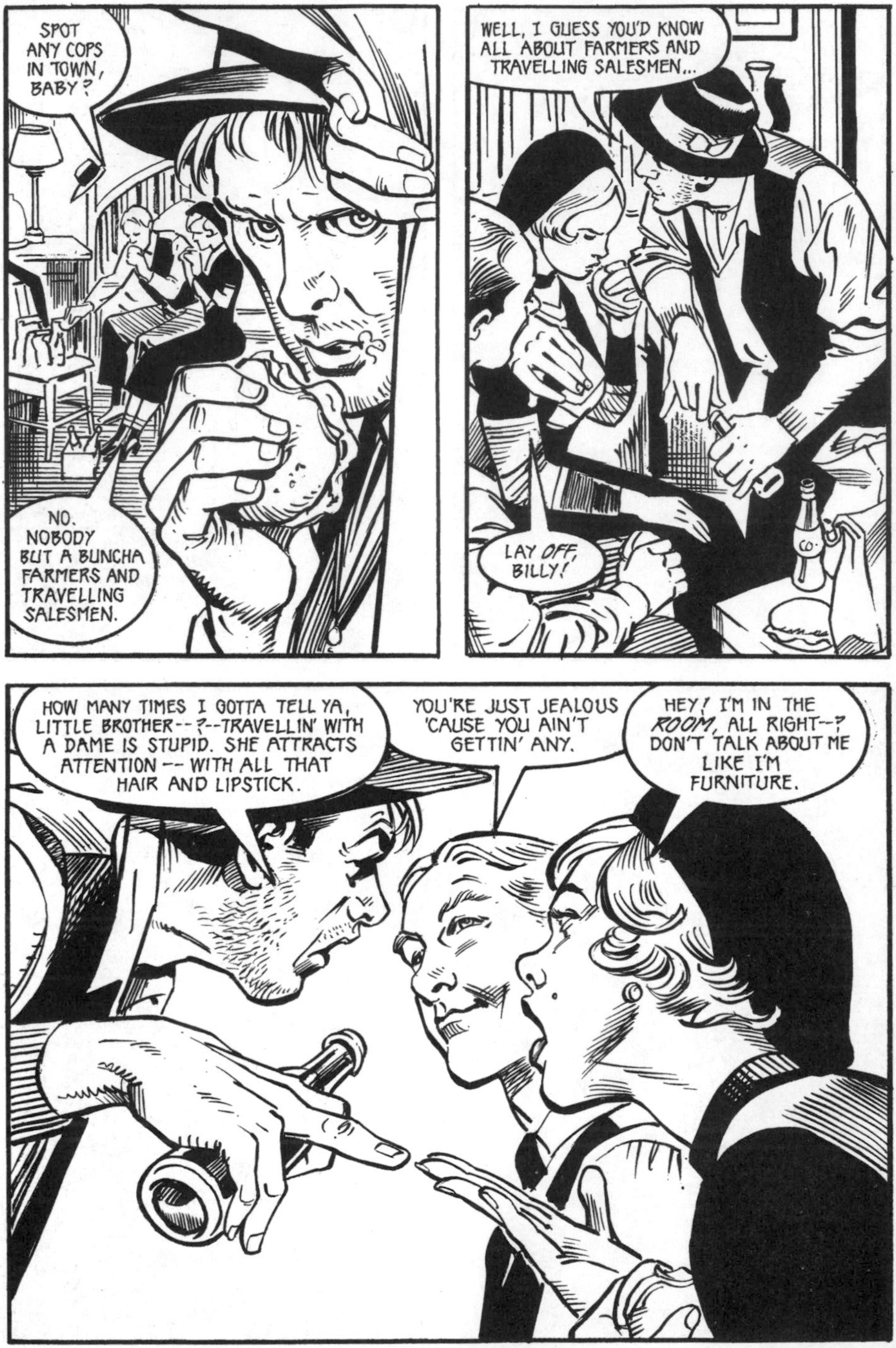
SPOT ANY COPS IN TOWN, BABY?
NO. NOBODY BUT A BUNCHA FARMERS AND TRAVELLING SALESMEN.
WELL, I GUESS YOU'D KNOW ALL ABOUT FARMERS AND TRAVELLING SALESMEN...
LAY OFF, BILLY!
HOW MANY TIMES I GOTTA TELL YA, LITTLE BROTHER--?--TRAVELLIN' WITH A DAME IS STUPID. SHE ATTRACTS ATTENTION -- WITH ALL THAT HAIR AND LIPSTICK.
YOU'RE JUST JEALOUS 'CAUSE YOU AIN'T GETTIN' ANY.
HEY! I'M IN THE ROOM, ALL RIGHT--? DON'T TALK ABOUT ME LIKE I'M FURNITURE.

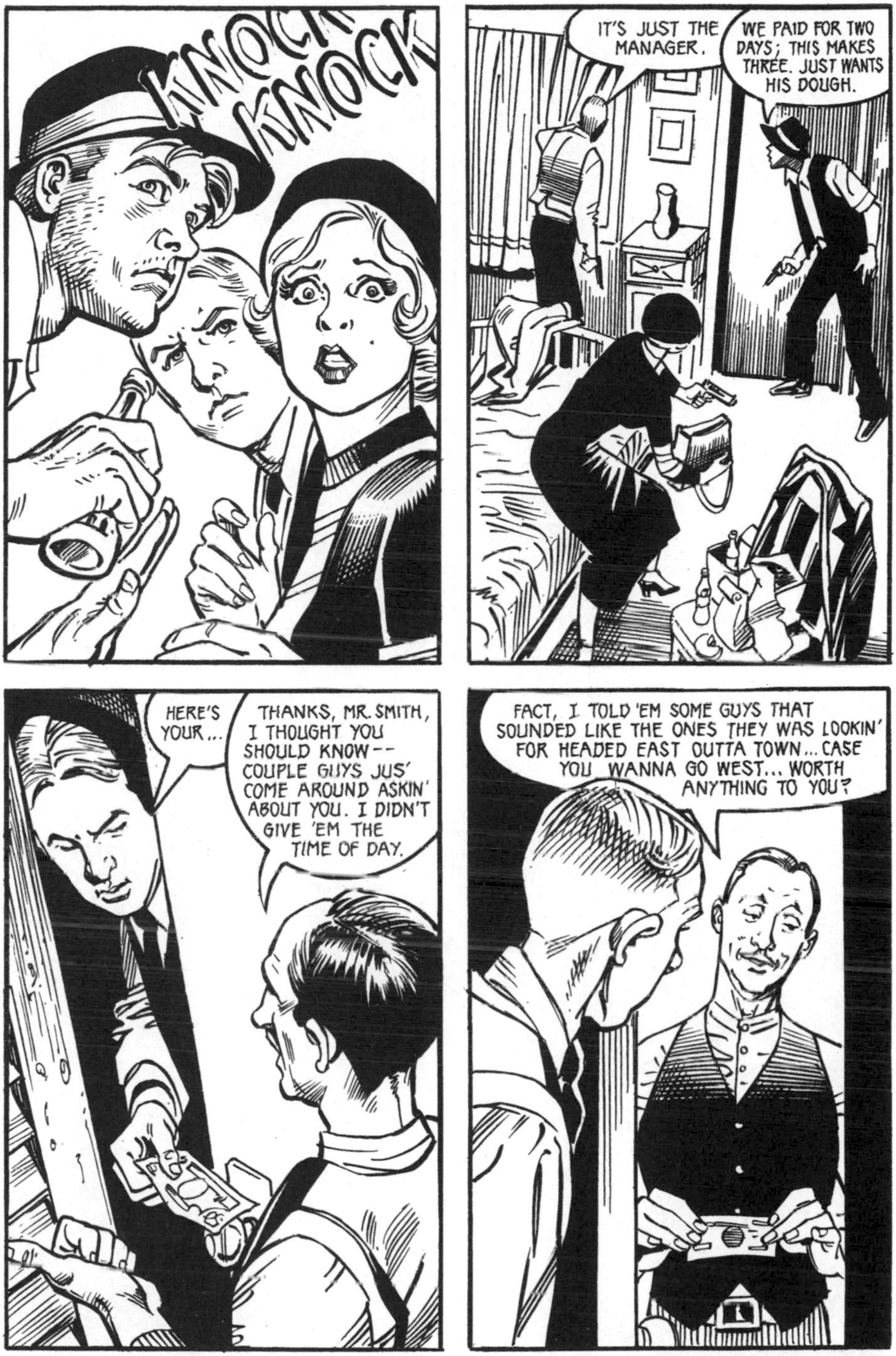

KNOCK KNOCK
IT'S JUST THE MANAGER.
WE PAID FOR TWO DAYS; THIS MAKES THREE. JUST WANTS HIS DOUGH.
HERE'S YOUR...
THANKS, MR. SMITH, I THOUGHT YOU SHOULD KNOW-- COUPLE GUYS JUS' COME AROUND ASKIN' ABOUT YOU. I DIDN'T GIVE 'EM THE TIME OF DAY.
FACT, I TOLD 'EM SOME GUYS THAT SOUNDED LIKE THE ONES THEY WAS LOOKIN' FOR HEADED EAST OUTTA TOWN... CASE YOU WANNA GO WEST... WORTH ANYTHING TO YOU?

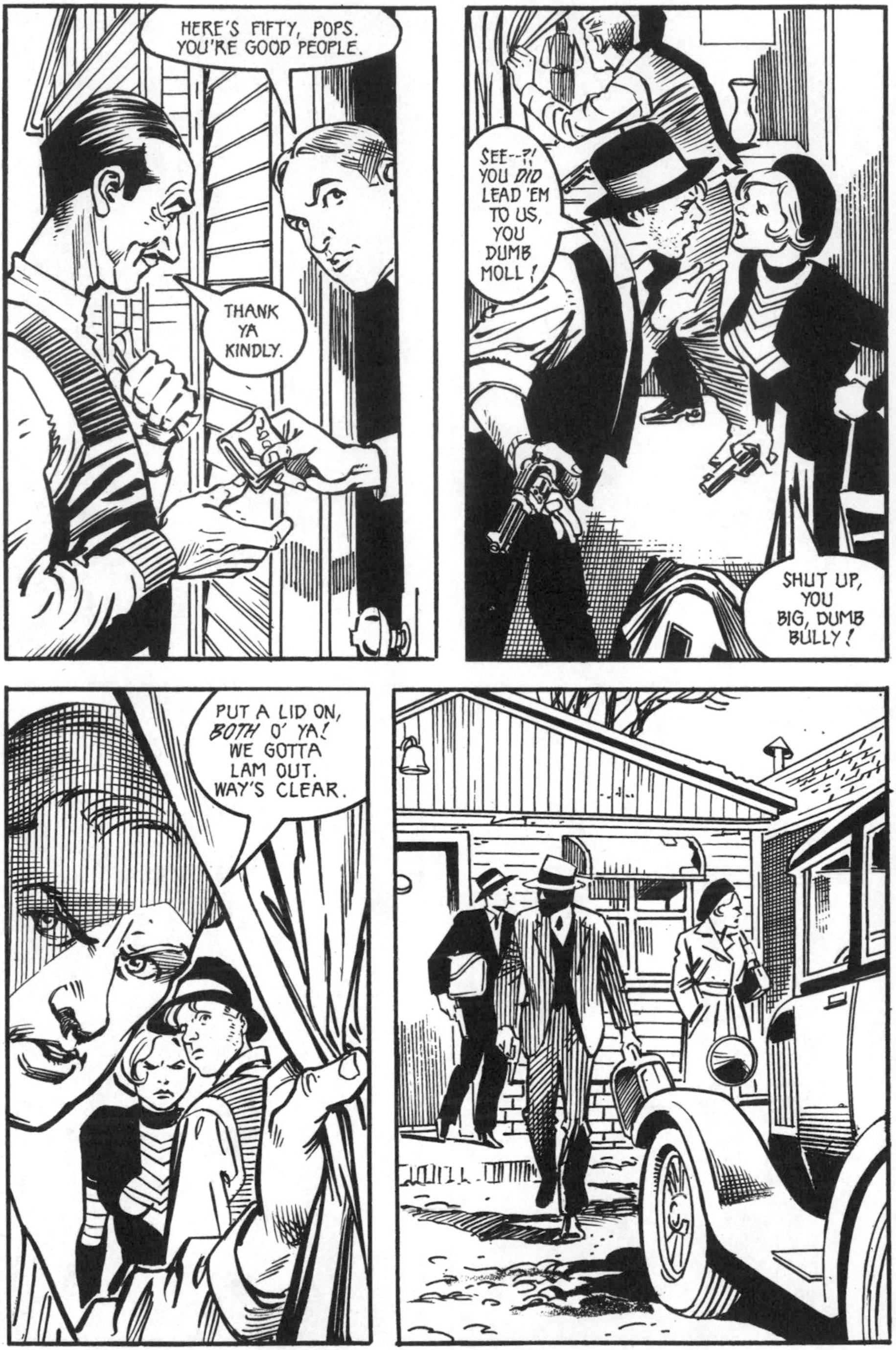
HERE'S FIFTY, POPS. YOU'RE GOOD PEOPLE.
THANK YA KINDLY.
SEE--?! YOU DID LEAD 'EM TO US, YOU DUMB MOLL!
SHUT UP, YOU BIG, DUMB BULLY!
PUT A LID ON, BOTH O' YA! WE GOTTA LAM OUT. WAY'S CLEAR.

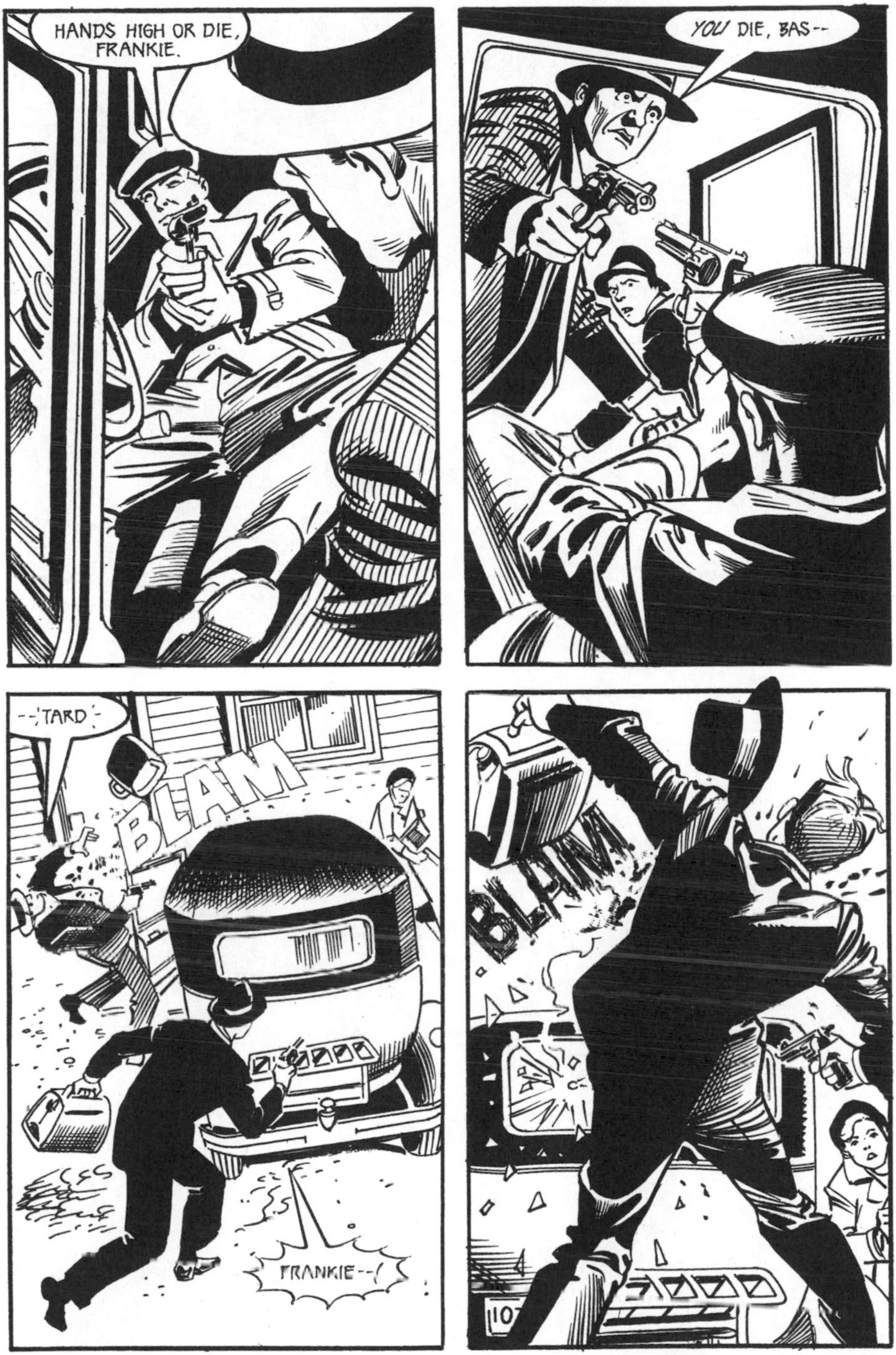
HANDS HIGH OR DIE, FRANKIE.
YOU DIE, BAS--
--TARD
BLAM
FRANKIE--!

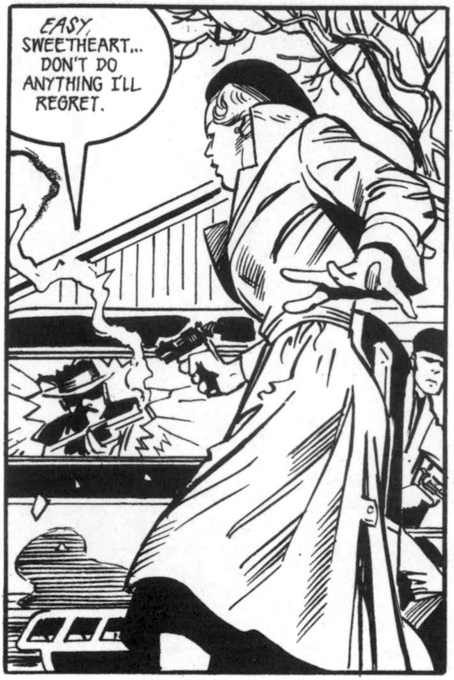
EASY, SWEETHEART... DON'T DO ANYTHING I'LL REGRET.

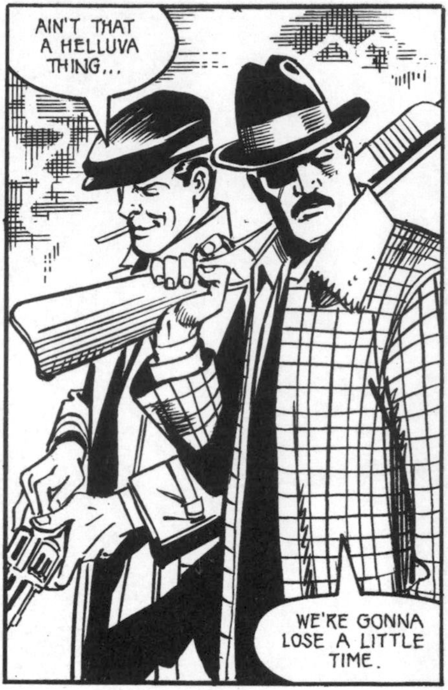
AIN'T THAT A HELLUVA THING...
WE'RE GONNA LOSE A LITTLE TIME.

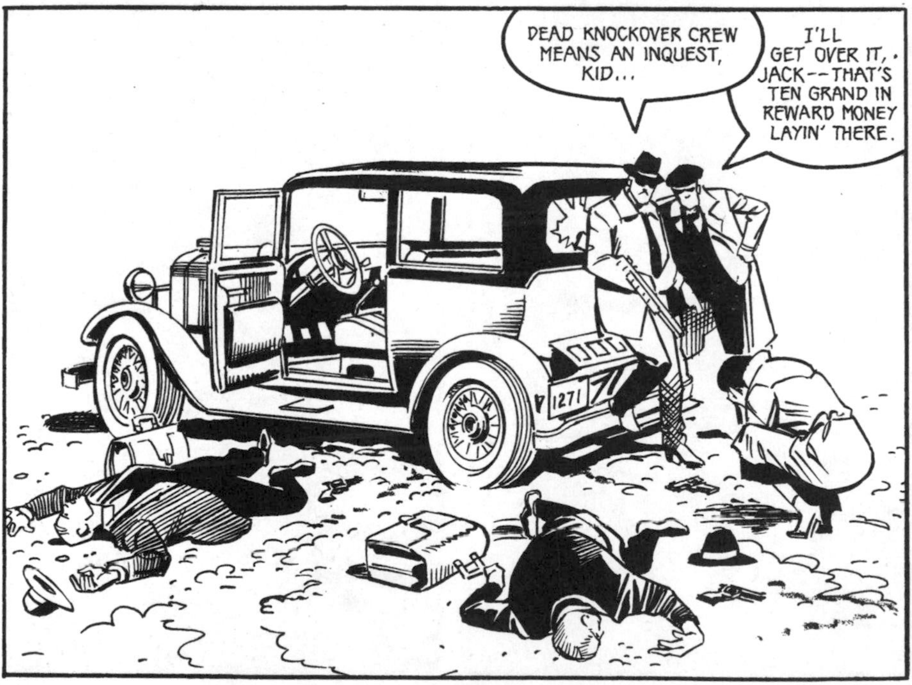
DEAD KNOCKOVER CREW MEANS AN INQUEST, KID...
I'LL GET OVER IT, JACK--THAT'S TEN GRAND IN REWARD MONEY LAYIN' THERE.
1271

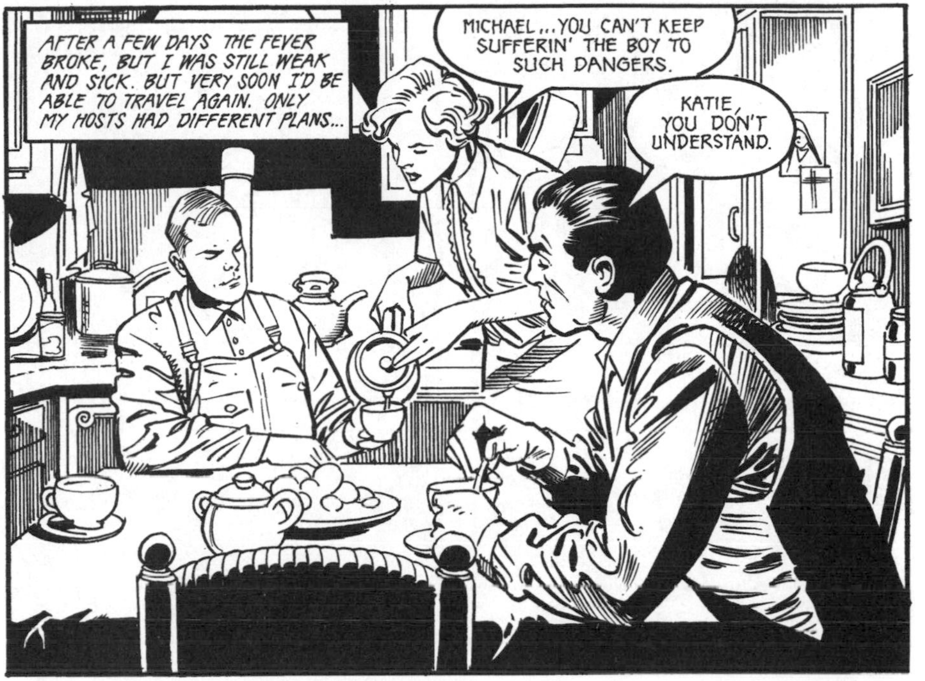
AFTER A FEW DAYS THE FEVER BROKE, BUT I WAS STILL WEAK AND SICK. BUT VERY SOON I'D BE ABLE TO TRAVEL AGAIN. ONLY MY HOSTS HAD DIFFERENT PLANS...
MICHAEL... YOU CAN'T KEEP SUFFERIN' THE BOY TO SUCH DANGERS.
KATIE, YOU DON'T UNDERSTAND.

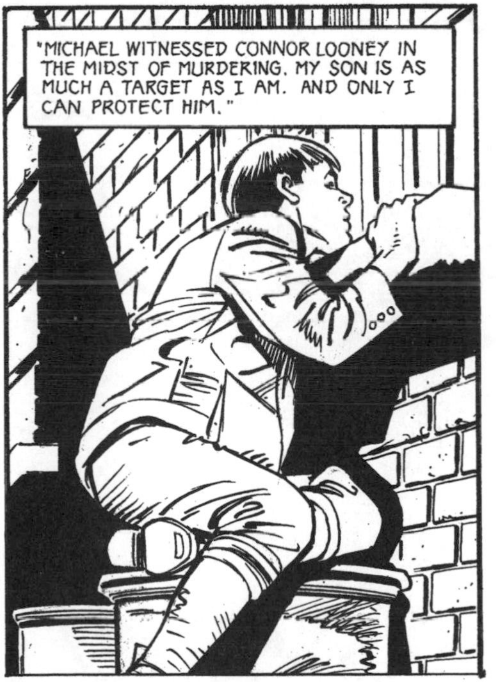
"MICHAEL WITNESSED CONNOR LOONEY IN THE MIDST OF MURDERING. MY SON IS AS MUCH A TARGET AS I AM. AND ONLY I CAN PROTECT HIM."

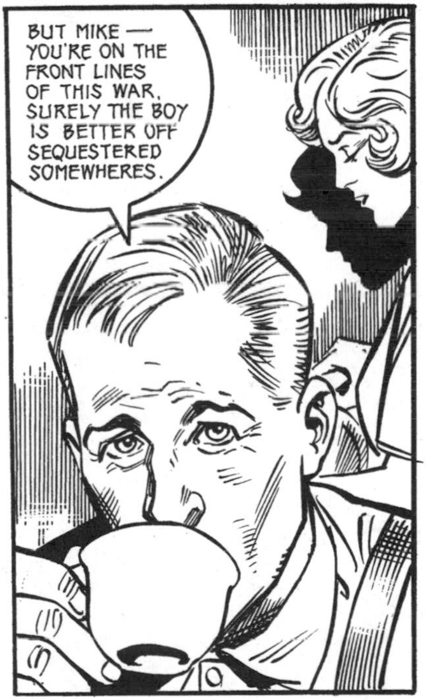
BUT MIKE — YOU'RE ON THE FRONT LINES OF THIS WAR. SURELY THE BOY IS BETTER OFF SEQUESTERED SOMEWHERES.

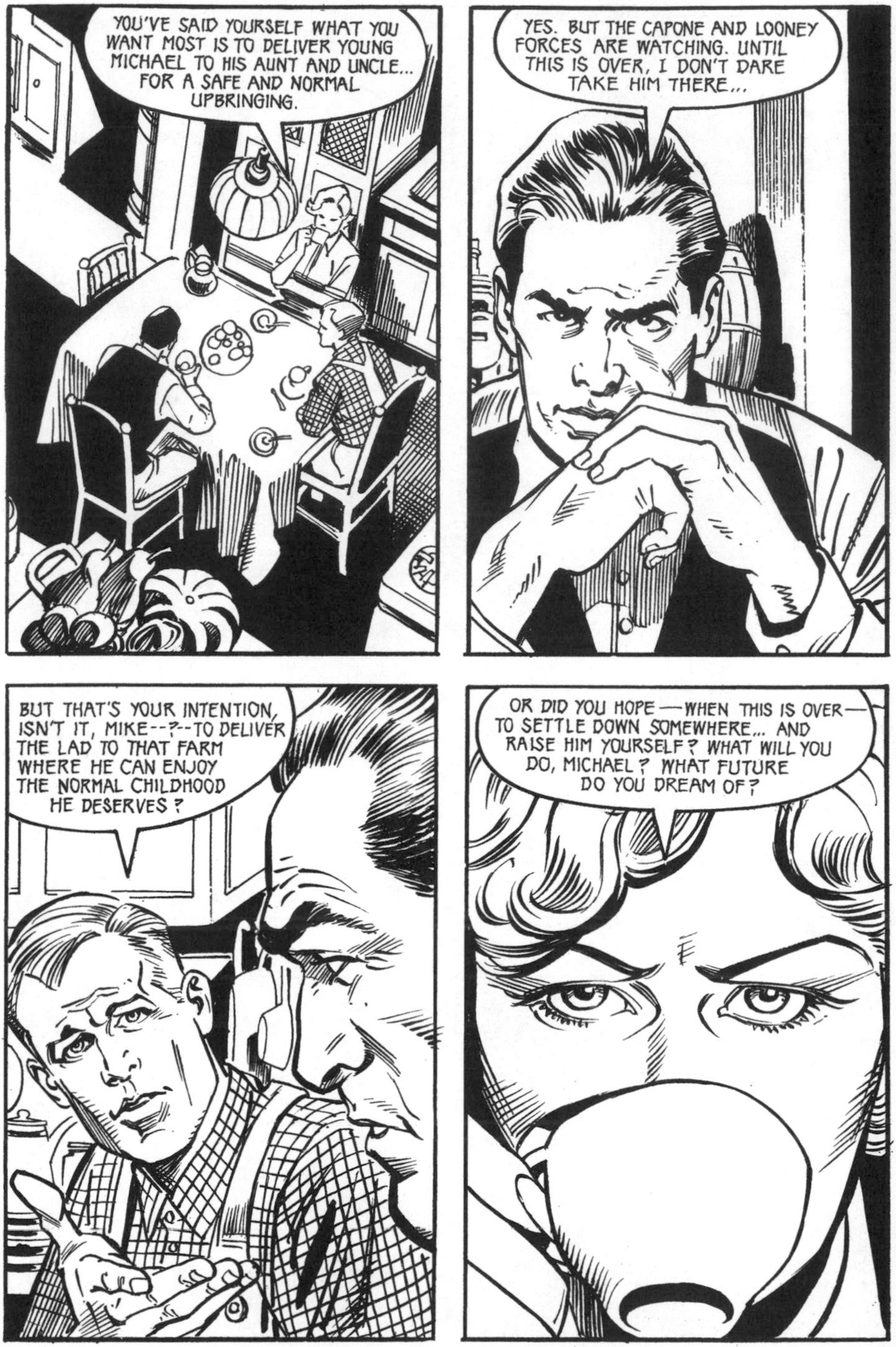
YOU'VE SAID YOURSELF WHAT YOU WANT MOST IS TO DELIVER YOUNG MICHAEL TO HIS AUNT AND UNCLE... FOR A SAFE AND NORMAL UPBRINGING.
YES. BUT THE CAPONE AND LOONEY FORCES ARE WATCHING. UNTIL THIS IS OVER, I DON'T DARE TAKE HIM THERE...
BUT THAT'S YOUR INTENTION, ISN'T IT, MIKE--?--TO DELIVER THE LAD TO THAT FARM WHERE HE CAN ENJOY THE NORMAL CHILDHOOD HE DESERVES?
OR DID YOU HOPE—WHEN THIS IS OVER—TO SETTLE DOWN SOMEWHERE... AND RAISE HIM YOURSELF? WHAT WILL YOU DO, MICHAEL? WHAT FUTURE DO YOU DREAM OF?

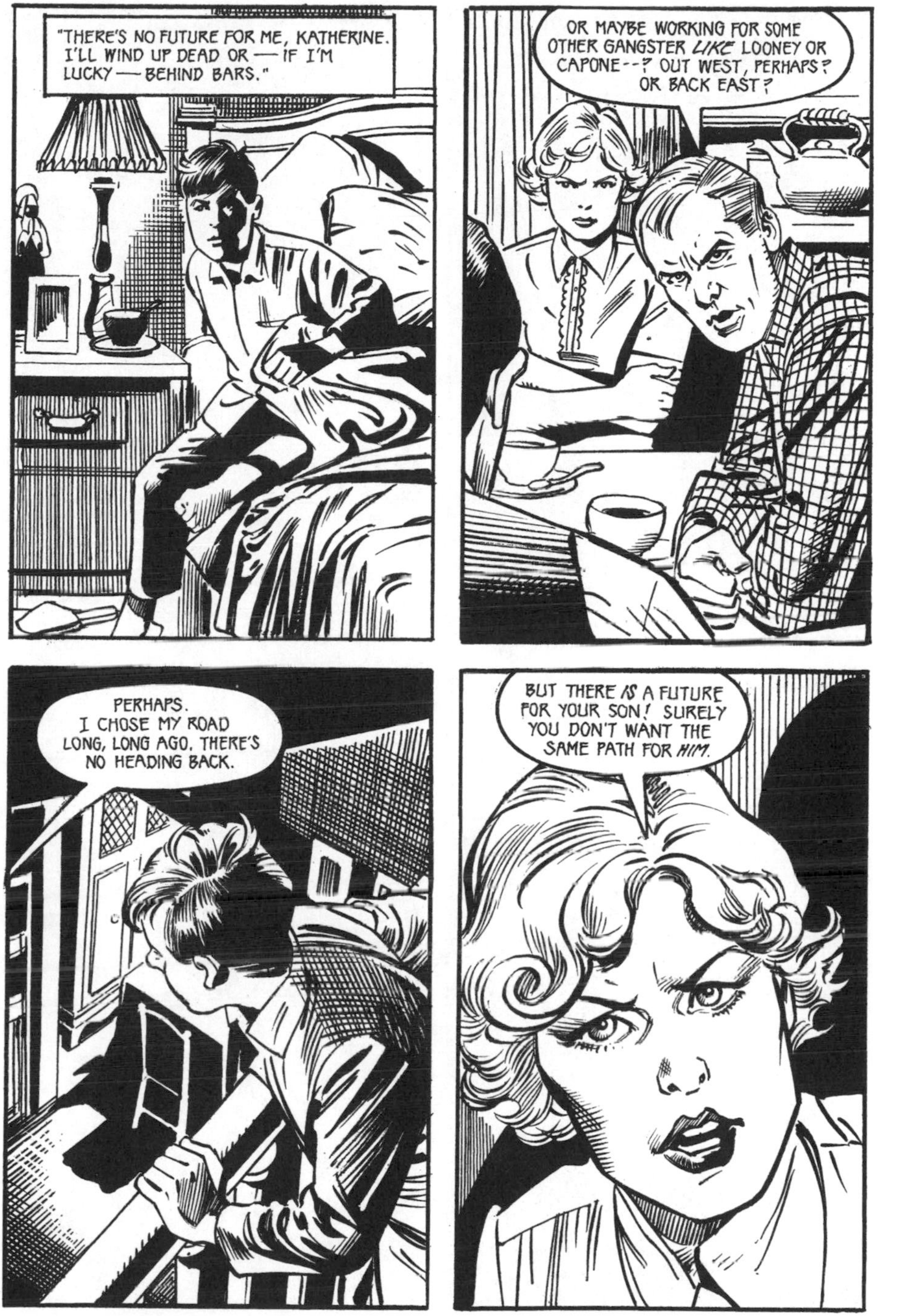
"THERE'S NO FUTURE FOR ME, KATHERINE. I'LL WIND UP DEAD OR — IF I'M LUCKY — BEHIND BARS."
OR MAYBE WORKING FOR SOME OTHER GANGSTER LIKE LOONEY OR CAPONE--? OUT WEST, PERHAPS? OR BACK EAST?
PERHAPS. I CHOSE MY ROAD LONG, LONG AGO. THERE'S NO HEADING BACK.
BUT THERE IS A FUTURE FOR YOUR SON! SURELY YOU DON'T WANT THE SAME PATH FOR HIM.

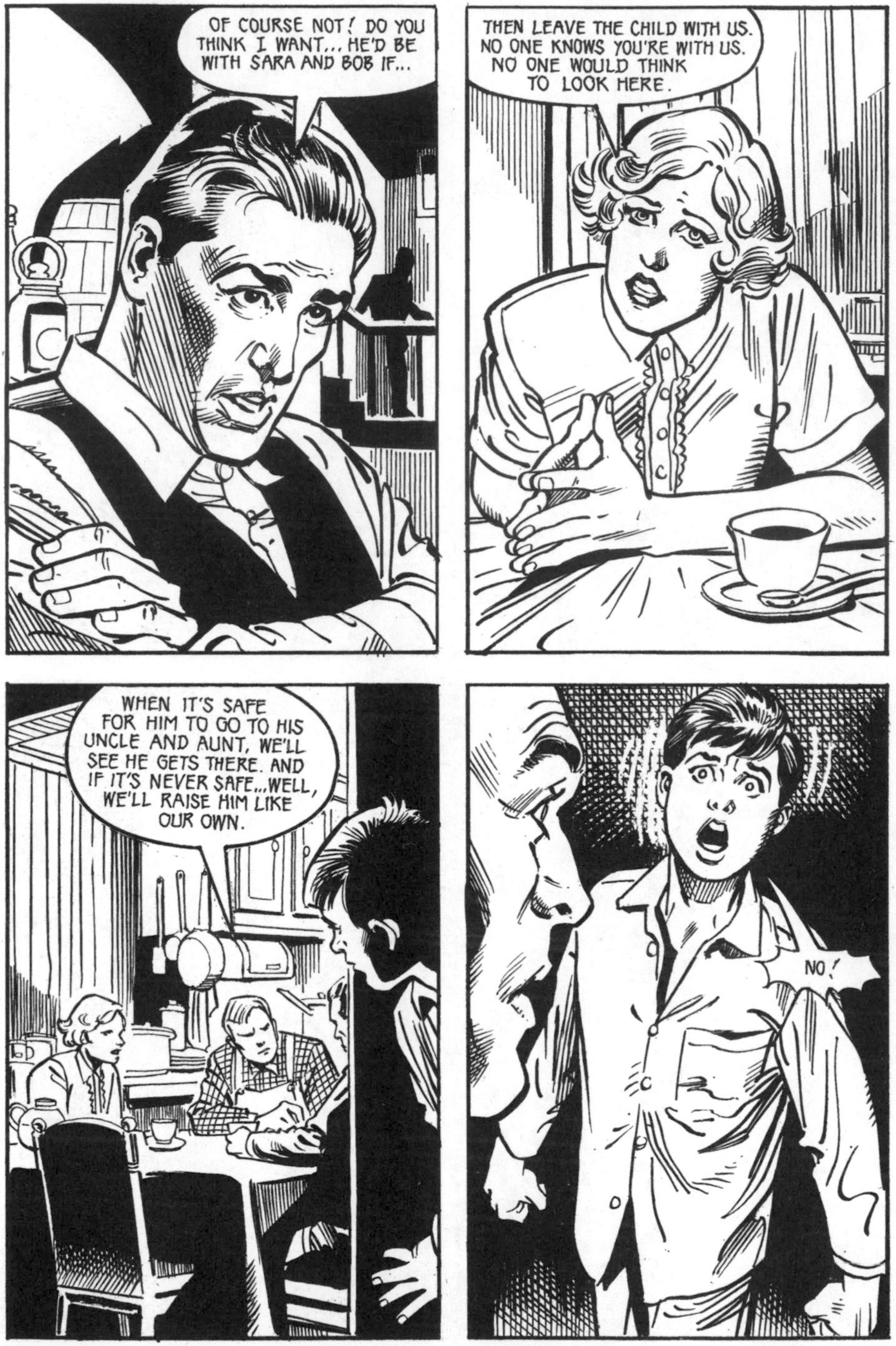
OF COURSE NOT! DO YOU THINK I WANT... HE'D BE WITH SARA AND BOB IF...
THEN LEAVE THE CHILD WITH US. NO ONE KNOWS YOU'RE WITH US. NO ONE WOULD THINK TO LOOK HERE.
WHEN IT'S SAFE FOR HIM TO GO TO HIS UNCLE AND AUNT, WE'LL SEE HE GETS THERE. AND IF IT'S NEVER SAFE...WELL, WE'LL RAISE HIM LIKE OUR OWN.
NO!

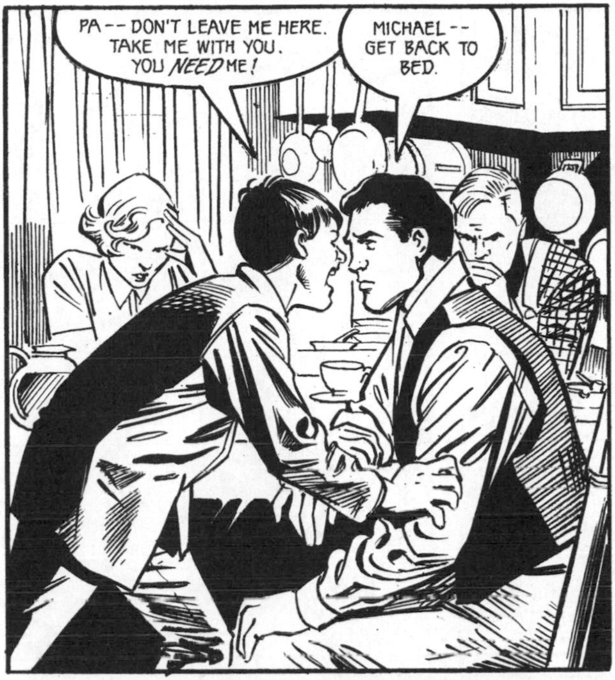
PA -- DON'T LEAVE ME HERE. TAKE ME WITH YOU. YOU NEED ME!
MICHAEL -- GET BACK TO BED.

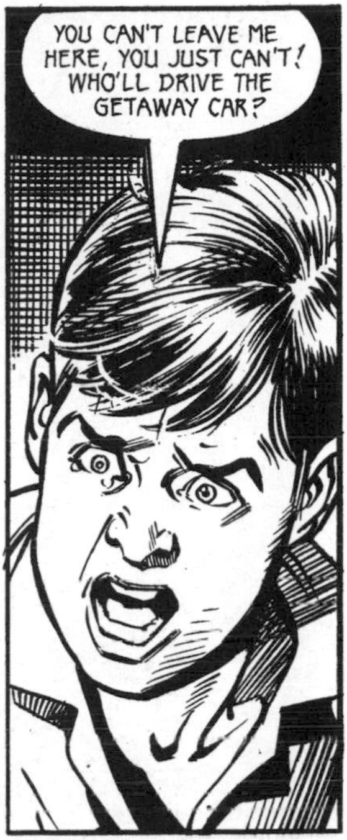
YOU CAN'T LEAVE ME HERE, YOU JUST CAN'T! WHO'LL DRIVE THE GETAWAY CAR?

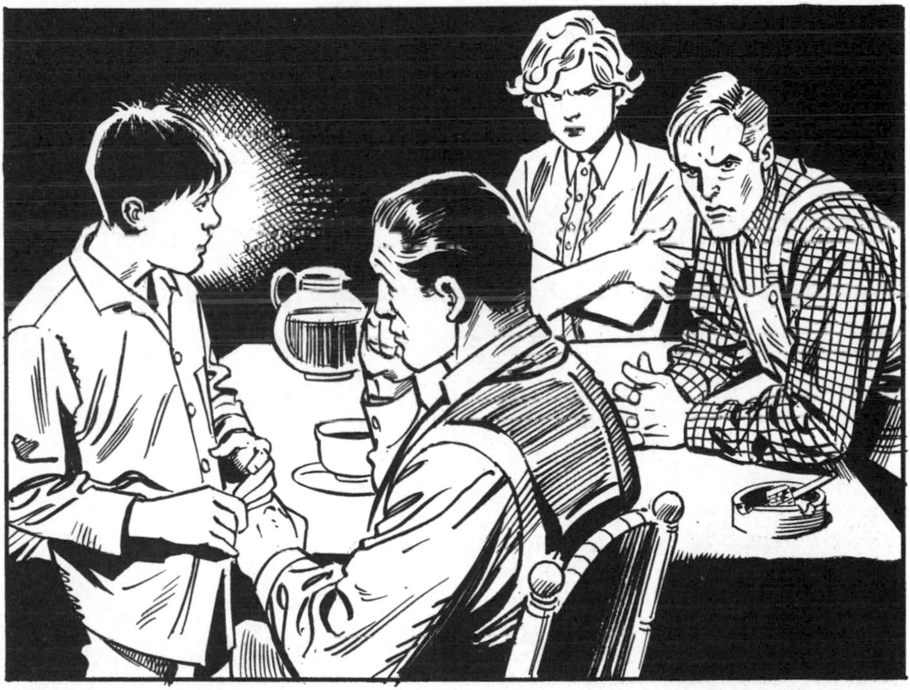

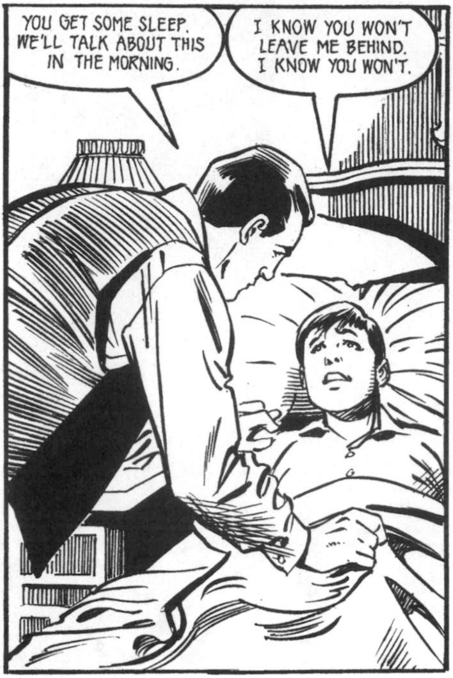
YOU GET SOME SLEEP. WE'LL TALK ABOUT THIS IN THE MORNING.
I KNOW YOU WON'T LEAVE ME BEHIND. I KNOW YOU WON'T.

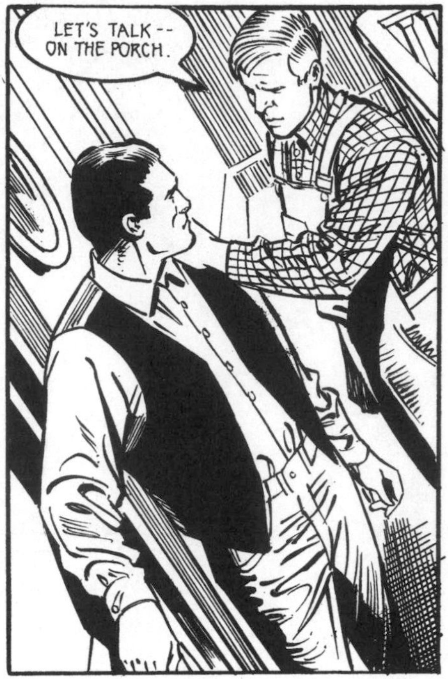
LET'S TALK -- ON THE PORCH.

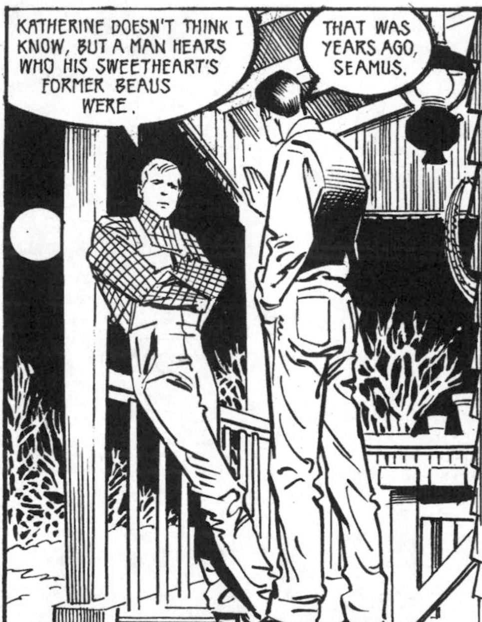
KATHERINE DOESN'T THINK I KNOW, BUT A MAN HEARS WHO HIS SWEETHEART'S FORMER BEAUS WERE.
THAT WAS YEARS AGO, SEAMUS.

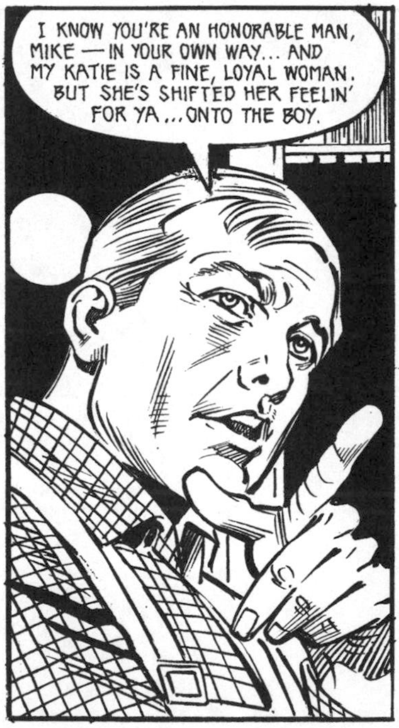
I KNOW YOU'RE AN HONORABLE MAN, MIKE — IN YOUR OWN WAY... AND MY KATIE IS A FINE, LOYAL WOMAN. BUT SHE'S SHIFTED HER FEELIN' FOR YA... ONTO THE BOY.

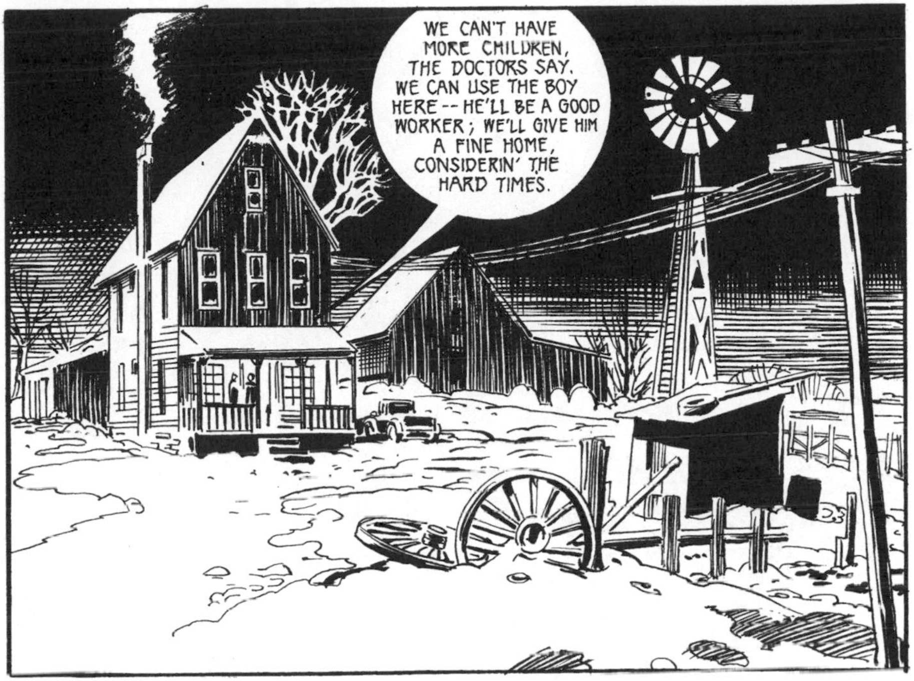
WE CAN'T HAVE MORE CHILDREN, THE DOCTORS SAY. WE CAN USE THE BOY HERE -- HE'LL BE A GOOD WORKER; WE'LL GIVE HIM A FINE HOME, CONSIDERIN' THE HARD TIMES.

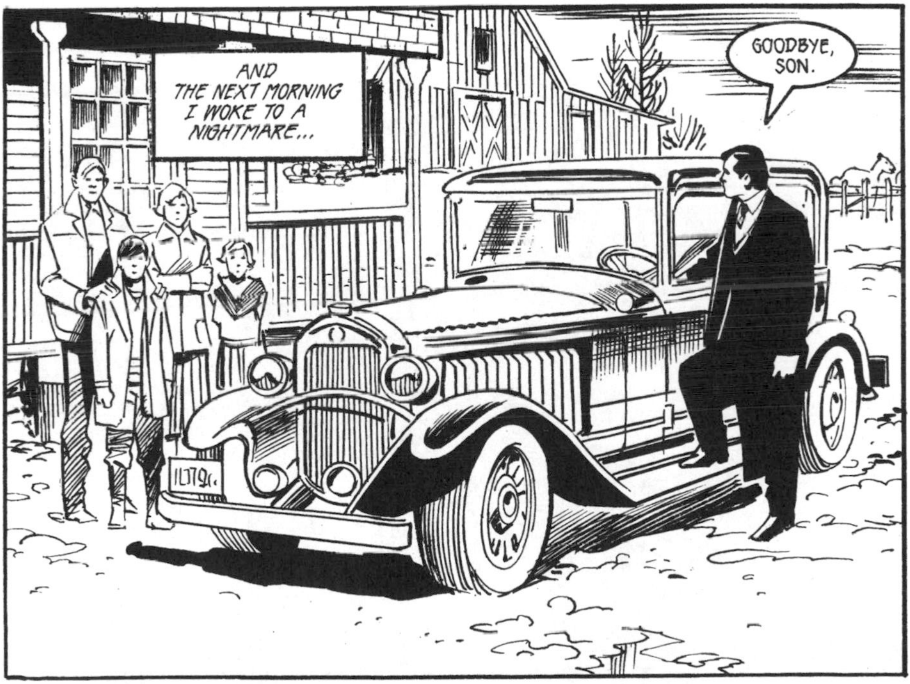
AND THE NEXT MORNING I WOKE TO A NIGHTMARE...
GOODBYE, SON.

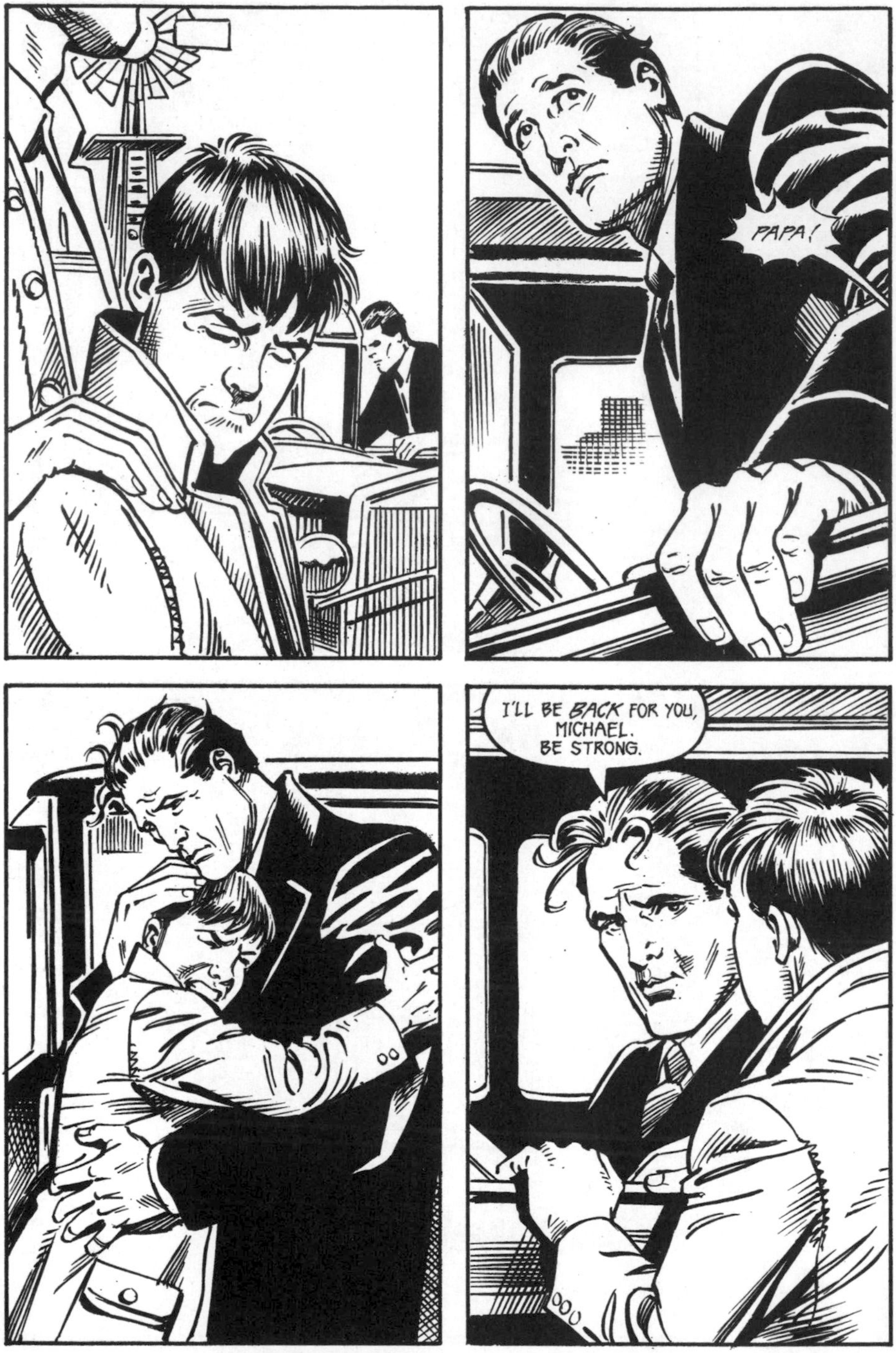
PAPA!
I'LL BE BACK FOR YOU, MICHAEL. BE STRONG.

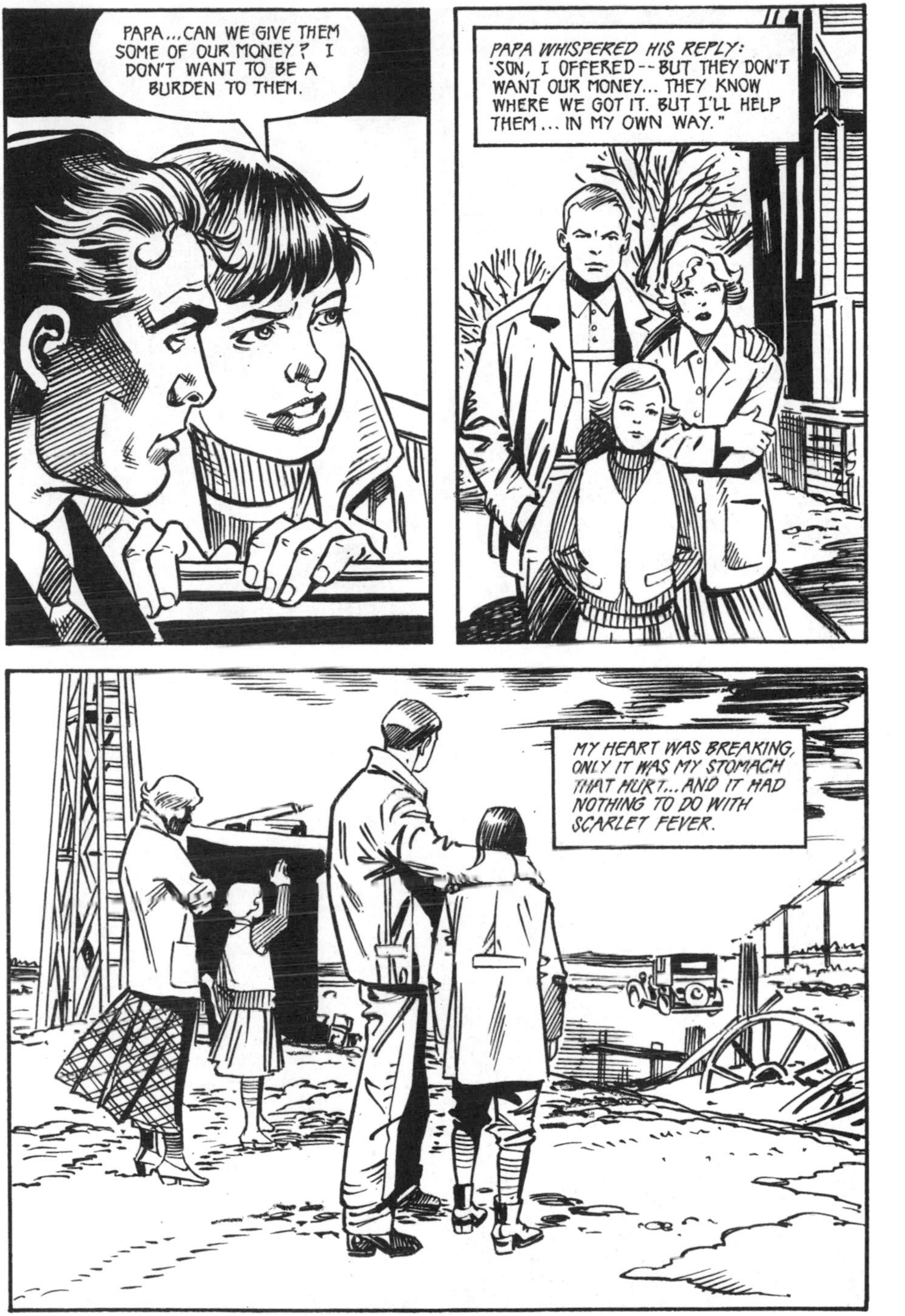
PAPA...CAN WE GIVE THEM SOME OF OUR MONEY? I DON'T WANT TO BE A BURDEN TO THEM.
PAPA WHISPERED HIS REPLY: "SON, I OFFERED--BUT THEY DON'T WANT OUR MONEY... THEY KNOW WHERE WE GOT IT. BUT I'LL HELP THEM... IN MY OWN WAY."
MY HEART WAS BREAKING, ONLY IT WAS MY STOMACH THAT HURT... AND IT HAD NOTHING TO DO WITH SCARLET FEVER.

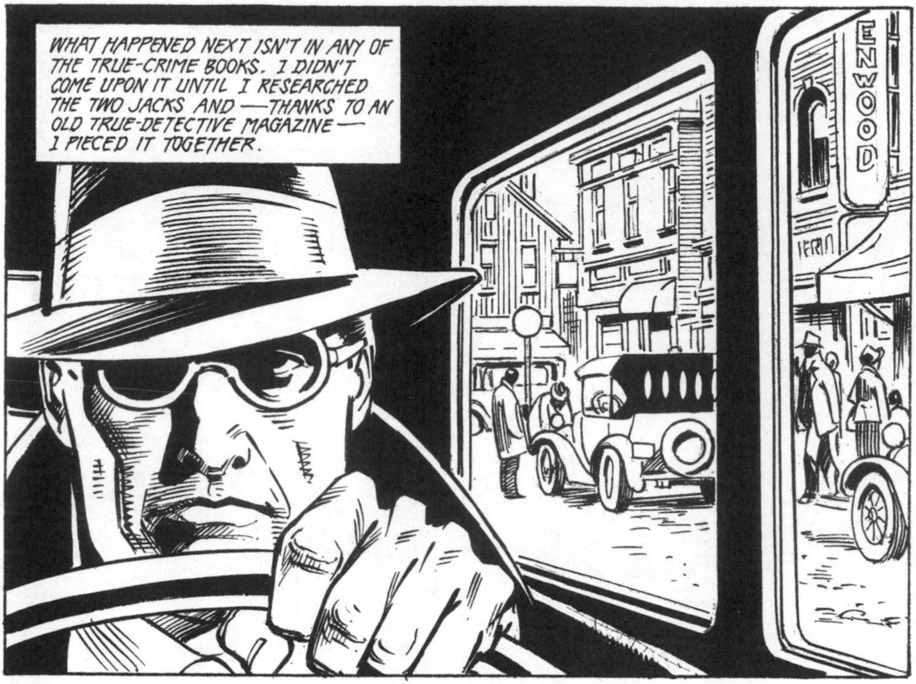
WHAT HAPPENED NEXT ISN'T IN ANY OF THE TRUE-CRIME BOOKS. I DIDN'T COME UPON IT UNTIL I RESEARCHED THE TWO JACKS AND —THANKS TO AN OLD TRUE-DETECTIVE MAGAZINE— I PIECED IT TOGETHER.
ENWOOD

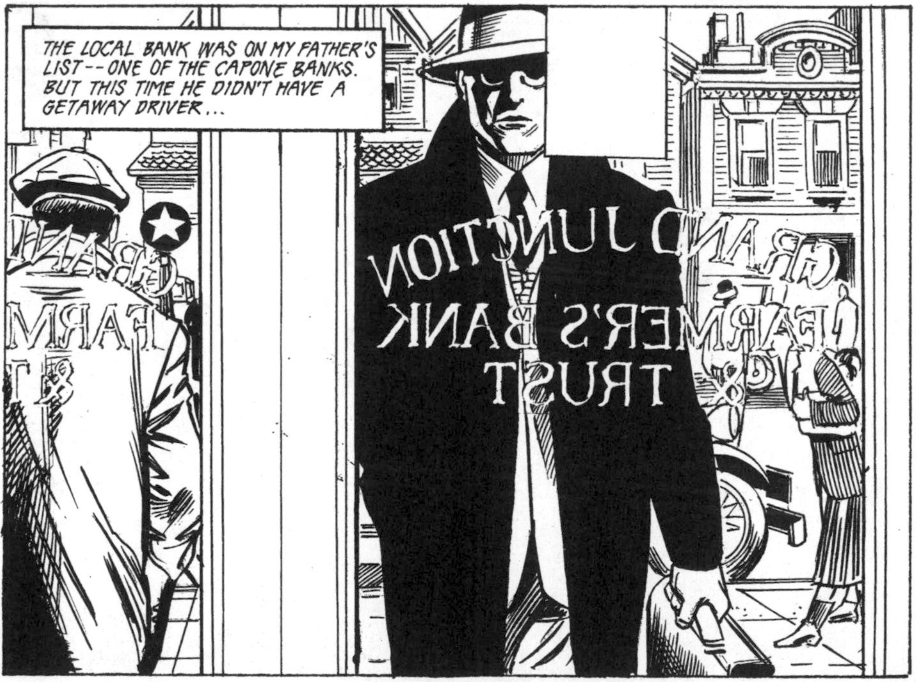
THE LOCAL BANK WAS ON MY FATHER'S LIST--ONE OF THE CAPONE BANKS. BUT THIS TIME HE DIDN'T HAVE A GETAWAY DRIVER...
GRAND JUNCTION
FARMER'S BANK
& TRUST

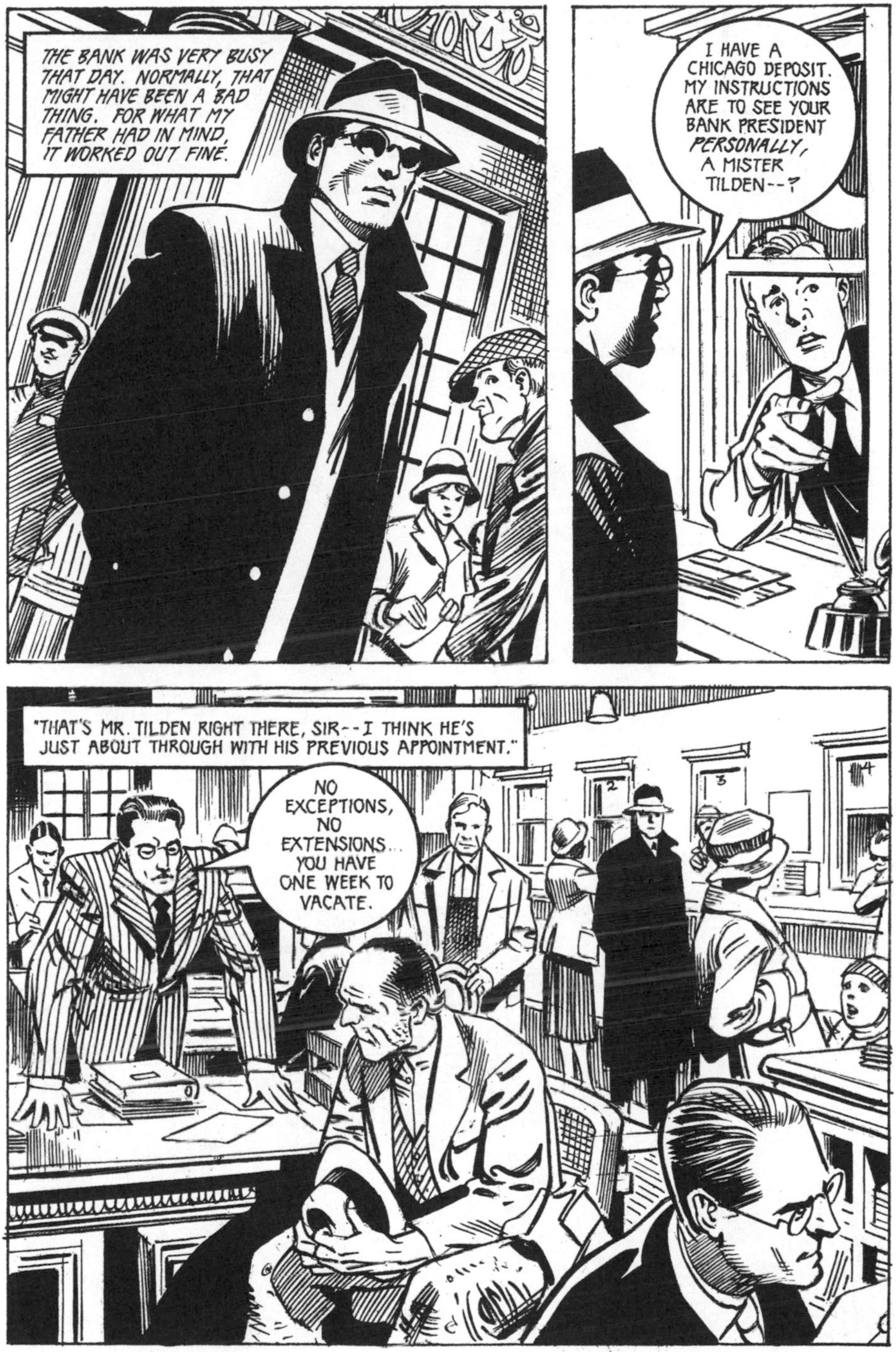
THE BANK WAS VERY BUSY THAT DAY. NORMALLY, THAT MIGHT HAVE BEEN A BAD THING. FOR WHAT MY FATHER HAD IN MIND, IT WORKED OUT FINE.
I HAVE A CHICAGO DEPOSIT. MY INSTRUCTIONS ARE TO SEE YOUR BANK PRESIDENT *PERSONALLY*, A MISTER TILDEN--?
"THAT'S MR. TILDEN RIGHT THERE, SIR--I THINK HE'S JUST ABOUT THROUGH WITH HIS PREVIOUS APPOINTMENT."
NO EXCEPTIONS, NO EXTENSIONS... YOU HAVE ONE WEEK TO VACATE.

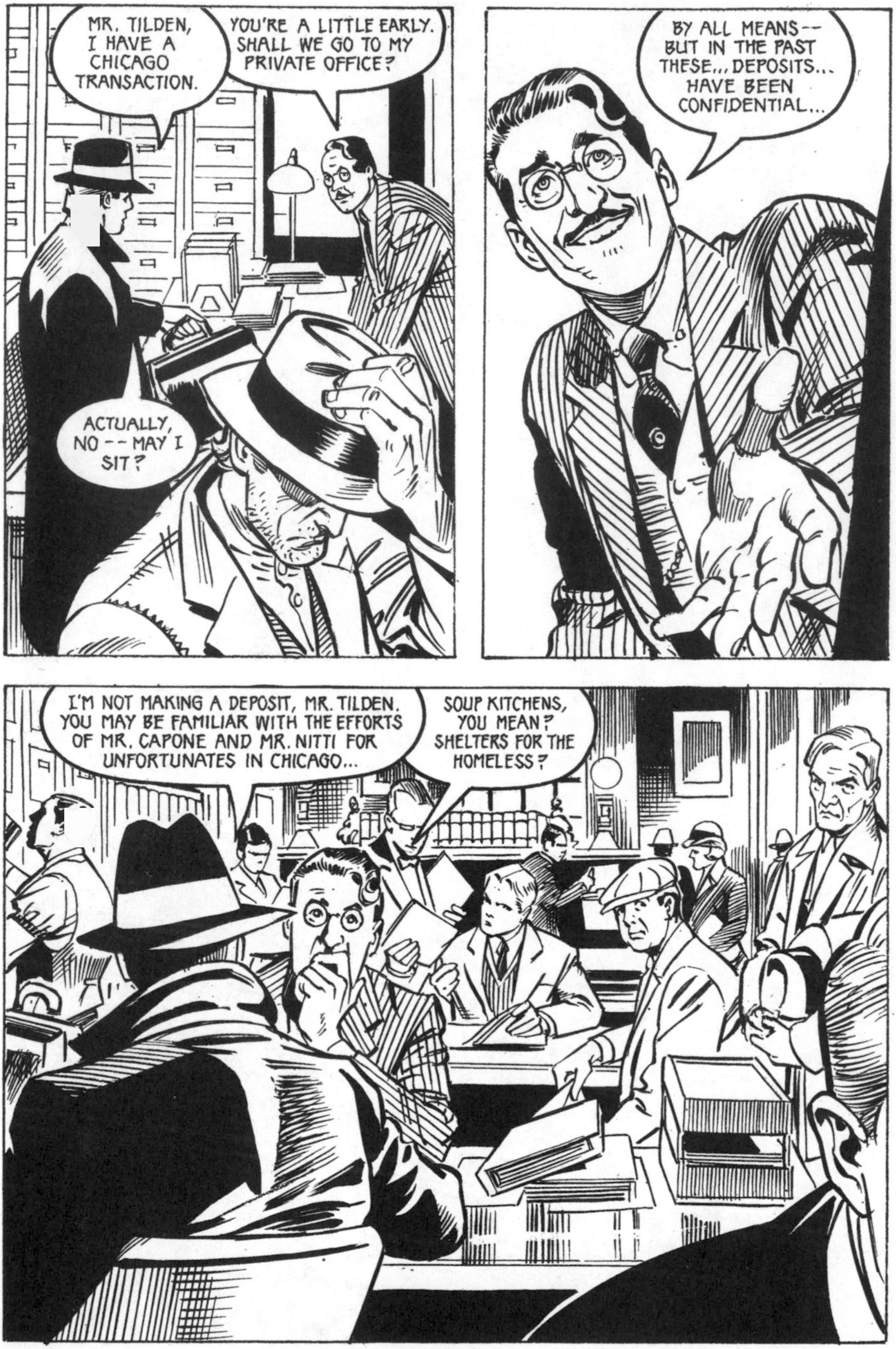
MR. TILDEN, I HAVE A CHICAGO TRANSACTION.
YOU'RE A LITTLE EARLY. SHALL WE GO TO MY PRIVATE OFFICE?
ACTUALLY, NO -- MAY I SIT?
BY ALL MEANS -- BUT IN THE PAST THESE... DEPOSITS... HAVE BEEN CONFIDENTIAL...
I'M NOT MAKING A DEPOSIT, MR. TILDEN. YOU MAY BE FAMILIAR WITH THE EFFORTS OF MR. CAPONE AND MR. NITTI FOR UNFORTUNATES IN CHICAGO...
SOUP KITCHENS, YOU MEAN? SHELTERS FOR THE HOMELESS?

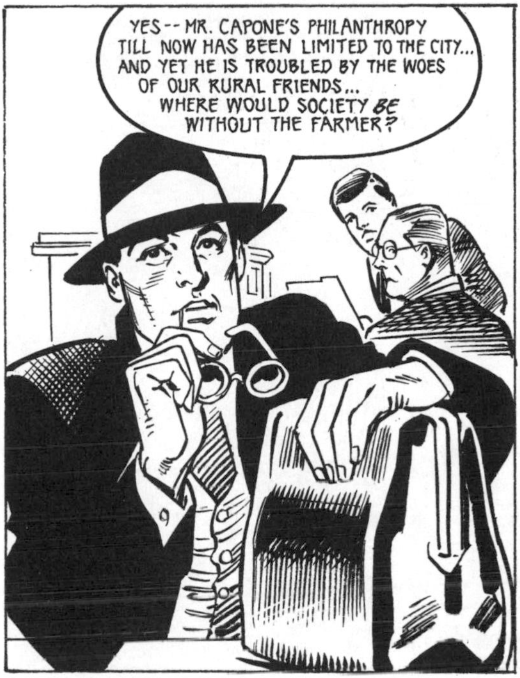
YES--MR. CAPONE'S PHILANTHROPY TILL NOW HAS BEEN LIMITED TO THE CITY... AND YET HE IS TROUBLED BY THE WOES OF OUR RURAL FRIENDS... WHERE WOULD SOCIETY *BE* WITHOUT THE FARMER?

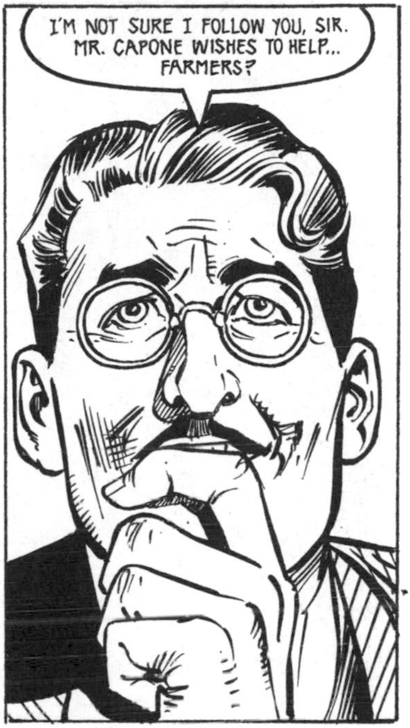
I'M NOT SURE I FOLLOW YOU, SIR. MR. CAPONE WISHES TO HELP... FARMERS?

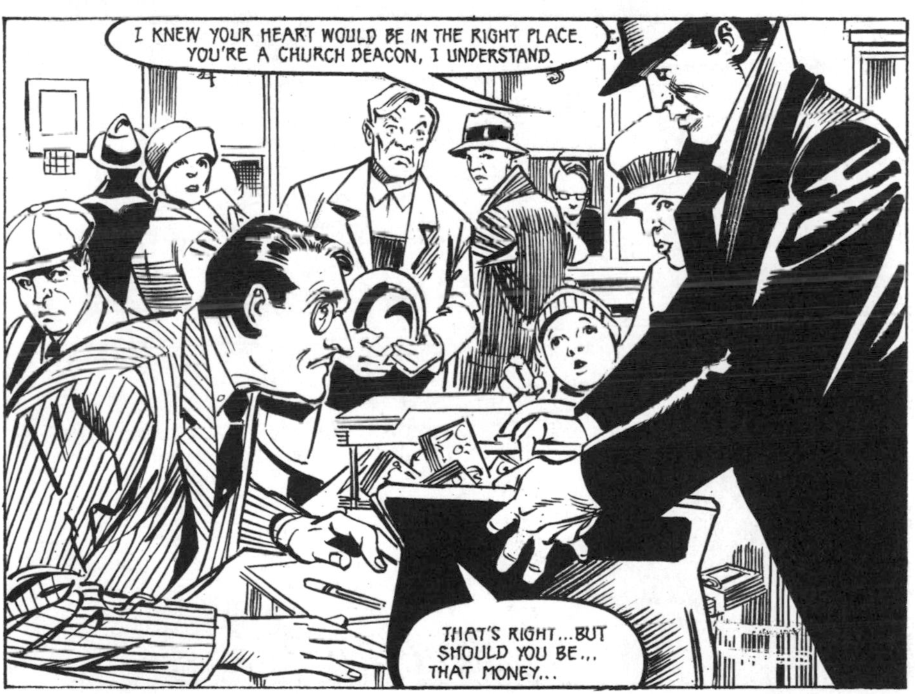
I KNEW YOUR HEART WOULD BE IN THE RIGHT PLACE. YOU'RE A CHURCH DEACON, I UNDERSTAND.
THAT'S RIGHT...BUT SHOULD YOU BE... THAT MONEY...

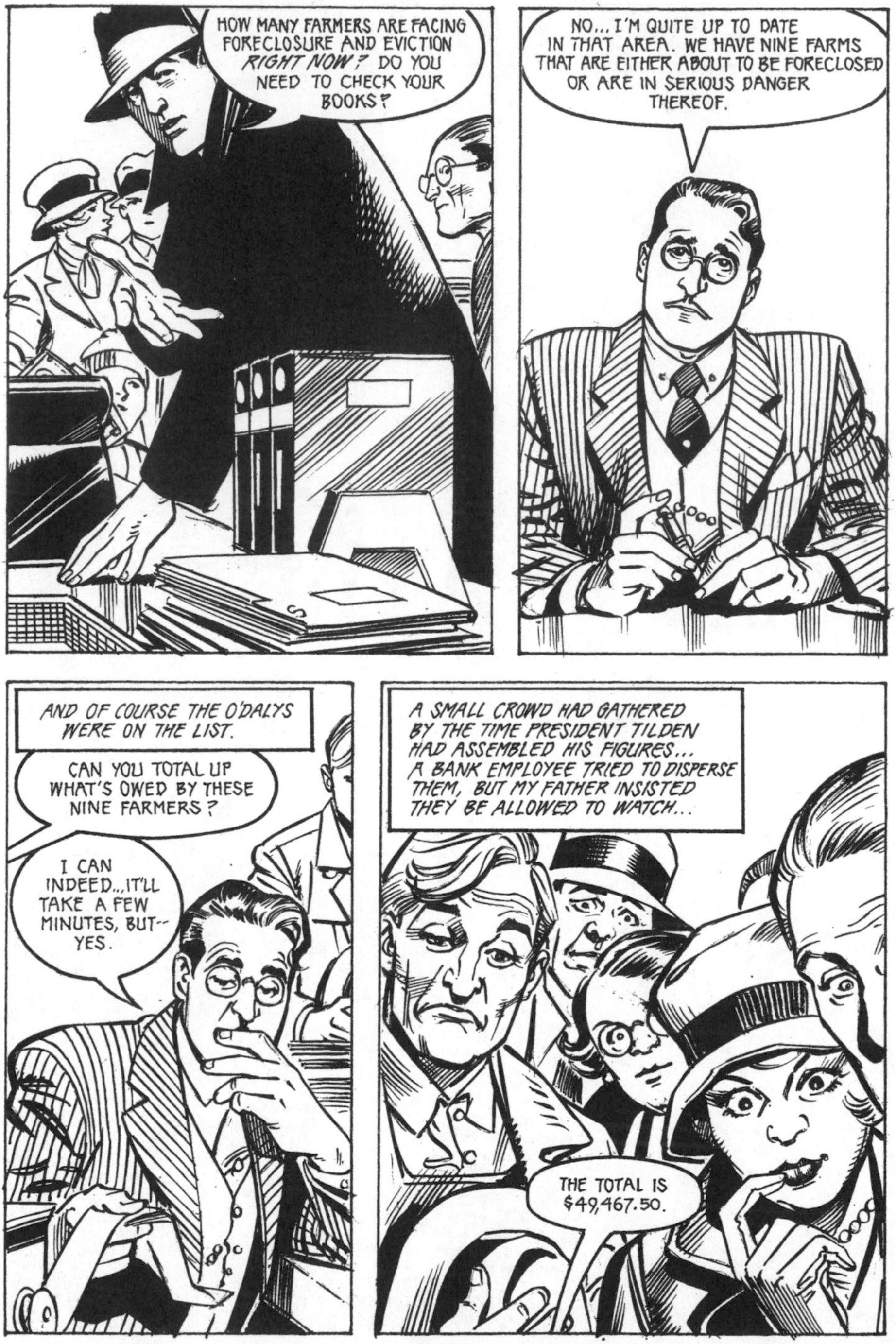
HOW MANY FARMERS ARE FACING FORECLOSURE AND EVICTION *RIGHT NOW?* DO YOU NEED TO CHECK YOUR BOOKS?
NO... I'M QUITE UP TO DATE IN THAT AREA. WE HAVE NINE FARMS THAT ARE EITHER ABOUT TO BE FORECLOSED OR ARE IN SERIOUS DANGER THEREOF.
AND OF COURSE THE O'DALYS WERE ON THE LIST.
CAN YOU TOTAL UP WHAT'S OWED BY THESE NINE FARMERS?
I CAN INDEED... IT'LL TAKE A FEW MINUTES, BUT-- YES.
A SMALL CROWD HAD GATHERED BY THE TIME PRESIDENT TILDEN HAD ASSEMBLED HIS FIGURES... A BANK EMPLOYEE TRIED TO DISPERSE THEM, BUT MY FATHER INSISTED THEY BE ALLOWED TO WATCH...
THE TOTAL IS $49,467.50.

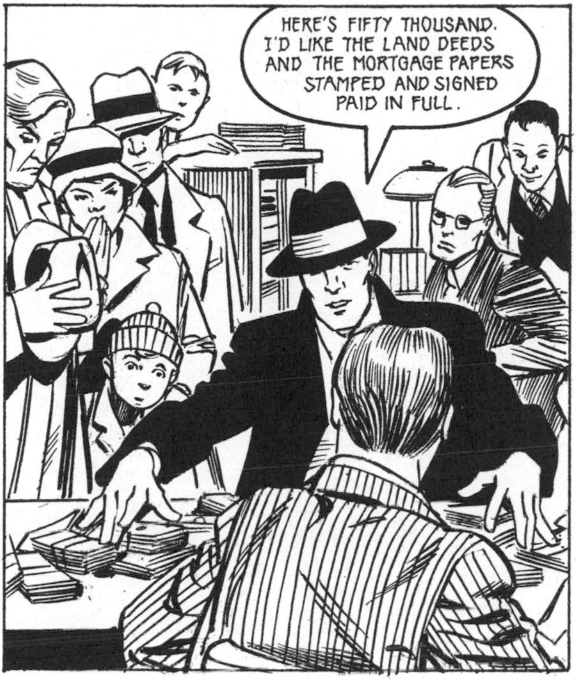
HERE'S FIFTY THOUSAND. I'D LIKE THE LAND DEEDS AND THE MORTGAGE PAPERS STAMPED AND SIGNED PAID IN FULL.

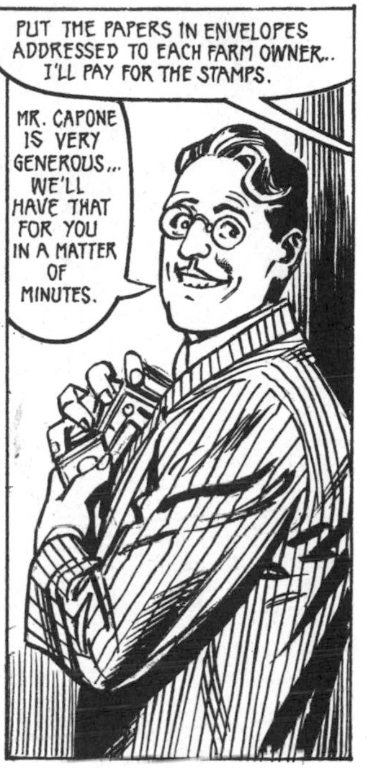
PUT THE PAPERS IN ENVELOPES ADDRESSED TO EACH FARM OWNER.. I'LL PAY FOR THE STAMPS.
MR. CAPONE IS VERY GENEROUS... WE'LL HAVE THAT FOR YOU IN A MATTER OF MINUTES.

AND THEY DID. AS IT HAPPENED, ONE OF THE FARMERS IN QUESTION WAS IN THE BANK.

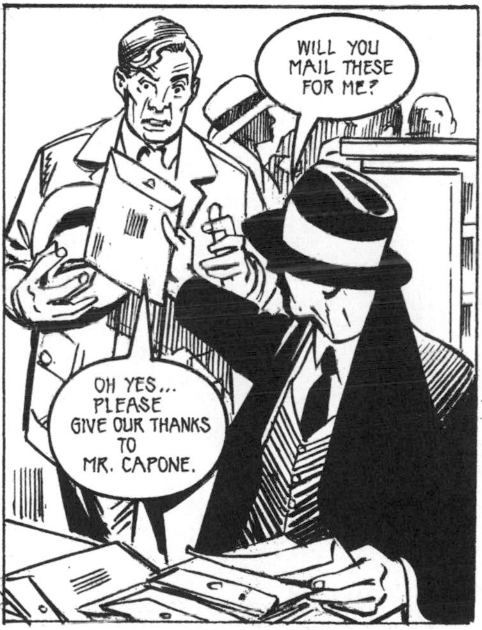
WILL YOU MAIL THESE FOR ME?
OH YES... PLEASE GIVE OUR THANKS TO MR. CAPONE.

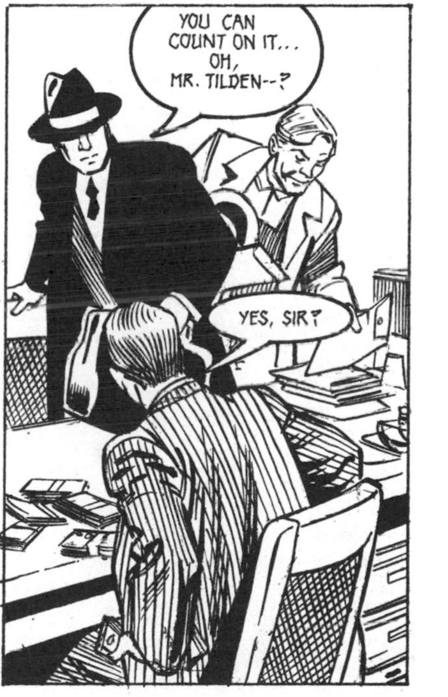
YOU CAN COUNT ON IT... OH, MR. TILDEN--?
YES, SIR?

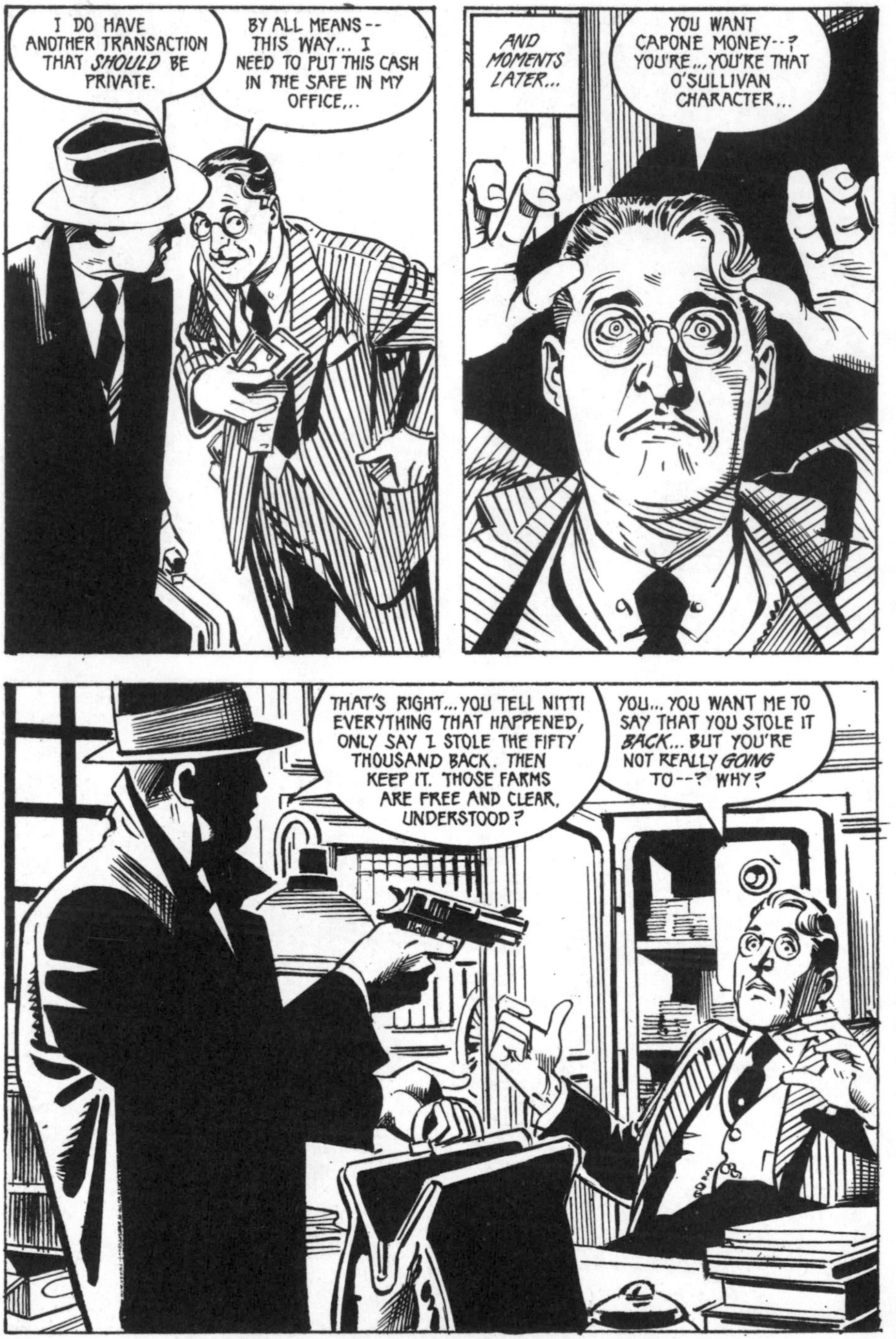
I DO HAVE ANOTHER TRANSACTION THAT *SHOULD* BE PRIVATE.
BY ALL MEANS -- THIS WAY... I NEED TO PUT THIS CASH IN THE SAFE IN MY OFFICE...
AND MOMENTS LATER...
YOU WANT CAPONE MONEY--? YOU'RE... YOU'RE THAT O'SULLIVAN CHARACTER...
THAT'S RIGHT... YOU TELL NITTI EVERYTHING THAT HAPPENED, ONLY SAY I STOLE THE FIFTY THOUSAND BACK. THEN KEEP IT. THOSE FARMS ARE FREE AND CLEAR, UNDERSTOOD?
YOU... YOU WANT ME TO SAY THAT YOU STOLE IT *BACK*... BUT YOU'RE NOT REALLY *GOING* TO--? WHY?

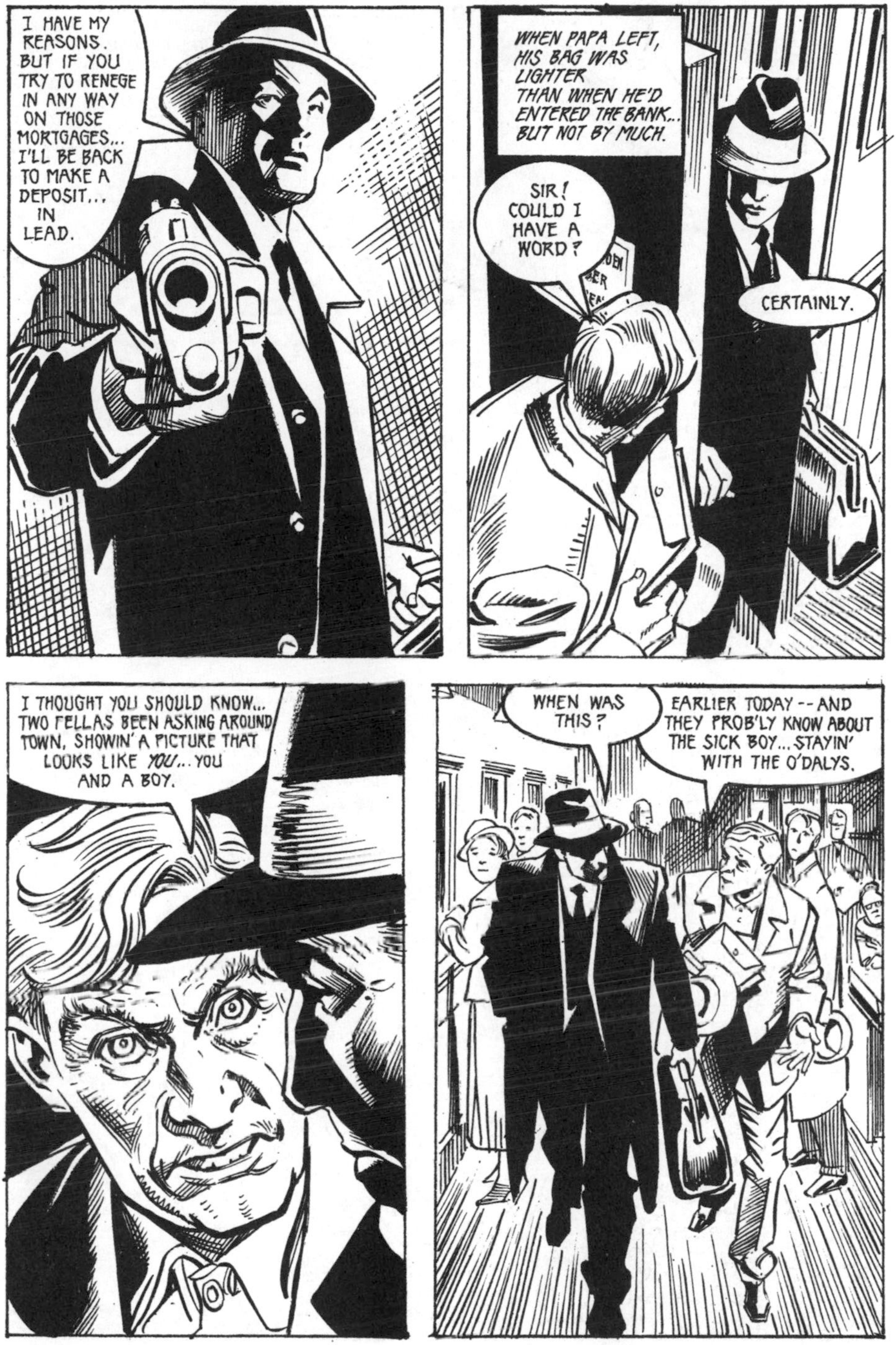
I HAVE MY REASONS. BUT IF YOU TRY TO RENEGE IN ANY WAY ON THOSE MORTGAGES... I'LL BE BACK TO MAKE A DEPOSIT... IN LEAD.
WHEN PAPA LEFT, HIS BAG WAS LIGHTER THAN WHEN HE'D ENTERED THE BANK... BUT NOT BY MUCH.
SIR! COULD I HAVE A WORD?
CERTAINLY.
I THOUGHT YOU SHOULD KNOW... TWO FELLAS BEEN ASKING AROUND TOWN, SHOWIN' A PICTURE THAT LOOKS LIKE *YOU*... YOU AND A BOY.
WHEN WAS THIS?
EARLIER TODAY -- AND THEY PROB'LY KNOW ABOUT THE SICK BOY... STAYIN' WITH THE O'DALYS.

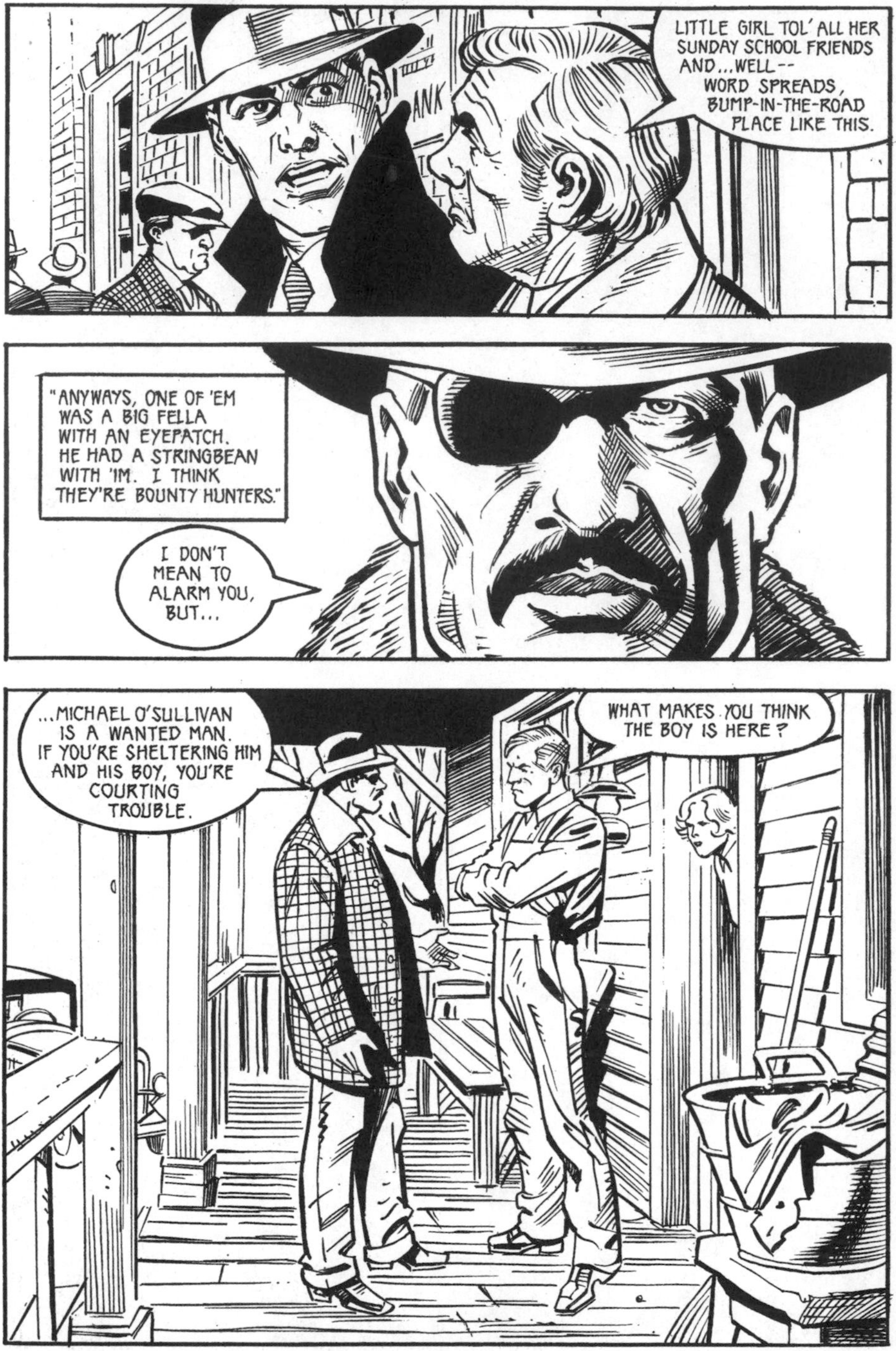
LITTLE GIRL TOL' ALL HER SUNDAY SCHOOL FRIENDS AND... WELL-- WORD SPREADS, BUMP-IN-THE-ROAD PLACE LIKE THIS.
"ANYWAYS, ONE OF 'EM WAS A BIG FELLA WITH AN EYEPATCH. HE HAD A STRINGBEAN WITH 'IM. I THINK THEY'RE BOUNTY HUNTERS."
I DON'T MEAN TO ALARM YOU, BUT...
...MICHAEL O'SULLIVAN IS A WANTED MAN. IF YOU'RE SHELTERING HIM AND HIS BOY, YOU'RE COURTING TROUBLE.
WHAT MAKES YOU THINK THE BOY IS HERE?

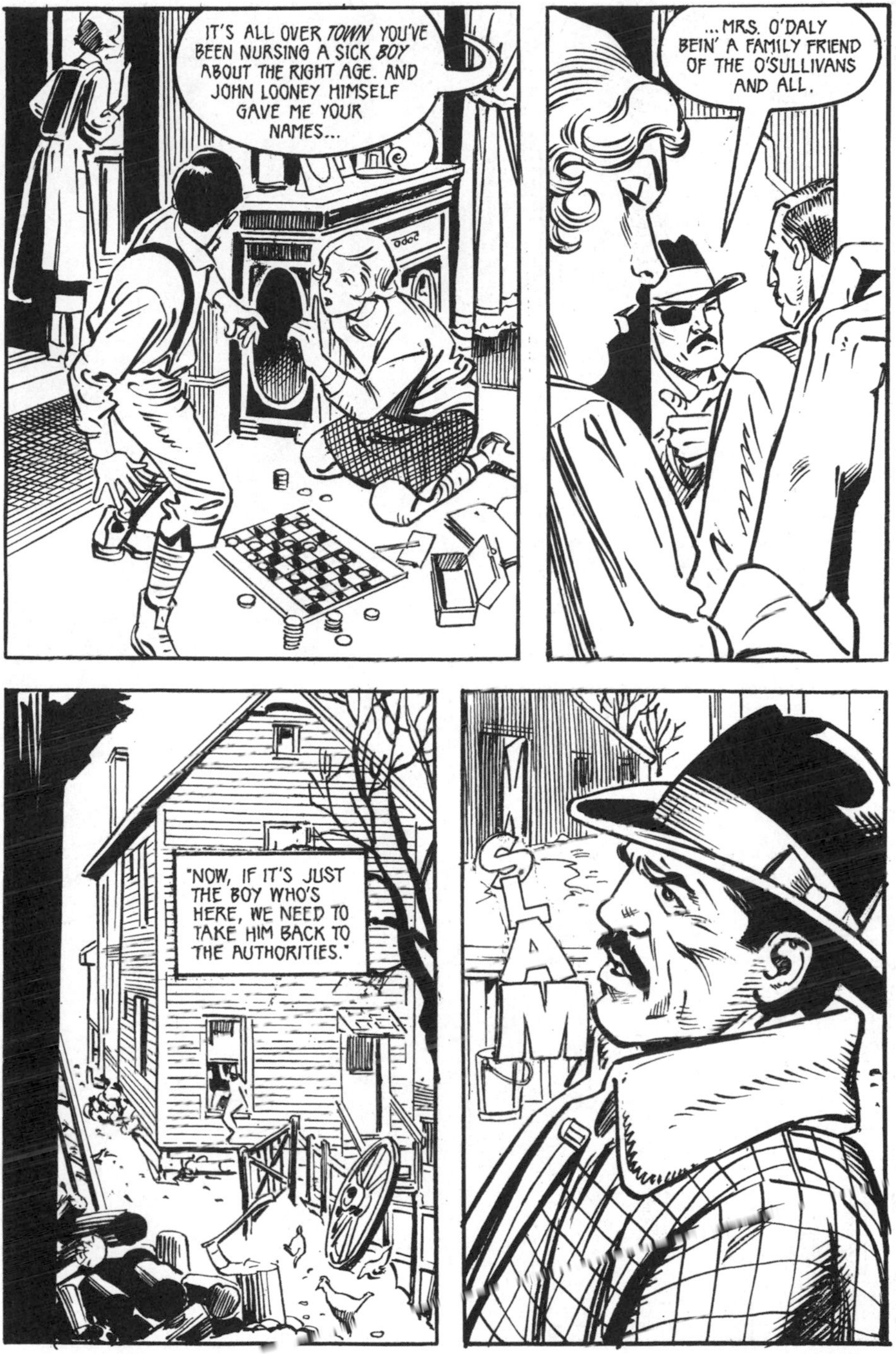
IT'S ALL OVER *TOWN* YOU'VE BEEN NURSING A SICK *BOY* ABOUT THE RIGHT AGE. AND JOHN LOONEY HIMSELF GAVE ME YOUR NAMES...
...MRS. O'DALY BEIN' A FAMILY FRIEND OF THE O'SULLIVANS AND ALL.
"NOW, IF IT'S JUST THE BOY WHO'S HERE, WE NEED TO TAKE HIM BACK TO THE AUTHORITIES."
SLAM

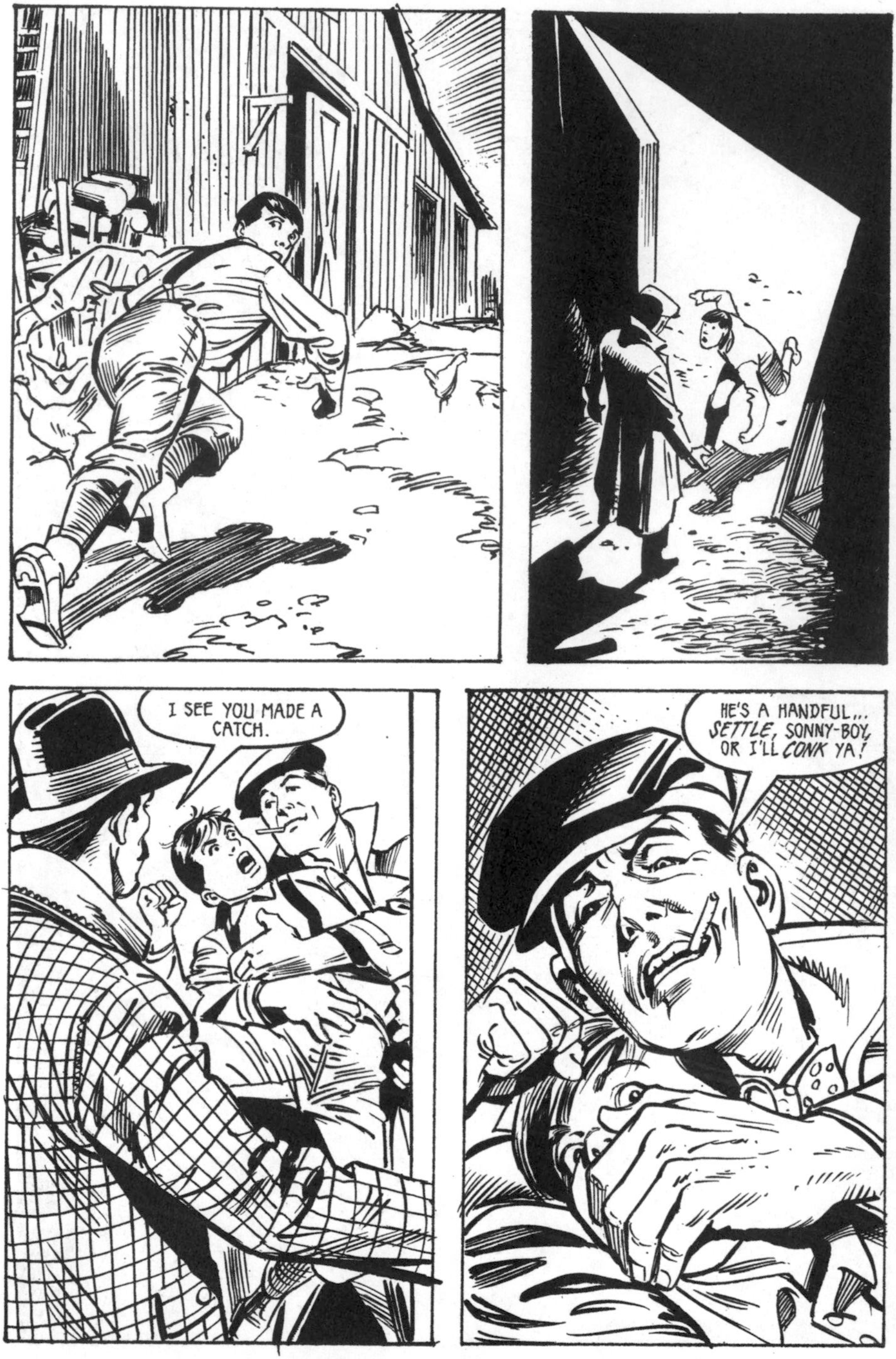
I SEE YOU MADE A CATCH.
HE'S A HANDFUL... SETTLE, SONNY-BOY, OR I'LL CONK YA!

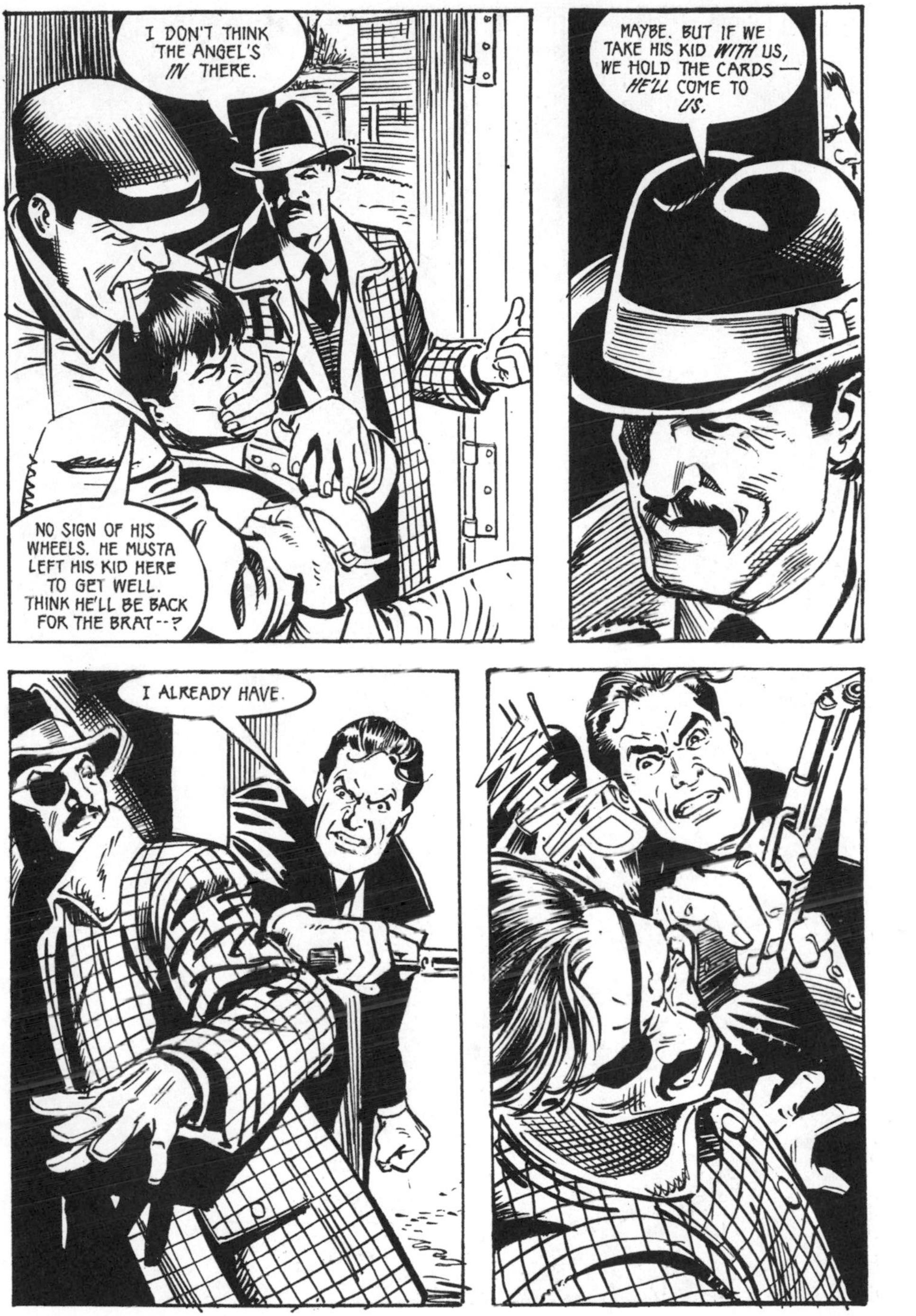
I DON'T THINK THE ANGEL'S *IN* THERE.
NO SIGN OF HIS WHEELS. HE MUSTA LEFT HIS KID HERE TO GET WELL. THINK HE'LL BE BACK FOR THE BRAT--?
MAYBE. BUT IF WE TAKE HIS KID *WITH* US, WE HOLD THE CARDS — *HE'LL* COME TO *US*.
I ALREADY HAVE.
WHAP

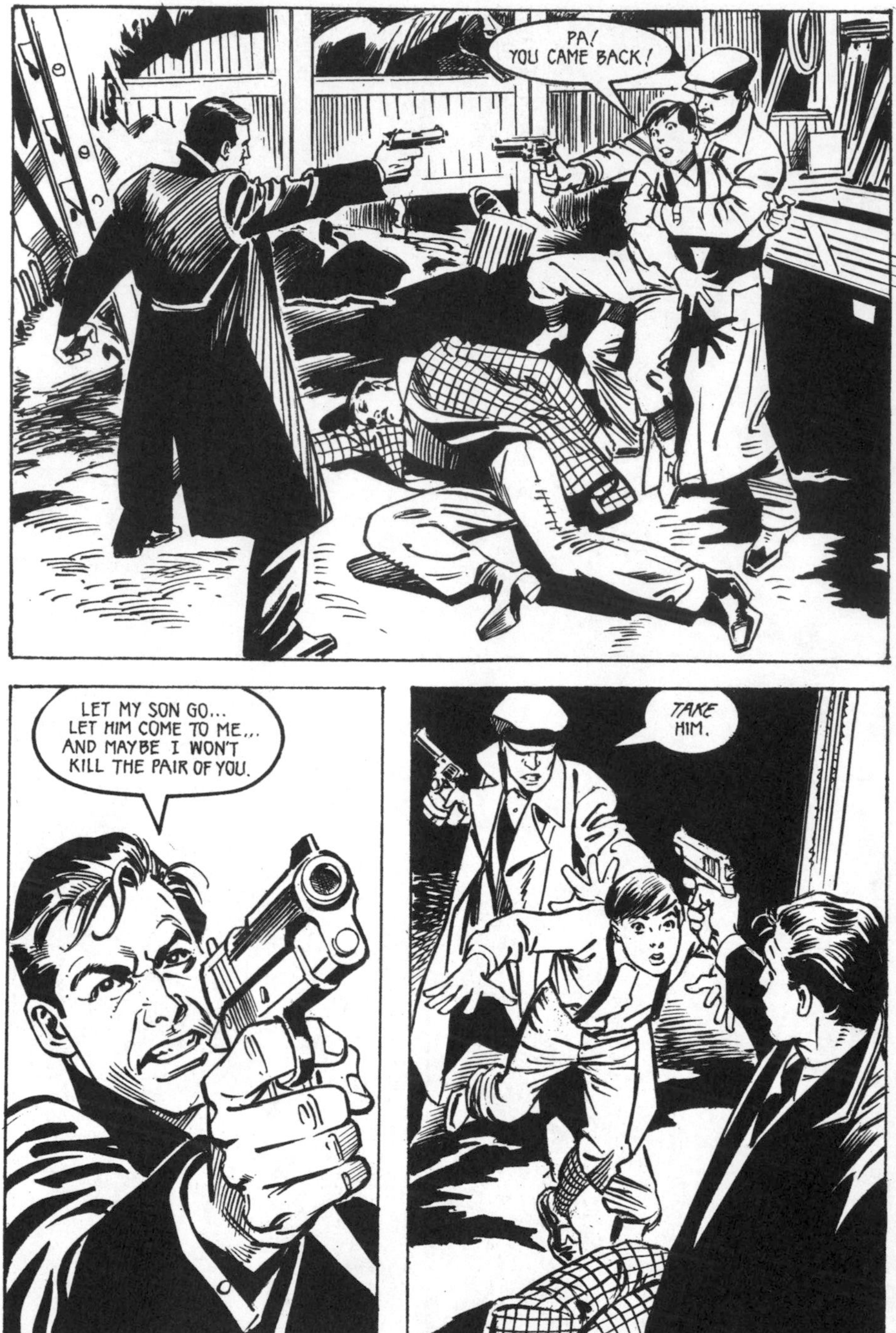
PA! YOU CAME BACK!
LET MY SON GO... LET HIM COME TO ME... AND MAYBE I WON'T KILL THE PAIR OF YOU.
TAKE HIM.

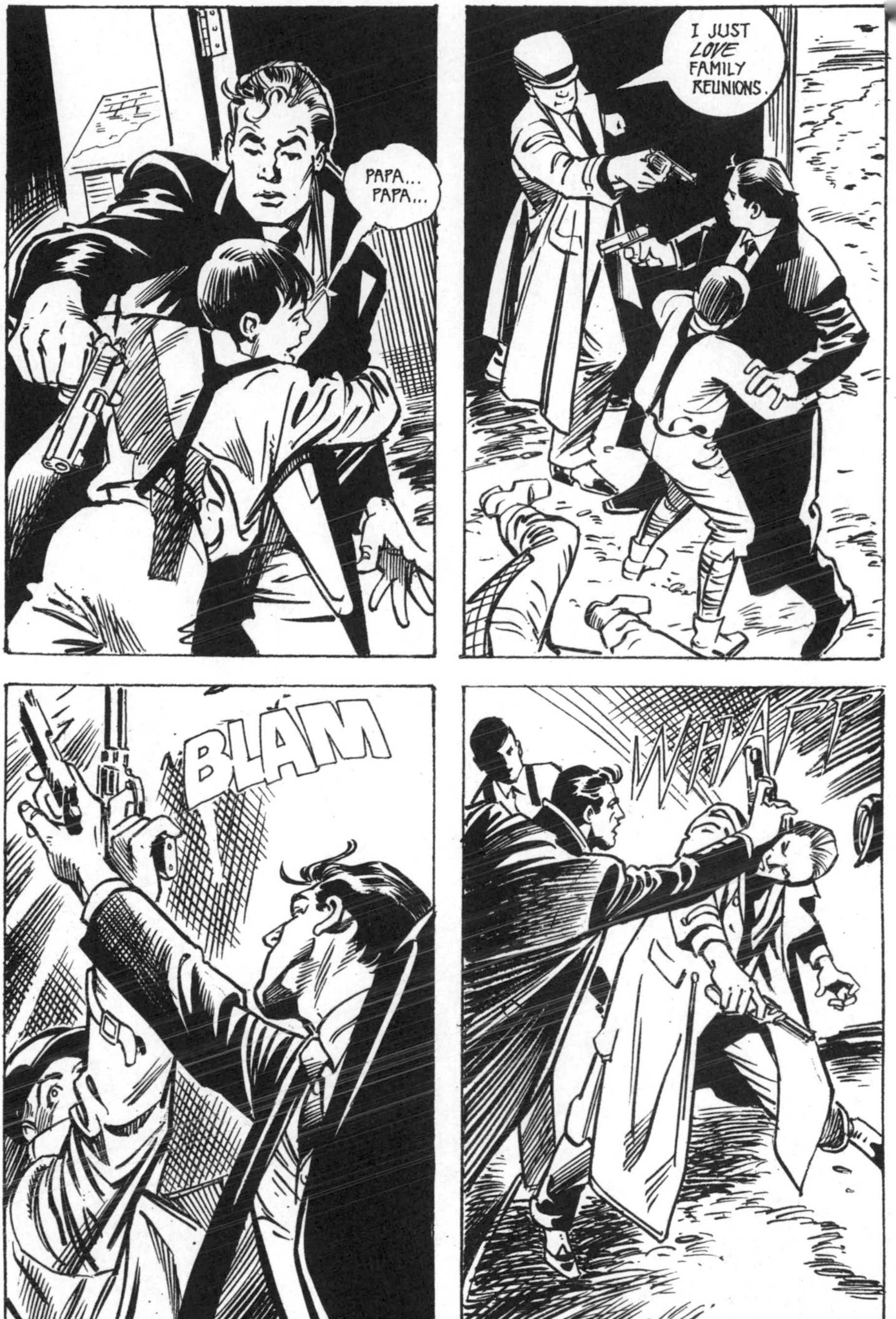
PAPA... PAPA...
I JUST *LOVE* FAMILY REUNIONS.
BLAM
WHAPP

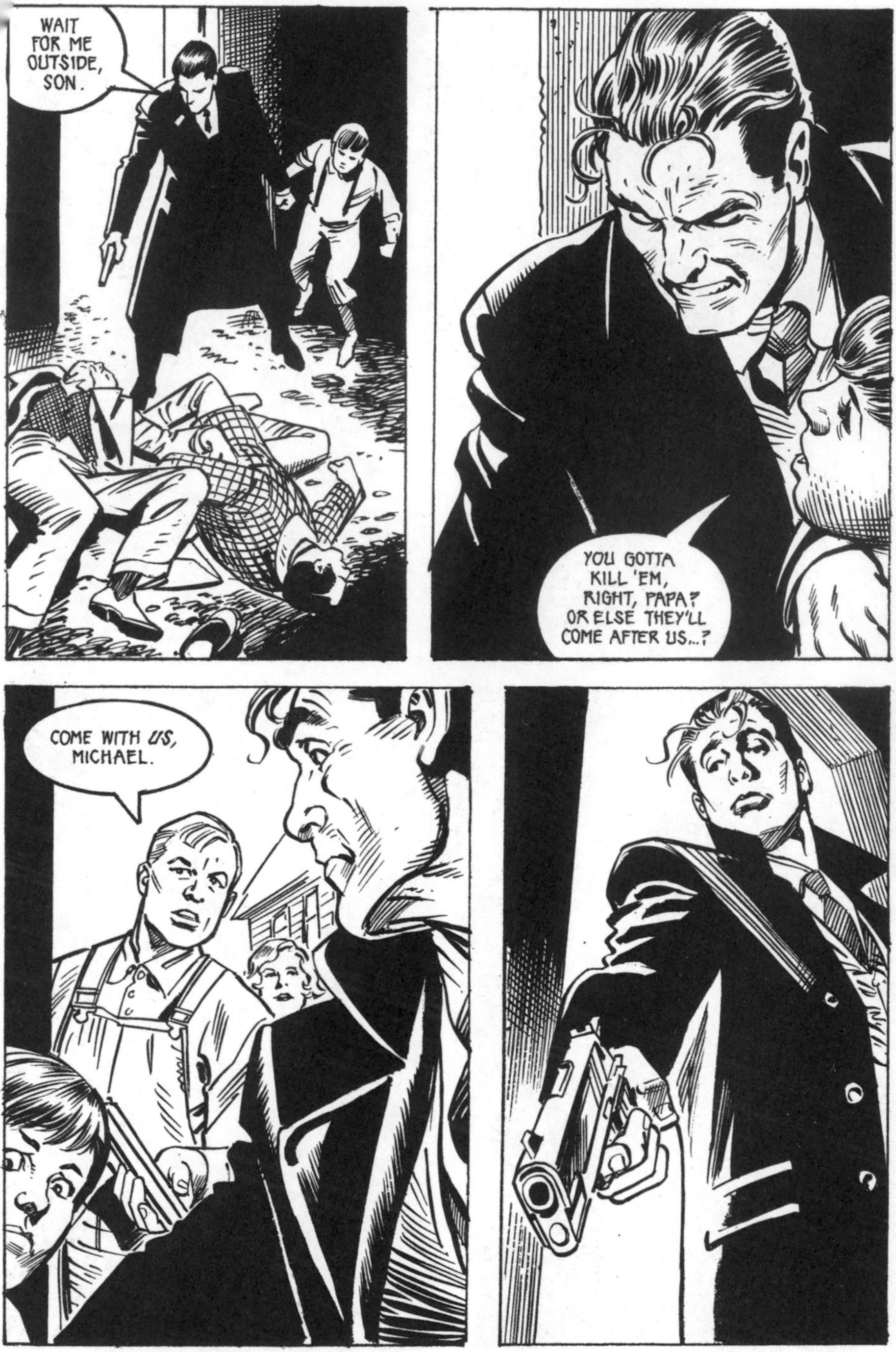
WAIT FOR ME OUTSIDE, SON.
YOU GOTTA KILL 'EM, RIGHT, PAPA? OR ELSE THEY'LL COME AFTER US...?
COME WITH *US*, MICHAEL.

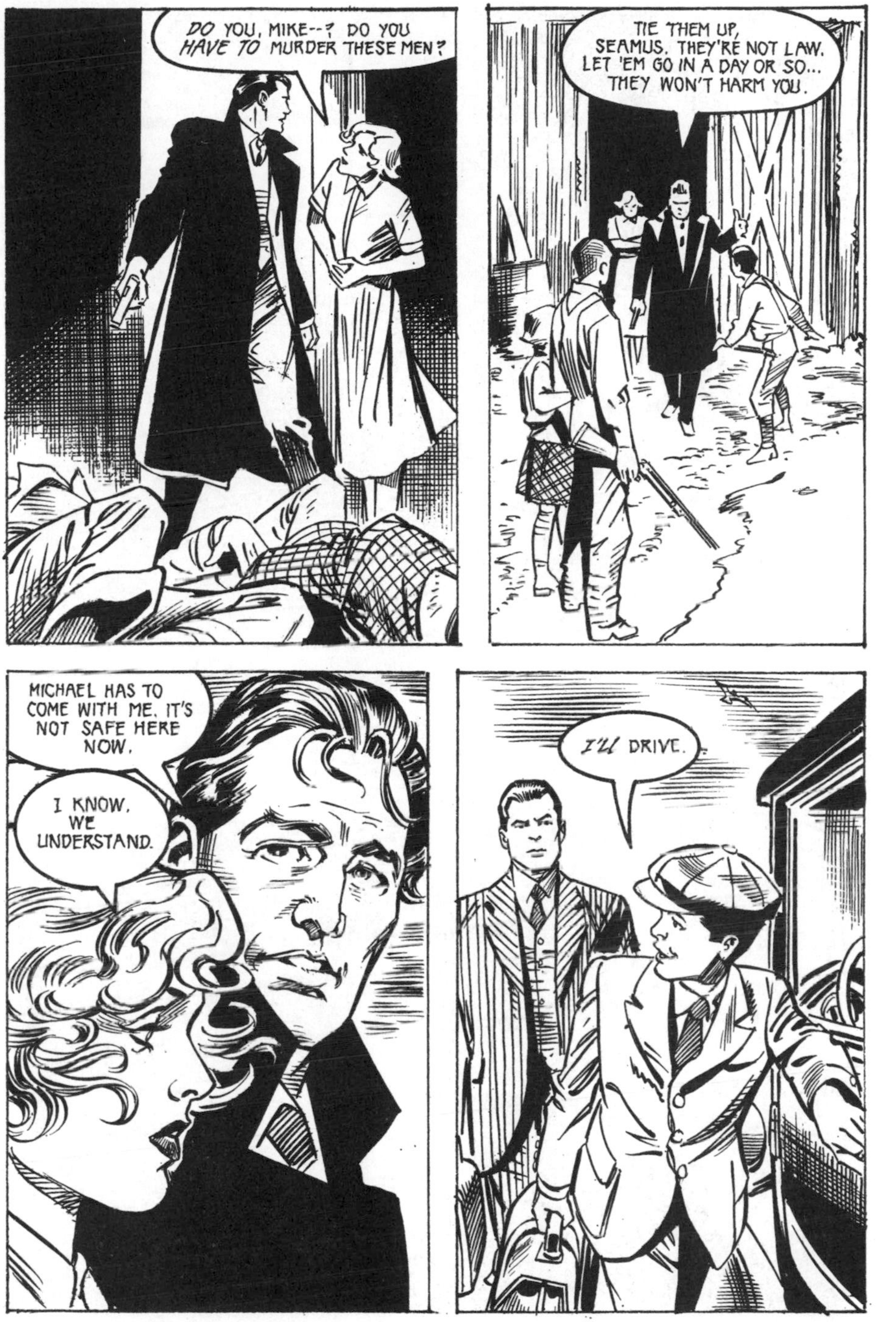
DO YOU, MIKE--? DO YOU HAVE TO MURDER THESE MEN?
TIE THEM UP, SEAMUS. THEY'RE NOT LAW. LET 'EM GO IN A DAY OR SO... THEY WON'T HARM YOU.
MICHAEL HAS TO COME WITH ME. IT'S NOT SAFE HERE NOW.
I KNOW. WE UNDERSTAND.
I'LL DRIVE.

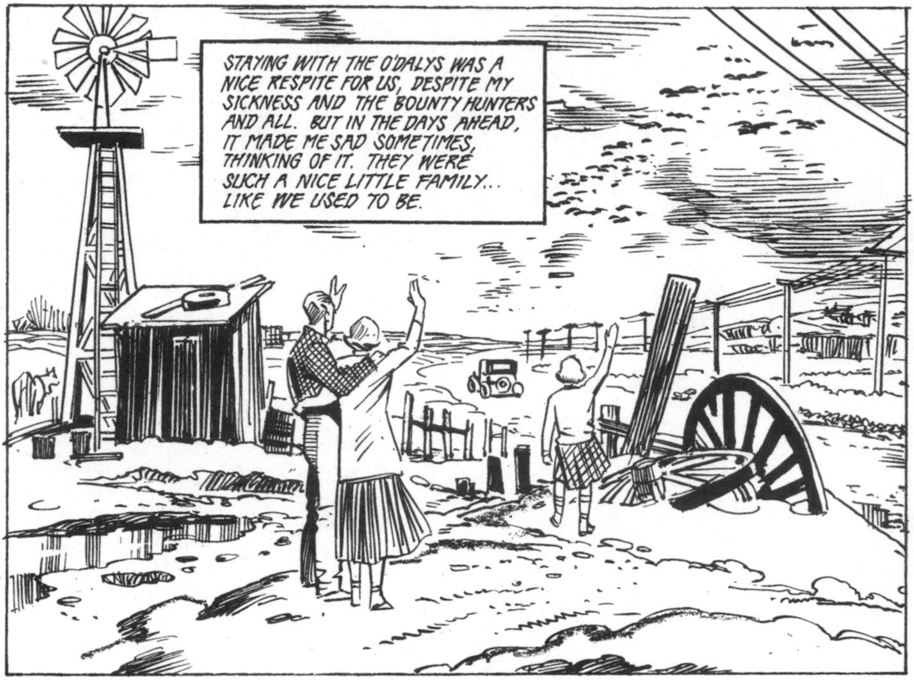
STAYING WITH THE O'DALYS WAS A NICE RESPITE FOR US, DESPITE MY SICKNESS AND THE BOUNTY HUNTERS AND ALL. BUT IN THE DAYS AHEAD, IT MADE ME SAD SOMETIMES, THINKING OF IT. THEY WERE SUCH A NICE LITTLE FAMILY... LIKE WE USED TO BE.

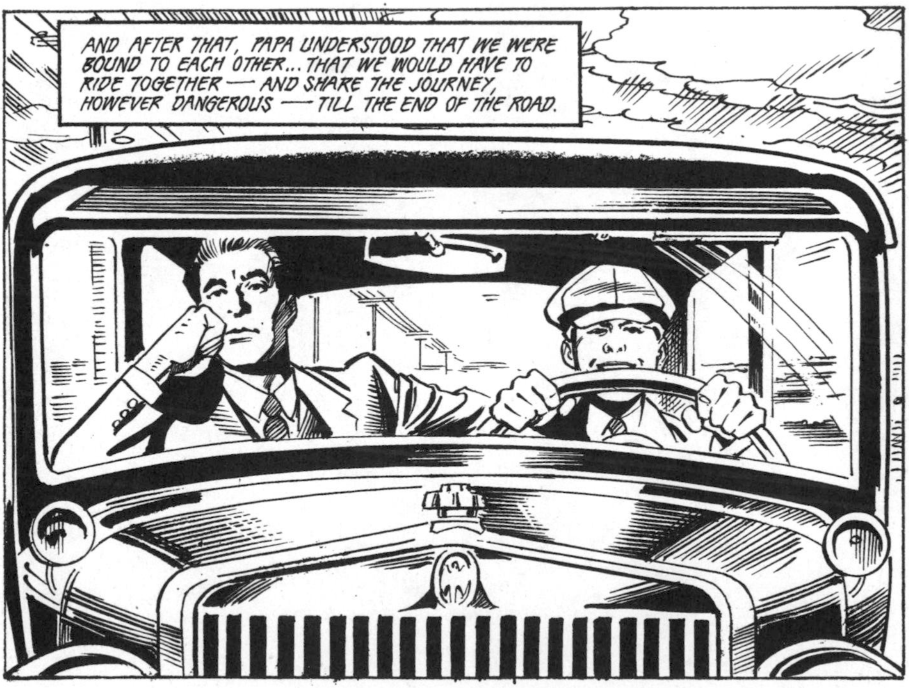
AND AFTER THAT, PAPA UNDERSTOOD THAT WE WERE BOUND TO EACH OTHER... THAT WE WOULD HAVE TO RIDE TOGETHER — AND SHARE THE JOURNEY, HOWEVER DANGEROUS — TILL THE END OF THE ROAD.